THROUGH
Green-Colored
GLASSES

THROUGH
Green-Colored
GLASSES

Environmentalism
Reconsidered

WILFRED BECKERMAN

CATO
INSTITUTE
Washington, D.C.

Library of Congress Cataloging-in-Publication Data

Beckerman, Wilfred.
 Through green-colored glasses : environmentalism reconsidered /
Wilfred Beckerman.
  p.   cm.
 Includes bibliographical references (p. 217-224) and index.
 ISBN 1-882577-35-3. — ISBN 1-882577-36-1 (pbk.)
 1. Environmentalism.   2. Economic development.   I. Title
GE195.B44   1996
333.7'2—dc20   96-30858
                                                                    CIP

Cover Design by Mark Fondersmith.

Printed in the United States of America.

CATO INSTITUTE
1000 Massachusetts Ave., N.W.
Washington, D.C. 20001

This book is dedicated to my publisher, the late Colin Haycraft, a man of outstanding intelligence and exceptional courage, integrity, and independence of spirit, who was not afraid to publish this very "politically incorrect" work.

Contents

Preface to the U.S. Edition

I ought to have known better. I was very much at the center of the environmental debate in Britain during the early 1970s, and as soon as I had published my 1974 book *In Defence of Economic Growth*[1] I got out of it. That was partly because I became bored—and sometimes disgusted—with the low intellectual level of most of the environmentalist arguments deployed to attack economic growth or to claim absolute priority for environmental concerns. But it was largely because I became exasperated by the emotional tone of the debate and the wild abuse hurled at me for my views. People would come up to me and say, in effect, "Oh, so you are that wicked fiend Wilfred Beckerman, are you? Well, what about the Minamata disaster, or the demise of the bald eagle?" as if I were personally responsible for those phenomena.

So after I had published my 1974 book I could reply to such people by saying, "Sir (or Madame), I think you are talking nonsense. But I don't wish to get down in the gutter and argue about it with you. I have just published a book setting out my views. If you can find any flaws in the logic or errors of fact, I hope you will write an article in one of the serious academic journals, since it would then no doubt come to my attention in due course and I could do my best to reply."

The challenge has never been taken up. This did not, of course, prevent one or two hostile reviews appearing in odd newspapers or in the environmentalist press, but those were vastly outnumbered by favorable reviews. This time, the English edition of my latest book, *Small Is Stupid*, which appeared last year, has met with more hostile reviews, although there have still been very favorable reviews in the most prestigious and serious outlets.

I do not put this down to any significant change in the nature of my message in this latest book, nor in the quality with which my

[1]Jonathan Cape, London. The U.S. edition, entitled *Two Cheers for the Affluent Society*, was published by St Martin's Press in 1975.

arguments have been presented. I put it down to the great strides that the environmentalist movement has made over the past two decades in mobilizing public opinion and gaining political support. It has been able to do so for a variety of reasons. One of these is that probably many more "environmental correspondents" are employed in the media, most of whom are committed ideologically to some of the environmentalist dogmas that I am attacking. But another reason is that environmentalism appeals to many quite different groups in society.

They include certain sections of the middle classes whose most immediate needs are satisfactorily met and whose priorities have moved now in the direction of environmental assets. For them it is morally satisfying to represent their preferences as a moral crusade against the crass materialism of modern industrial society. Also on the environmentalist bandwagon are certain politicians who find that catering to popular, if misplaced, fashions that have a high moral tone helps them on the road to political power. Other groups with a vested interest in extreme environmentalism include even many scientists whose research budgets depend on their claims that their research is needed to save humanity from impending environmental catastrophe. The media, too, have a part to play. A threat of environmental disaster is always good for attracting the attention of readers. And one must not forget the bureaucrats. In addition to the explosion of international and national commissions and committees to implement the agreements reached at the vast Rio de Janeiro "Earth Summit" of 1992, new rules and regulations to be imposed in the name of saving the world from the exhaustion of "finite resources" or some other exaggerated environmental threat.

Finally, there is the appeal of environmentalism to modern-day radical revolutionaries. Socialism now has been visibly discredited throughout most of the world. Everybody has been able to see that, instead of ushering in a society characterized by equity, justice, and comradely love, it led to the imposition of monstrous and incompetent regimes in many parts of the world. So the radical revolutionaries have turned to environmentalism as their rallying cry and their justification for acts of eco-terrorism and defiance of democratic processes of decisionmaking. Like most anti-democratic movements in the past they defend their activities by appeal to vague and meaningless slogans—like "sustainable development" or "the precautionary principle"—and muddled mystical pseudo-philosophizing about the intrinsic value that nature would have even in the absence of human beings or the wonderful symbiotic relationship that existed between humans and nature in the Stone Age.

Taken together, these various passengers on the environmentalist bandwagon represent a formidable influence on society. They are behind the intrusion of bureaucratic regulation in our lives and livelihoods, behind pressures to restrict international trade or punish countries that do not share the same relative preferences for the environment as do the more prosperous nations, behind a disrespect for law and order in environmental policy, and behind a contempt for rational argument on the subject. Their propaganda at all levels, particularly among impressionable children who are particularly attached to animals, constitutes an obstacle to serious and balanced debate over environmental policy.

Of course, there is always a grain of truth—and sometimes more than a grain—in the current concern with the environment. I became interested in the environment, and was made a member of the newly created Royal Commission on Environmental Pollution, back in 1970 because of my concern with preserving the environment from excessive abuse. Concern with the environment reflects many of the best instincts of human beings, whether it is spiritual appreciation of the environment, or concern with future generations, or compassion for other creatures. But the environmentalist pressure groups advocate policies that are often inimical to the true interests of the environment or future generations. There are three reasons for this.

First, if economic growth were to be slowed down or stopped it would be impossible to improve the environmental conditions of most people in the Third World. Second, the widespread resort to regulations, instead of some market mechanism, to prevent excessive pollution, would only make environmental protection even more expensive, so that society would do less of it. Third, pursuit of the objective of "sustainable development" would, in fact, only reduce the welfare of future generations.

As I said earlier, I ascribe the more widespread hostility aroused by my latest attack on extreme environmentalism to the rapid advance that the environmentalist movement has made during the last two decades. One common feature of the hostile reviews is wonderfully characteristic of the abysmal level of environmentalist debate. That is that they like to accuse me of attacking "straw men" when I refer to the anti-economic growth sentiments of the environmentalists. For example, Jonathan Porritt, a leading British Green activist, wrote of my book that "[he] sets up a whole gallery of antediluvian straw men specifically to incinerate them with his withering scorn." And the reviewer in *New Scientist* wrote that I attribute "extreme statements or policies to environmentalist and 'ecodoomsters,' and to politicians who have fallen under their sway. But he doesn't attrribute specific statements to specific people."

I sent the following letter to *New Scientist*: "I am sorry to learn that Jonathan Porritt, Sir Crispin Tickell, Lester Brown, and Jeremy Leggett, all of whom I quoted, are not, after all, "specific people." I have met three of them in person and got the distinct impression that they were. Have they even been misleading us all about that as well?" Needless to say, the letter was not published. The humorless zealots that tend to proliferate in environmentalist circles are not easily amused.

Fortunately, the serious press has been on my side. The editor of *Nature* wrote that "environmentalists tempted to ignore Wilfred Beckerman's latest book had better think again; there is no better way of 'knowing your enemy,' and no more mordant enemy," and that "Beckerman has written a thoughtful book as well as an entertaining one."[2] A later reviewer in *Nature* wrote that "I cheer when Beckerman takes on, in turn, the myth that we are running out of resources, those groups who would have developing countries sacrifice economic growth for the developed countries' ideas of environmental protection, those advancing the notion that sustainable development is really a new and better substitute for the economist's 'tired refrain' of maximizing social welfare. . . ."[3] In like vein the *Times Literary Supplement* reviewer said that "there is much to ponder and admire in Beckerman's book,"[4] and *The Economist* wrote that "contrary to the image he cultivates, Mr. Beckerman is not antigreen. He is just sensible."[5]

[2]March 23, 1995.
[3]May 11, 1996.
[4]September 8, 1995.
[5]April 8, 1995.

But even more gratifying is the fact that the book has been praised also in journals that represent specific environmental concerns of one kind or another. For example, the *Commonwealth Forestry Review* stated that the book ''. . . should be required reading for environmentalists. . . .''[6] The *Safe Energy Journal*'s reviewer thought that "this is a valuable contribution to the environmental and equity debates. . . . All of those who seek to influence the policy agenda for the coming millennium and beyond would be well advised to familiarize themselves with the arguments he [Beckerman] presents.''[7] Even the British Ecological Society's *TEGNews* review stated that "this book goes against much of the current orthodoxy but in so doing it puts up a compelling case backed with some important factual material. It deserves a wide audience because such stimulating texts as this are rare.''[8]

So there is still some hope that the voice of reason and hard factual evidence will continue to be heard. It may well be that the publishers of my 1974 book found, this time round, that the views I expressed were no longer likely to appeal to "right-on" people who subscribe to political correctness. But at least the book is published, and even some of my natural adversaries are honest and generous enough to recognize that, after all, there may be something in my arguments. I must now let the readers judge for themselves.

[6]Vol. 74, no. 4, 1995.
[7]December 1995.
[8]Winter 1995.

Preface

It is often asserted that "Oxford is the home of lost causes." I have also heard it said that this is because I have been associated with them. It is true that people who don't know me might imagine from the title of this book that I have a confrontational style that only equips me to write a book on how to make enemies and antagonize people. But, as a result of my position on environmental issues, I have made so many enemies over the last 20 years that a few more or less now makes no difference. The chief thing is that I have also made a few friends, some of whom have helped me sort out my views on the issues covered in this book. It would be an act of gross ingratitude to reveal all their names here.

However, I am indebted for specific assistance with rather technical aspects of chapters 9, 10 and 11 to some people who do not necessarily subscribe at all to the general theme of the book. These include, notably, John Broome, Ian Little, Joanna Pasek, John Pezzey, and Maurice Scott.

But, as my dedication will indicate, my greatest debt is to the late Colin Haycraft, who had no hesitation about publishing a book that would raise the hackles of many members of the environmental establishment. I am also indebted to him for his personal contribution to the editing of the book, which went far beyond the call of duty, as well as to the staff of Duckworth who took over the burden after his sudden and tragic death in September 1994.

I am also grateful to Balliol College and the University of Oxford for granting me a term's sabbatical leave during which I made considerable progress on this book. For this I am prepared to forgive them the fact that, shortly afterwards, I was forced to retire on the flimsy pretext that I had been born in 1925. Like anybody else who has had the great fortune and privilege of being a Fellow of Balliol, I am also deeply indebted to the members of that College—colleagues and students—for providing such a friendly and stimulating working environment over very many years. I am also grateful to the Rockefeller Foundation for inviting me to spend time at their Bellagio Center, where I worked on a different problem but where I met another academic whose chance remarks brought me back into the battle against the self-righteous obscurantism of the environmental extremists that I thought I had left forever back in 1975. I knew then that I had lost the battle, and I have no illusions that my feeble and inadequate efforts in this book will be more successful than was my 1974 book on the same subject. But this is the spirit that keeps Oxford the home of lost causes.

Finally, I am indebted to the editors of *Environmental Values* for allowing me to reproduce, substantially unchanged, my article " 'Sustainable Development': Is It a Useful Concept?'', which appeared in the issue of Autumn 1994; to the World Bank for permission to reproduce material that I prepared for the Bank in connection with its 1992 *World Development Report*; to Oxford University Press for permission to reproduce some of the material I contributed to *The International Politics of the Environment* (edited by A. Hurrell and B. Kingsbury); and to Blackwell Publishers for permission to reproduce some of the material I contributed to *Economic Policy Towards the Environment* (edited by D. Helm).

Introduction

The Age of Meaningless Slogans Has Arrived—Alas!

During the last decade the environmentalist movement has renewed its attack on the desirability of economic growth, and has redoubled its call for drastic measures to ward off environmental catastrophe. Environmentalist pressures eased off in the middle 1970s, when the sudden rise in the oil price led to deflationary policies in most Western countries, so that the public was more concerned with the lack of economic growth than with the fear that economic growth was harmful. But since the early 1980s various developments have provided fresh ammunition for alarmists to predict environmental disaster, and calls for tough measures to protect us from them have been very much back on the agenda.

One of the most important of these developments has been the alleged longer-term effects of global warming, but damage to the ozone layer or the apparent loss of biodiversity have also played a part. These alleged threats have led environmentalists to adopt some so-called "precautionary principle." In addition, the old myth that we would run out of supplies of so-called "finite resources" has given rise to a call that we should pursue only "sustainable development."

These two new catch-phrases, "the precautionary principle" and "sustainable development," are repeated parrot-fashion by environmental policymakers. Commissions and committees, national and international, are set up to supervise and report on the adoption of policies to promote "sustainable development" and to implement the "precautionary principle." Any politicians or opinion-formers who fail to pay due lip service to them do so at their peril. Environmentalists, many scientists, media commentators, politicians and public figures, all eager to demonstrate their sense of social responsibility, as well as many genuinely concerned members of the public, treat the injunction to pursue "sustainable development" and the

1

"precautionary principle" with reverential respect without realizing that both are fundamentally confused. Continued invocation of these catch phrases can only pressure governments into hastily devised, inefficient, and expensive environmental regulatory policies that usually involve an unwarranted intervention in the operation of the market.

To begin with, the "precautionary principle" interpreted sensibly is nothing new at all. It is something that motivates us all in ordinary life—for example, when we install smoke alarms in our dwellings. I discovered it for myself when, as a young man, weighing up the risk that my bicycle might be stolen, the loss that this would impose on me, and the cost of buying a padlock to prevent it, I decided that it was worth my while buying the padlock. If the bicycle had been almost worthless, the chances of its being stolen negligible, and the cost of the padlock very high, I would not have bought it. But to apply a principle that is taken to mean that, irrespective of the chances of future loss, the scale of the loss and the costs of preventing it, one must incur those costs, would be simply stupid. Yet the "precautionary principle" is constantly invoked as if it meant that, as long as there is the remotest possibility of serious harm in the distant future, we should take drastic action now when it is very expensive and may soon be found to be unnecessary, rather than wait until (i) we know more about the phenomenon in question, and (ii) it would be cheaper anyway to take action if it is still found to be desirable. As explained in Chapter 6, the attempt to blind the layman with science by attributing this interpretation of the "precautionary principle" to "game theory" is quite unwarranted.

As for "sustainable development," society's proper objective should be to obtain the highest feasible welfare. The time period over which welfare is to be maximized is debatable, as is the definition of what "welfare" comprises. But if "sustainable development" is to provide some new alternative objective its proponents should make clear in what way it differs from it. For example, if "sustainable development" is interpreted—as it sometimes is—as implying that all other components of welfare are to be sacrificed in the interests of preserving the environment exactly in the form it happens to be in today, then it is morally indefensible. If, instead, it is after all no different from the goal of maximizing society's welfare, it is totally redundant; hawking the concept around as if it constituted some important new insight to guide environmental policy merely creates confusion. And, as this book shows, in the longer run economic growth is still the best means of achieving the old-fashioned goal of maximizing society's welfare over whatever time period is thought relevant.

In this book I demonstrate that economic growth is still a necessary condition for remedying most of the serious environmental problems facing the world, particularly in developing countries. I show that if appropriate policies are adopted there is no real conflict between economic growth and the environment, let alone between man and the environment. There is widespread conflict between man and man (or between woman and woman, or even man and woman). But that is nothing new and its analysis lies way outside my competence.

I then challenge the widespread assertion that we are on course toward environmental catastrophe. Finally, I try to expose the hollowness of the environmentalists' claim to occupy the moral high ground by their insistence on the virtue of "sustainable development" and its greater concern for the interests of future generations.

The Real Environmental Problems

It has been clear for at least 30 years that the world is facing serious environmental problems. In advanced countries these include urban air pollution and traffic congestion, pollution of beaches and rivers, and the disposal of the mountains of ordinary garbage produced in affluent societies, not to mention the disposal of radioactive waste. Pioneering books such as Ed Mishan's *The Costs of Economic Growth* or Schumacher's *Small is Beautiful* brought home to a wide public the importance of the growth-environment relation.[1] It may come as a surprise to many people to learn that the authors of both books were economists. But it is not really surprising. Economists were already well aware that the market mechanism would not always ensure adequate protection for the environment unless special steps were taken to improve, or supplement, its operation.

For the environment exhibits certain technical characteristics that hamper the operation of market forces—such as the absence of clearly defined property rights and, often, the sheer technical impossibility of allocating legally enforceable property rights. Allied to this is the "public good"—or rather "public bad"—character of many environmental services. For example, it is rarely in the interests of an individual to do anything to reduce air or water pollution, although it may be in the collective interest of society to do so.

The challenge facing policymakers therefore is to design policies to enable market forces to operate in the environmental sphere, or to mimic the operation of the market—for example, by some system of pollution charges where property rights cannot be applied. But this is an extremely difficult task. And it is to this that policymakers should pay attention rather than to vast international jamborees to discuss the latest fashion in apocalyptic predictions. By contrast, pressures to take drastic action to save us from imminent environmental disaster only push governments in the direction of regulations and controls, like those used in Soviet economies with the disastrous effects that are now well known. For such "command and control" policies are much easier to devise. They also suit the bureaucratic instinct to regulate things rather than help markets operate more efficiently within an appropriate legal framework.

But the worst environmental problems are those found in the Third World. These are problems of lack of access to clean drinking water or to sanitation, not to mention the intolerable air pollution and urban squalor of most of the main cities in developing countries. In the Third World these environmental problems persist largely because of poverty. One of the gurus of the environmentalist movement most deserving of respect and admiration, Edward O. Wilson, points out that conventional conservation measures, such as the establishment of national parks in the United States or Europe, are of little use in poor countries where ". . . the poorest people with the fastest-growing populations live next to the richest deposits of biological diversity. One Peruvian farmer clearing rain forest to feed his family, progressing from patch to patch as the soil is drained of nutrients, will cut more kinds of trees than are native to all of Europe. If there is no other way for him to make a living the trees will fall. . . . Only new ways of drawing income from land already cleared, or from intact wildlands themselves, will save biodiversity from the mill of human poverty."[2]

There are also serious international environmental problems— such as the threat to fish stocks, or the transmission of acid rain, or the possibly serious loss of biodiversity, and so on. Progress in dealing with these problems has been very slow because the problem of reaching mutually satisfactory agreement among sovereign states, all of which seek to protect their own interests, is enormously complex. Reaching agreement among sovereign states on measures that may well be to the benefit of humanity as a whole but meanwhile may hit the interests of powerful groups inside individual countries is inevitably a colossal task.

These various problems—market imperfections in advanced countries, poverty in developing countries, and the conflict between national and international interests in environmental matters—are difficult enough already. Society should not be distracted from them by the attention paid to phony disaster scenarios. It is right that we should be concerned with the real environmental issues. It is also right that we should be concerned with the sort of world that we bequeath to our descendants. At the same time we should not be taken for a ride by the environmentalist movement's predictions that we are on the verge of environmental catastrophe, and that governments must be pushed into taking far more drastic action than they appear to be taking. For alarm bordering on hysteria is no guide to balanced policy.

Of course the environmentalist movement must be given some credit for the fact that the public and many governments have taken seriously the genuine environmental problems that face us. But some of the credit should go to economic growth. For the resulting rise in incomes leads to a shift in people's priorities from the satisfaction of basic needs to concern with their environment and a greater willingness to devote resources to environmental protection. However, governments will not willingly take action to remedy any environmental problem unless constantly pressed to do so by the weight of public opinion. And this opinion needs to be channeled through organized groups, among which environmentalist organizations have a valuable part to play. But they should play their part in a responsible manner.

False Alarms Are Fun—And They Pay Off Too

Not surprisingly the public tends to believe that the most acute environmental problems facing the world today are dramatic problems, such as global warming or the exhaustion of the world's supply of finite materials, or some other environmental catastrophe. After all, the media have an understandable interest in publicizing disaster stories. Scare stories about catastrophic climate change resulting from economic activity are almost daily fare in our newspapers and on our TV screens. Such stories provide far better photo opportunities than features showing that the world's most acute environmental needs are clean drinking water and better sanitation in the Third World.

According to Andrew Kenny: "Interest in the environment among the general public is minimal, and editors believe it can only be sustained by photographs of cuddly animals and predictions of doom. Editors like the drama of Chernobyl . . . they like warnings that an ice age is about to freeze us or that global warming is about to roast us. . . . It is the difficult modern duty of scientists to reach the public through this sensational and distorting medium."[3] Of course, as Kenny also says: "In times of tightening science budgets, and in an age where scientists feel misunderstood and unloved, some of them are being seduced by money and popularity to encourage, or at least acquiesce in the latest well-funded, well-publicized Green scares. . . . Predicting catastrophe is a good way of getting money to continue your research and showing what a compassionate scientist you are."

Predicting catastrophe is also the best strategy for the environmentalist movements to adopt if they are to increase their revenues and boost their bureaucracies. People will more readily send a donation to an outfit that promises to save the planet from imminent catastrophe than to one that merely wants to spend more money on drains in the Third World.

And the incessant publicity for the main alarmist environmental threats, which are usually blamed on economic growth, probably also appeals to the subconscious desire of most of us—ranging from radical youth to public figures—to indulge in ego trips that reassure us of our moral fiber, our concern for the welfare of future generations, our compassion for the natural world, our aesthetic sensibilities, and our ability to see through the hollowness of the consumer society. But in fact, as this book tries to show, these dramatic issues are not the most important environmental problems facing the vast majority of the population, in rich and poor countries alike.

Of course it is difficult not to sympathize with those who take a far more apocalyptic view of the environment than I now do myself. Until the early 1970s I firmly believed that the environment was in serious danger as a result of defects in the market economy. (I wrote

6

a favorable review of the Mishan book when it appeared in 1967.) It was my concern with the environment that led the late Anthony Crosland, to whom I had frequently expressed it, to appoint me, in 1970, to the newly establihed Royal Commission on Environmental Pollution.

However, within a few weeks of taking up my appointment and studying the evidence, I discovered, somewhat to my embarrassment, that the impression I had gained from the media, and from much environmentalist literature about pollution trends or the exhaustion of finite resources, was quite false. Almost every indicator of pollution that I looked at showed that, in Britain at least, there had been a steady improvement for at least a decade. For example, in Britain total smoke produced in factories had fallen from 2.3 million tons in 1953 to 0.9 million in 1968, and the total quantity of sulphur oxides emitted into the air began to decline around 1962. As a result, during the 1960s average smoke concentrations in urban areas in Britain fell by 60 per cent, and sulphur oxide concentrations fell by 30 per cent, despite increasing population and industrial output. In the principal cities, such as London or Sheffield, where action was taken early, the improvement in the ambient air quality was even more noticeable. For example, over the same decade the average hours of winter sunshine in London doubled; in 1958 average visibility was one mile, and by the early 1970s winter visibility averaged four.[4]

And I soon found ample historical evidence to show that past dire predictions of imminent exhaustion of finite resources had all been falsified and that, in fact, the whole notion of exhaustion of finite resources was riddled with absurdities. My disillusionment with the wilder claims of the environmentalists and with the related anti-growth school of thought led me to write my 1974 book, *In Defence of Economic Growth*.[5] I then abandoned the whole subject and switched to other research.

But about 15 years later I had the privilege of spending time at the Rockefeller Foundation's Center at Bellagio. One day a distinguished professor of civil engineering, who specialized in water supplies, irrigation, and so on, arrived to work at the Center. To my great surprise and satisfaction, he said that he had read and approved of my 1974 book. I replied that, while naturally gratified by his approval, I was apparently mistaken back in 1974, having failed to recognize the terrible new threats facing us, notably from climate change as a result of the increasing amounts of carbon dioxide being pumped into the atmosphere. For I had the impression, from casual acquaintance with the media and other sources of information, that there was a serious threat of global warming. To my astonishment, he said: "Oh no, Wilfred, that's all just as exaggerated as the scare stories you were attacking back in 1974."

So I decided to do a little research into this area, and I quickly found he was right. But the moral of the story is that if I, who had discovered once before that I was seriously misled by alarmist environmentalist and anti-growth propaganda and was therefore in general very skeptical of their claims, could be taken in once again by it, what hope was there for the vast majority of the public? It is true that I may be more gullible and naive than most. But at least I had been bitten once already.

Many people and institutions are engaged in the analysis of genuine environmental problems. They produce a flow of information that is important in the design of environmental policies. Members of the public who are concerned with these and innumerable other environmental problems throughout the world should resist the diversion of funds and energy away from such serious research and toward the glamorous issues that catch the headlines and dominate the debate.

The Plan of the Book

The balance that needs to be restored to the environmental debate is not just a balance between competing environmental needs. For this is partly the outcome of competing group interests. The nature and severity of most, though not all, environmental problems is very different according to whether we are concerned with richer or poorer groups in advanced countries, or with richer or poorer countries. Part I therefore begins with some discussion of this clash of interests.

This is related to the fact that, in the early stages of economic development, economic growth can have catastrophic effects on local environments. This was the case in the industrial revolution in Britain and other countries in the 19th century, when urban conditions were appalling. And it is still the case in many developing countries today, particularly in the fast-growing cities. How effectively and quickly countries can protect themselves against these terrible environmental effects of growth depends very much on the policies they adopt. Concern with the implementation of the right policies—not with the fashionable disaster scenarios—is the test of whether we are serious about the environment or just want to strike poses and make fine gestures. Part I shows that fashionable global issues, such as climate change or the exhaustion of finite resources, are grossly exaggerated by comparison with the acute environmental problems of the Third World today. It also is demonstrated that the best—and no doubt the only—route by which these countries can overcome their appalling environmental problems is to become richer.

Part II considers the implications of these factual findings. In particular, we have to ask ourselves whether there really is any case for abandoning the conventional goal of economic growth. The economist's approach to the question of the desirability of economic growth and the limitations on this approach are explained. Few economists would claim nowadays that their economics training enables them to answer the grand questions that are frequently put to them, such as how to reconcile full employment with stable prices. But economics, which is sometimes known as "the logic of choice," does provide a few basic lessons—such as how to distinguish between means and ends, and between what is desirable and what is optimal given the opportunities open to us, and, in the light of this, how to recognize that the best choice usually involves some compromise between competing objectives—that is, striking a balance.

As indicated above, much is heard nowadays of the desirability of switching to some other overriding objective of policy, namely the notion of "sustainable development." Part II therefore contains a detailed explanation of why the value of this concept is vastly overrated. Of course, its popularity and its emphasis on the rights of future generations bring us to tricky ethical questions. One of these is the question how far we have obligations to future generations. It is widely asserted that we have, and I believe that this is true in some sense. But it is not as simple a matter as is usually supposed. The problem of why we have obligations to future generations, if any, and what form they take, is discussed at some length in Part II, together with the question of how to make future costs and benefits comparable with those that may have to be incurred today in order to implement a particular environmental policy.

The conclusion of all this is that while it is quite right that we should continually seek to improve and implement policies that give *due* attention to the environment in particular, and to the interests of future generations in general, we should not be panicked into drastic action that would impose unnecessary burdens on the poorest sections of the present generation. The "posh" global environmental issues that capture the headlines are not those that concern, or that ought to concern, the vast majority of the world's population. They are not even the concerns that should be given top priority by the citizens of affluent countries. They should not be ignored, but we have time to think.

We also have time to continue with serious research into a wide variety of genuine environmental problems, such as those mentioned above. Of course, serious thought, careful study, and balanced appraisal of the evidence is not as much fun as going around making apocalyptic prophecies of imminent doom if we do not repent and abandon our wicked ways and our desire for increased material prosperity. It does not ensure reverential respect for the nobility of one's sentiments. But, if we are genuinely concerned with adopting a balanced approach to the impact of the environment on the future welfare of the human race, it is this in the long run that is our best bet.

PART I

THE CHOICE OF PRIORITIES

1. Whose Growth? Whose Environment?

Changing Concerns in the Environmental Debate

In my 1974 book I gave detailed figures to show the improvements that had taken place in the quality of life of most people in developed countries, notably in their environments, their health, and their living and working conditions. I also showed that the widespread fears concerning the exhaustion of mineral and other nonrenewable resources were groundless. In my characteristically naive and simple-minded way I had hoped that the book's publication would effectively put an end to the debate about the conflict between economic growth and the environment. The weight of the detailed evidence and the arguments I presented in favor of economic growth seemed to me to be so overwhelming that no objective reader could fail to be convinced. Alas, my hopes were not fulfilled.

However, while the environmental debate has persisted—albeit with fluctuating intensity—it has changed its character in some important respects. First, with some exceptions, the environmental pressure groups do not simply attack the objective of economic growth. They have shifted their ground and advocate replacing it by the goal of "sustainable development." But while many environmentalists may have muted their hostility to economic growth they by no means have abandoned it. The leading environmentalist Jonathan Porritt has recently written that ". . . in the current state of the planet, the idea that economic growth is necessarily and automatically a good idea is no longer tenable."[1]

A second change in the character of the debate—and a further reason for its persistence—has been the change in the character of the environmental threat facing us. The environmental concerns that were in the forefront of the debate in the advanced countries in the early 1970s were relatively local (though serious) issues, such as pollution of rivers, or of beaches as a result of discharges from the rivers or neighboring urban conglomerations, or poor air quality in towns and cities. These problems were important, but it seemed to many—including me—that excessive pollution of this kind was a relatively straightforward matter of the misallocation of resources at a given point in time. The economic principles governing the corrective measures needed, therefore, seemed to be familiar in principle, though raising difficult problems in practice.

I also underestimated the reluctance of most governments to embark on the appropriate measures to deal with these forms of mainly local pollution. Hence, although there has been progress in many cases, local environments are often still excessively polluted, even in relatively wealthy countries. Of course, this no more constitutes an argument against economic growth today than it did 20 years ago. Bringing growth to a halt is the last thing that would encourage governments to spend more money on environmental protection.

In the last decade or so, however, environmental issues of a more global character have come to the forefront of attention. Until relatively recently the impact of the human race on the physical environment was trivial by comparison with large natural changes in ecosystems. But this impact now seems to be becoming significant. It is true that in the early 1970s some concern was also expressed over international environmental problems, notably acid rain, ocean pollution from oil tankers, or depletion of certain fish stocks. But acid rain has increased in many parts of the world, and other global problems, such as climate change, or deforestation, or the threat of species extinction—including threats to species, such as whales, that are rightly valued by many people for more than their economic value—have also become much more serious recently and hence have figured prominently in the growth-versus-environment debate.

The Threefold Conflict of Interest

The Intergenerational Conflict

The emergence of global issues, particularly those whose effects will be felt in the more distant future, has meant that there is a major conflict of interest today between present and future generations. As a result, one of the main differences between the growth-versus-environment debates of the early 1970s and today is our increased awareness that we must sort out our moral intuitions about what we owe to future generations. In the early 1970s the ethical problem

14

of our obligations to future generations had not been been given much attention. However, during the last decade or so a few economists and philosophers have tried to fill this gap in their analysis of the relevant environmental issues.

It would be difficult enough to find an equitable balance between the interests of present and future generations even if each generation could be regarded as being, within itself, more or less homogeneous and sharing common concerns and preferences. But this is not the case. There are also major conflicts of interest between different groups within each generation. Thus the tradeoff may not be between, say, rich people in a hundred years' time and less rich people today. It may be between rich people in 100 years' time and poor—or even destitute—people today. For it may be the world's poorest people who would have to bear the burden of any major sacrifice made today in the interests of posterity. And how rich will posterity be?

It is impossible to predict very confidently how much more prosperous future generations will be, because it is not possible to predict very confidently how far the average world growth rate of the last few decades will be maintained. One can think of various reasons why it may slow down. On the other hand, there are three strong reasons to believe that it may speed up:

(i) The mainspring of growth is technological progress, which depends, in turn, on scientific and technological research and development. And since the proportion of the population in most countries receiving education in general and higher education in particular is rising, as is the quantity of resources worldwide devoted to scientific and technical research, this constitutes a powerful force in favor of faster economic growth.

(ii) Another new factor on the scene is the recent emergence of dynamic economies in Asia and some Latin American countries. Freed of dogmatic adherence to anti-market-oriented policies these economies have been "taking off" at a remarkable rate, and the spillover effects of fast growth in China and other Asian countries, as well as of economic reform in most other hitherto "planned" economies in the world is certain to be favorable.

(iii) World population growth is slowing down. This means that it is becoming easier to raise capital per head without raising the share of resources devoted to investment.

15

In the light of all these factors it seems most unlikely that the average world growth rate will slow down significantly. Indeed it seems more likely that it will speed up. And over the period 1950 to 1985 the average per capita gross national product of the world as a whole rose by 2.1 percent per annum. A very conservative assumption therefore would be that, in the longer-run future, it may rise by only, say, 1.5 percent per annum. This would mean that per capita income levels in 100 years' time would be 4.4 times as great as they are now! And, as will be shown in Chapter 6, it has been estimated that, if nothing is done to stop it, global warming would cut the average income level in 100 years' time by about 1 or 2 percent. Suppose this is a grossly optimistic estimate, and that climate change reduces the future income level by as much as, say, 10 percent. This would mean that, instead of being 4.4 times as rich as we are today, the population around the year 2100 would be only 4 times as rich. How much sacrifice should we impose on current generations in order to avoid this eventuality?

Some of us can, no doubt, easily make some sacrifice and would be willing to do so—even if it is not clear why. But some groups in society are not in a position to make any sacrifice. As will be shown in detail in Chapters 2 and 3, the most acute environmental problems today are those in the Third World, and it is those countries whose prospects would be most damaged by any prolonged failure to achieve steady economic growth in the more affluent countries.

Conflicting Interests within Any Society

In fact, the importance of the conflict of interest between different groups within any given society at the same point in time is one feature of the growth-versus-environment debate that has not changed much in the 20 years since my earlier book was published. Different interests in the growth-versus-environment debate still correspond closely to differences in relative incomes. The alleged conflict between economic growth and the environment often reflects a conflict between the interests of the rich and of the poor. Surveys of how far members of the Sierra Club—one of the oldest of all environmental pressure groups in the United States—were concerned with the interests of future generations showed not only that this concern was ". . . decidedly urban and upper-middle class in its composition," and that ". . . its membership has clearly indicated in surveys (60 percent in agreement) a complete disinterest in the environmental problems of the urban poor or disadvantaged ethnic majorities in non-urban settings." One study concluded: "The environmentalist movement is a rich man's cause. . . . The Club of Rome discovered the limits to growth while gathered on the terrace of a villa overlooking the hillside belonging to its founder."[2]

Many of the middle-class concerns with some aspects of the way that economic growth was harming their particular environment were brilliantly formulated in Mishan's justly famous 1967 book.[3] Environmental pollution was only one. Others were congestion of travel facilities and holiday resorts. And there were less tangible effects, such as the subordination of nobler social values to the pursuit of materialist objectives and the consequent deterioration in society's moral standards.

It is true that for the more affluent groups in society economic growth brought some deterioration in certain components of their standards of living. Economic growth means change, and when the world changes some people tend to lose out. Servants tend to get uppity, or even difficult to get at all. And what were once the favorite holiday resorts of the middle classes—the Bahamas, Greek islands, Italian hill towns, and so on—were being transformed by the millions of less affluent tourists on cheap package holidays.

Of course, all the newer classes of tourist were much better off as a result of the changes that allowed them to travel to such places, and the local inhabitants were also much better off. And presumably it became less congested in the holiday resorts back home where the working classes had previously been forced to spend such holidays as they could afford. But the middle classes deplored the destruction of picturesque untouched villages abroad, quaint native customs, and empty beaches. To the middle classes in the advanced countries, therefore, it might well appear that, on balance, economic growth was bad for their welfare. (The really rich did not mind, of course. On their private yachts or personal estates or remote islands they were immune to the changes taking place in what had hitherto been the preserve of the middle classes. And they could still afford the domestic servants.)

In fact even in the advanced countries it was never clear that the conflict between economic growth and the environment was on the agenda for most of the population. The vast majority of the working classes in the developed countries appreciated only too well the benefits of the improvements in their living standards that techno-logical advance could bring. For them the washing machines and automobiles that some environmental groups affected to despise represented a release from drudgery and an opening up of mobility. And the virtual elimination of malnutrition and many fatal diseases associated with poverty in the advanced countries undoubtedly made a major contribution to the welfare of most of the working population in these countries. Insofar as this section of the population was concerned with the environment at all, it was their inadequate housing, or the dirty, noisy, and dangerous conditions in which many of them worked, that they worried about. But the noise levels or safety precautions in factories never have appeared in the lists of environmental concerns that are prominent in the environmentalist literature, and improvements in these aspects of the environment have been obtained largely by pressure from trade unions.

By the end of the 1960s, almost all the most prominent components of the environment in the more advanced countries were improving, as I show in detail in Chapter 3. These and other changes in Britain and some other countries were, of course, partly the result of chang-ing social and economic conditions that both raised environmental concern in the hierarchy of priorities of the population in advanced countries and increased the means available to deal with the environ-ment.[4] Without economic growth, the environments in most of the Western world would have remained as bad as they had been in the 19th century and as bad as the environments that were—and are still—found in most of the poor cities of the world. And as I shall show in Chapter 3, the favorable effect of economic growth on the environment is not limited to what are now the developed countries of the world. There is overwhelming statistical evidence of the favorable effect of higher income levels on those ingredients of the environment that are now of most importance to the developing countries—namely access to clean water supply, sanitation, and the urban environment in general.

The International Conflict of Interest

One manifestation of the widespread concern with the impact of economic growth on the environment in the early 1970s was the UN World Conference on the Environment in Stockholm in 1972. But at this conference the developing countries made it perfectly clear that development was given greater priority in their objectives and policies than preservation of the environment. In countries where most of the population were worried about where the next square meal was coming from, the level of sulphur dioxide concentration in the atmosphere in Pittsburgh or the level of carbon monoxide and nitrous oxides in Tokyo—let alone the concentration of carbon dioxide in the atmosphere in the year 2050—was of little importance. Slowing down economic growth in the interest of protecting the environment might appear to be a worthy cause to the more affluent groups in the rich countries but was certainly not on the agenda of the developing countries.

Today, the conflict of interest between rich and poor countries is probably still the predominant real conflict of interest. There has been rapid population growth in the Third World, often accompanied by a race for industrialization that has paid no attention to environmental consequences. As a result the most acute environmental problems facing the world's population today are in the Third World. They are the scarcity of access to safe drinking water and sanitation, or urban squalor and degradation in most cities in developing countries. True, some advocates of the concept of "sustainable development" make passing reference to the need to take account of the problems—environmental and other—of the poorer countries for whom economic growth is an absolute necessity.[5] But it is not these problems that are in the forefront of Green publicity. The main reason for this, according to Andrew Kenny, is that "the Greens need environmental scares as arms manufacturers need wars. A scare must satisfy two essential requirements. The first is financial: it must attract funding. The second is ideological: it must demonstrate the evil of modern industry."[6] As he proceeded to explain, the worst threat to the environment arises largely from poverty in the Third World, but "this is of no interest to the Greens. It satisfies neither requirement."

As the UN *Human Development Report 1991* put it, "The Third World's environmental priorities can be different from those of the industrial countries. . . . These differences have two implications for the international community. The first is to recognize that the way to save the environment is to tackle poverty. Developing countries do not need lectures on the global commons. They need the resources to finance environmentally sound development."[7]

19

Unfortunately, it is not the environmental concerns of the developing countries that capture the headlines today or are quoted in order to scare the public into taking drastic action to reduce global warming, or to change radically our whole way of life and give up the vulgar pursuit of better standards of living. Calls, such as those of Edward Goldsmith, that "what we must aim for is not growth but negative growth, or economic and demographic contraction,"[8] may go down well with sections of the population who do not desperately need further growth, or who are on the lookout for what may appear to be new noble causes to espouse, but they are hardly likely to be appreciated by the poverty-stricken masses in developing countries. As Nobel Laureate Robert Solow put it: "Once you think about sustainability, you are almost forced logically to think about equity, not between periods of time but equity right now. There is something inconsistent about people who profess to be terribly concerned about the welfare of future generations but do not seem to be terribly concerned about the welfare of people today. The only reason for thinking that sustainability is a problem is that you think that some people are likely to be shortchanged, namely in the future. Then I think you are obligated to ask whether anybody is being shortchanged right now."[9]

Do We Need a New Approach?

It may well be true, as Jonathan Porritt has said, that "Politically, the world is too far gone. It is not a question of nearing the abyss. We daily look down into it if we choose to open our eyes, and millions are already at the bottom of it."[10] But the present awful state of the world is not, as he suggests, mainly the result of economic growth and its accompanying environmental degradation. It is not environmental change that has been responsible for vicious and brutal civil war in what was Yugoslavia, or the murderous communal strife that is endemic on the Indian subcontinent, or the bitter ideological struggles that have ravaged Cambodia for decades, or tribal conflict in Rwanda, Somalia, and the Sudan.

Nor is it likely to be the case—as many environmentalist pressure groups would have us believe—that we need to abandon our basic assumptions, or change our modes of thought and vocabularies, or accept different cultural values.[11] What is really needed is good old reliance on scientific standards of logic and research. This means that we have to accept the enormous complexity and difficulty of the problems facing the world today. This is the only way we can arrive at balanced solutions involving compromises between conflicting objectives. Many people dislike this prospect. They prefer simple answers and melodramatic appeals. But there are no simple answers. And simple answers like "Stop economic growth," or "Incur any cost in order to stop any risk of climate change or preserve every single existing species," are of no more help than vague appeals that we should change our vocabulary or our modes of thought. Existing modes of thought will do very well. What is needed is that we use them.

Most criticisms of economic growth not only contain errors of logic or fact. They are also divorced from political reality. Even if it could be demonstrated that economic growth does not lead to a rise in welfare, it would still not follow that we should try to bring growth to a halt. For, in the absence of some transformation in human attitudes, the like of which has never been seen in spite of constant admonitions by powerful religions for thousands of years, human nature has not yet abandoned the goal of increased prosperity. To some people this goal is a denial of holiness. But to others it is a testament of the infinite variety of the human spirit. And to some it is an opportunity to rid the world of poverty and drudgery. This means that if growth were to be abandoned as an objective of policy, democracy too would have to be abandoned. And, as the experience of the 1980s has demonstrated, even totalitarian regimes cannot, in the end, survive if they fail to deliver the increase in living standards to which their populations aspire.

But, as I shall show in later chapters, there is no conflict between economic growth and an improved quality of life. In the long run economic growth is the surest—and probably the only—route to a general improvement in the quality of life and in the environment. But the compatibility between economic growth and "development," defined more widely and with due respect for the environment, will not be achieved automatically. It depends on the adoption of appropriate policies. The necessary policies are often complex and expensive, and in some cases they will involve the cooperation of a large number of countries with conflicting interests. When it comes to reaching agreement on rational policies for the whole human race, comprising nearly 200 nations with conflicting pressure

21

groups within each nation, not to mention a conflict of interests between present and future generations, the notion that there can be some simple answer is totally fatuous.

Melodramatic appeals to a total revolution in people's aspirations of the kind that have been the stock-in-trade of evangelical prophets of imminent doom throughout the ages are usually based on warnings that we shall otherwise be doomed to imminent disaster on account of the "greenhouse effect" or some other global environmental catastrophe. We are warned that, unless governments implement draconian measures without delay we are threatening the existence of future generations. But if the world's policymakers were to believe these prophecies and take hasty and drastic action to insure against the threatened environmental catastrophes, it would make it more difficult to devote time, energy, and resources to tackling the more serious environmental problems in advanced countries, not to mention the far more acute environmental problems facing billions of people in the Third World. For there are limits to the amount of aid that the richer countries are prepared to extend to the developing countries, not to mention the amount of energy and attention that will be devoted to environmental issues in general.

On account of the widespread hysteria over the alleged imminent effects of global warming, a group of 226 distinguished members of the scientific and intellectual community, including 52 Nobel Prize winners, presented a petition—known as the "Appel de Heidelberg"—to the heads of state attending the Rio summit in June 1992. In this they stated:

> We are . . . worried, at the dawn of the twenty-first century, at the emergence of an irrational ideology which is opposed to scientific and industrial progress and impedes economic and social development. . . . We fully subscribe to the objectives of a scientific ecology for the universe whose resources must be taken stock of, monitored and preserved. But we herewith demand that this stock-taking, monitoring and preservation be founded on scientific criteria and not on irrational preconceptions. . . . We intend to assert science's responsibility and duties toward society as a whole. We do however forwarn the authorities in charge of our planet's destiny against decisions which are supported by pseudo-scientific arguments or false and non-relevant data. . . . The greatest evils which stalk our Earth are ignorance and oppression, and not Science, Technology and Industry whose instruments, when adequately managed, are

indispensable tools of a future shaped by Humanity, by itself and for itself, overcoming major problems like overpopulation, starving and worldwide diseases.[12]

I welcome this, and other, appeals by eminent scientists to eschew some of the pseudo-scientific environmental scare stories that proliferate. But I am a mere economist, and I must stick to what economists are best at. This includes emphasizing that all-or-nothing solutions to problems of choice are very rarely rational. The whole problem is to bring out into the open the difficulties of identifying clearly, in the environmental field, which objectives may conflict and what are the facts concerning the tradeoffs between them. The conflicts that are relevant here are conflicts between the interests of different generations, between different claims on our resources, and between different groups in society, including different nations. If we can begin to see more clearly which conflicts are real and which are fictitious we can move toward a greater balance between our genuine objectives.

However, I cannot claim to have attempted here to write a fully balanced book. In the Preface to my 1974 book, I wrote:

> As the title indicates, this book is not an attempt to present a survey of all the pros and cons of economic growth. The prosecution case has been put to the public over and over again in numerous forms; here I want to put the case for the defence—at least as I see it. I did not want to write a balanced *book*, for what is needed is a balanced *debate*, and so far the field has been occupied largely by the anti-growth cohorts. Some statement of the case for the defence will go some way to restore the balance of the discussion.

I believe that, with minor amendments, this position is as valid today as it was 20 years ago. True, the environmental debate now is less an attack on economic growth than a call for drastic action to save the Earth from ecological disaster. But what I wrote in 1974 about the balance of the debate still holds good. The public is exhorted to support a policy of "sustainable development," which is frequently presented as requiring us to stop using up nonrenewable resources or to take expensive steps to cut carbon dioxide emissions. This one-sided and oversimplified presentation of the problem needs to be balanced by a presentation of a different point of view. As one sympathetic reviewer of a recent pro-environmental economics book put it:

> The really worrying thing is that the presumption seems to be that because green economists are on the side of the angels with regard to the global environmental crisis (which I for one am convinced they are) it is not necessary to be accurate, or to work out careful, rigorous arguments; all that is necessary is to come out of the corner with fists flying, secure in the knowledge that since you are against the destruction of the planet, anyone who disagrees with you is likely to be not just wrong but villainous with it.[13]

I know that for some time I have been widely regarded by many environmentalists as a terrible villain, but in this book I have attempted to control my natural instinct just to hit back. I appreciate that for some readers it may be less fun following careful argumentation if it is not enlivened from time to time by a good slanging match. But I hope that these readers will not be put off by this warning. For I can assure them that my attempts to control my natural instincts rarely succeed.

2. Poverty and the Environment in the Third World

"Needs" and Welfare in Developing Countries[1]

In the richer countries of the world it is at least understandable that important sections of the community should question whether priority should be given to further increases in the output of goods and services. But for the vast majority of the world's population it does not require much imagination or knowledge of their terrible poverty to rule out the question of whether further economic growth is desirable for them. Nevertheless it is often argued that the developing countries should not make the same "mistakes" as were made by the now advanced countries. They are advised not to pursue economic growth in spite of its adverse social or environmental effects, and not to fall into the trap of "rising expectations." Furthermore, we often hear that if the developing countries seek to achieve standards of living comparable with those now enjoyed by the advanced countries there simply will not be enough resources to go round.

One conclusion that might appear to follow from these pessimistic doctrines is that, because the rich countries of the world can hardly be expected to reduce their levels of material prosperity, the poor countries must not be encouraged to believe that they too can aspire to such levels of prosperity. They must therefore accustom themselves to the idea of giving priority to environmental preservation rather than economic growth. Of course, it is bad luck for them that the point at which economic growth has to stop should just have arrived near the end of the 20th century, when other countries have already achieved a certain affluence but before they have had the opportunity to do likewise themselves.

This view, not surprisingly, has always been rejected by the developing countries. As far back as 1972, the so-called "Founex report," drawn up by a group of experts convened by the United Nations to prepare a report on Development and the Environment for the

1972 UN World Conference on the Human Environment, pointed out that, although "the developing countries would clearly wish to avoid, as far as is feasible, the mistakes and distortions that have characterized the patterns of development of the industrialized countries . . . the major environmental problems of developing countries are essentially of a different kind: they are predominantly problems that reflect the poverty and very lack of development of their societies. They are problems, in other words, of both rural and urban poverty. In both the towns and in the countryside, not merely the 'quality of life' but life itself is endangered by poor water, housing, sanitation and nutrition, by sickness and disease."[2]

Though the truth of these statements was clear to anybody who had direct contact with environmental conditions in developing countries, they were not as well documented in 1972 as they are today. In the intervening years the state of the environment has moved up sharply in the hierarchy of concerns in national and international bodies. One of the side effects has been the vast increase in our knowledge of the state of the environment in the Third World. Hence it is now possible to document this in a manner that was not previously possible. And the evidence overwhelmingly confirms the general picture painted by the experts who wrote the Founex report quoted above. This chapter is devoted to surveying some of this evidence.

The environmental conditions in most of the Third World are now particularly well documented in sources produced by various international agencies, such as the World Health Organization, the Global Environmental Monitóring System, and the World Bank. For example, the World Bank's *World Development Report 1992: Development and the Environment* provides an authoritative survey of the relationship between economic development and the environment. In this chapter, therefore, we shall be concerned mainly with establishing two simple facts. These are (i) that poverty is usually the worst enemy of the environment, and (ii) that the ingredients of the environment that are of vital interest to the billions of people living in developing countries are not the ones that are most in the public eye, such as global warming or the depletion of the ozone layer or the demise of the bald eagle. They are lack of clean drinking water and sanitation, and poor air quality in the big cities.

In the next chapter we shall survey the statistical relationship between economic growth, as conventionally measured, and these particular environmental media, as well as longer-run historical data on how the environment has changed over the last century or more in advanced countries and the relationship to human welfare. In short, the message of this chapter and the next is that if you want a better environment in general and, in particular, reasonable access to clean drinking water, adequate sanitation, and an acceptable urban air quality, you have to become rich.

This does not mean that, for the world as a whole, or for future generations, other ingredients of the environment—such as biodiversity, soil erosion, deforestation or global pollution of the atmosphere or the oceans—are considered unimportant. Nor does it mean that other facets of economic "development" defined more widely and including, for example, equality or political freedom, are unimportant. It is simply that (i) the environmental problems selected here are crucial in developing countries, and (ii) they can be reasonably well captured by statistical data. If the scope of the enquiry is extended to the other variables or to wider concepts of economic development, the problems of data and their interpretation become formidable and can only be tackled in the context of a major long-range research project.

The Overall Situation

Water Supply, Sanitation, and Health

Although gaps in the data rule out calculations, it is possible to obtain some idea of the overall situation, particularly as regards access to safe drinking water and reasonable sanitation arrangements. Three points can be firmly established.

First, water supply and sanitation are still a major problem. At least a billion people in developing countries have no access to safe drinking water, and at least two billion have no access to proper sanitation.[3] Other estimates put the numbers without safe drinking water or sanitation much higher.

Second, the reason is partly that although during the 1980s water supply was provided for an extra 730 million or so people in developing countries, and sanitation for an extra 400 million, this was barely enough to keep pace with the increase in population in these countries. Indeed, if we include rural areas, the number of people without satisfactory sanitation in developing countries rose by about 400 million in the 1980s. Given the expected future growth of population,

---

BOX 2.1 - WATER SUPPLIES AND DISEASE
IN DEVELOPING COUNTRIES

Surveys by international experts show that between one and
one-and-a-half billion people are affected in some way by
water-related diseases—notably schistosomiasis, hookworm,
diarrhea, ascariasis, guinea worm, and trachoma.[6] And infant
mortality alone from diarrhea, which has a strong relationship
to clean water supplies and sanitation facilities, is reckoned to
be about 5 million per annum.[7] For example, in Algeria, where
the relationship between water-related disease and the degradation of water supplies is well documented, about a third of
all infant deaths are attributed to diarrhea. In fact in the areas
most affected by worsening water supplies water-related diseases account for about three quarters of all reported sickness.[8]
In Pakistan, nearly half of infant deaths are attributed to the
same cause. And it is not only children who are at severe risk
from diarrhea. For example, in Bangladesh diarrheal diseases
also account for about one in five deaths in all age groups over
five years.[9]

---

by the year 2000 there could still be well over a billion people without
adequate water supply and more than twice as many without sanitation, chiefly in Africa and Asia.[4]

Third, because the rise in population was fastest in the urban
areas it is in these areas that the absolute number of people lacking
in water supply or sanitation has risen most. During the 1980s an
extra 90 million or so people were without access to safe drinking
water in urban areas and an extra 210 million were without satisfactory sanitation. And some estimates suggest that the absolute levels
of deprivation are even greater than those given above.[5] But whatever the precise figures, they do not change the conclusions either
about the scale of the problem or about the failure of the increase
in supply of both drinking water and sanitation to do more than keep
pace with the population increase, particularly in the urban areas.

The serious welfare effects on developing countries of inadequate water and/or sanitation supplies are indisputable—in spite of much uncertainty concerning the precise relationship between water supplies and health. True, the relationship between the diseases concerned and water supply is far from simple, and numerous other variables are usually implicated. For example, it is well known that personal and domestic hygiene, access to health care, and other factors—above all adequate nutrition—will influence the vulnerability of any group to diseases associated with water supplies. On the other hand, these estimates of the incidence of the disease probably understate the true incidence, because hardly any countries have an incentive to institute large-scale reporting systems for morbidity, and a large amount of disease no doubt goes unreported and is not identified in any surveys.

An adequate supply of clean drinking water, or of water suitable for sanitation purposes, is not always a sufficient condition for immunity to water-related diseases, but it is almost certainly a necessary condition in most situations. Thus, for example, a recent study of Bangladesh found that although other variables, particularly malnutrition, were partly responsible for infant mortality from diarrhea, projects designed to improve water supplies in rural areas led to a cut of about 50 percent in the incidence of diarrhea among children, as well as a reduction by about one third in the incidence of ascariasis.[10] Similarly, inadequate sewage and water supply has been found to be the primary cause of the rising infant mortality rates in Sao Paulo in the 1960s. But there is also evidence of the role of the other variables, as in Indonesia, where it is reported that such reduction as has taken place in mortality rates "cannot be attributed to water supply and sanitation but to improved health services, primary health care programs, and use of oral rehydration agents."[11]

Air Pollution

Similar conclusions can be drawn concerning air quality in developing countries. One of the best known cases is, of course, Sao Paulo, where by the early 1970s air pollution had become so severe that there were noticeable increases in mortality. There was even worse air pollution in Cubatao, resulting from a combination of the mix of industries located there and unfavorable meteorological conditions.[12]

Unfortunately, there is no simple and reliable way of measuring air pollution that corresponds closely with the extent to which it reduces welfare. For example, ideally we would like to take account of the number of people exposed to it (and also of the duration of their exposure). For a foul smell on some totally isolated and uninhabited remote island caused by rotting vegetation would have no welfare significance at all. Like sin, pollution requires victims.[13]

Furthermore, once we try to allow for the degree of human exposure to air pollution we have to account for indoor air pollution, partly because sometimes this is far worse than outdoor air pollution and partly because most people spend much of their time indoors.[14] In the more advanced countries there are important indoor pollutants such as are emitted from certain types of gas appliances and cooking stoves, from various furnishings and household cleaning products, or are introduced, or aggravated, by air conditioning, ventilation, or heating systems in modern buildings.

But in most developing countries severe indoor air pollution is caused by the pollution-intensive character of traditional cooking and heating techniques (notably reliance on biomass fuels, such as wood, agricultural waste, or dung).[15] Hence, inhabitants of developing countries account for about 88 percent of total human exposure to "SPM" (roughly speaking, dirt, soot, smoke), or over seven times that accounted for by developed countries.[16] This is believed to be partly responsible for the fact that more than 5 million children die every year from acute respiratory illness that is most prevalent in rural areas of developing countries.[17] This is about as many as the number of children who die every year from diarrhea on account partly of inadequate water and sanitation services.[18]

Furthermore, as I show in Chapter 3, outdoor air pollution tends to be either worse in developing countries or increasing or both, whereas in developed countries it tends to be either better or at least decreasing, or both. If allowance is also made for the difference between indoor air pollution in developing and developed countries we cannot escape the conclusion that "for some important pollutants, urban ambient air pollution appears to be inversely related to income. In other words, poorer cities have more air pollution, in part because of the coexistence of modern and traditional pollution sources, that is, household and neighbourhood use of dirty solid fuels such as wood and coal combined with high-emission industrial and vehicular sources. This interaction exemplifies 'risk overlap,' which can occur during the transition from traditional to modern risk that is inherent to economic development."[19]

30

Rapid urbanization, increasing numbers of vehicles, plus the particular pollution-intensive character of most vehicles in developing countries mentioned above, mean that as well as experiencing the growth of air pollution experienced in the past in what are now advanced countries, the fast-growing cities there are also suffering from acute vehicle-based air pollution. For example, according to a World Bank report, "Urban air pollution in Thailand, especially with regard to diesel particulates, is already quite acute and is reaching chronic levels . . . carbon monoxide and ambient lead levels periodically exceed internationally accepted limits." In Indonesia: "The combination of densely congested traffic, poor vehicle maintenance, and large numbers of diesel vehicles and two-stroke engined (smoky) motorcycles has contributed to elevated air pollution levels in Jakarta and other large urban centers." In the Philippines "it appears that particulate, lead, carbon monoxide, and possibly ozone levels exceed internationally accepted standards. . . . Motor vehicles are estimated to account for approximately 50 percent of particulates, 99 percent of carbon monoxide, 90 percent of hydrocarbons, and 5 percent of sulphur dioxide."

In other words, at an early stage in their development cities in some countries may get the worst of both worlds. On the one hand, their old-fashioned machinery and techniques and industrial structures make them highly pollution-intensive and, on the other, economic growth brings with it newer forms of pollution—particularly those associated with the automobile and with urban congestion and waste disposal—before they have adequately reduced their exposure to the more traditional pollutants.

The Poverty-Environment Nexus

Economic development can damage the environment in so many well-known ways that it would be superfluous to enumerate them here. We hardly need to spell out the poisoning of the air and rivers from industrial effluent that took place in the past in what are now advanced countries, and the urban air pollution that is still taking place in some of them and in most developing countries. But these harmful effects of economic growth are often inextricably mixed with local favorable effects, so that a net balance is difficult to strike.

For example, poverty has contributed to deforestation in various countries, notably in Thailand, the Philippines, and Brazil. But in the same countries modernization of agricultural techniques sometimes causes further environmental degradation. This is the case, for example, with *caboclo* agriculture in the Amazon region, which is a traditional form of agriculture that respects the need for sustainability and regeneration. But when the farmers are supplied with credits to buy powerful machinery, chemical inputs, and so on, the longer-term sustainability of the areas in question tends to be destroyed.[20] And numerous other instances of the same process can be found all over the world. However, in these and other cases it is often difficult to distinguish between the effect of low incomes per se on environmental damage and the effect of rising population.

Urbanization

This distinction is particularly difficult to make in the analysis of urbanization, which is one of the most striking mechanisms by which economic growth contributes to environmental degradation. This is as much, if not more, the result of population growth as of a rise in incomes per head, although the ultimate sources of the population growth may well be found in the dynamics of the incomes-population relationship. For a rise in incomes per head usually leads to a rapid population growth for a period, during which mortality rates are declining, and is then followed by a much slower population growth when birth rates also begin to decline significantly.

Of course, the net effect on welfare of fast urbanization is not a simple matter. On the one hand, people migrate to the cities presumably because they believe they will be better off as a result; on the other, their arrival in the cities may reduce the welfare of people already in the cities. Migrants will move into the cities when the benefits they expect to obtain themselves exceed what they perceive as the costs to themselves of moving. They will not take account of adverse effects on the existing inhabitants of the cities any more than automobile drivers take account of the costs imposed on others by their decision to drive into town. And it is clear that the rapid inflow of migrants imposes strains on the capacity of recipient cities to meet the fast-rising needs for housing, waste management, sewerage, and water supply, not to mention the more indirect effects on air quality and other aspects of the environment.[21]

The pace of urbanization in developing countries is much faster than in developed countries. And until very recently it was accelerating, whereas in developed countries it was slowing down.[22] In 1985

8 of the 12 cities with 10 million or more inhabitants were in developing countries, and it is expected that, by the year 2000, there will be about 23 cities of that size, of which 17 will be in developing countries.[23]

BOX 2.2 - THE CASE OF SAO PAULO

Sao Paulo, according to a World Bank report, is a clear example of the price paid by rapid growth and industrialization. "Water pollution in Sao Paulo, as elsewhere, is the result of a combination of increasing industrial effluents and raw domestic sewage discharged into local rivers and other water bodies. Air pollution, in turn, is associated with the rapidly growing number of motor vehicles and the emission of a variety of substances by industrial sources." The same report adds: "Although water and air pollution are probably the most serious urban environmental problems . . . they are by no means the only ones. Other areas of concern are solid waste—including hazardous industrial and nonindustrial waste collection, storage and/or disposal, and frequently associated soil and subsoil contamination, stormwater drainage, and related phenomena such as flooding, erosion, and land or mudslides, as well as noise pollution."[24]

Rapid urbanization has many effects. In most countries they include poor housing conditions, inability to handle waste disposal, contaminated water supplies, and effects particular to individual cities. For example, in Thailand they are reported to include contaminated food and recurrent floods (worsened by land sinking from the digging of deep industrial wells and construction of new building). In fact, land subsidence caused by falling groundwater levels is a common feature of many fast-growing areas.

Poverty, Urbanization, and Automotive Air Pollution

Paradoxically, even the role of the automobile in adding to air pollution in fast-growing cities is an illustration of the poverty-environmental degradation nexus. For in addition to fast-growing

33

populations and vehicle numbers, low incomes are associated with less stringent measures to reduce the pollution generated by automobiles. Whereas most rich countries have been able to cope, up to a point, with the growth of automobile numbers by means of successively more stringent, albeit expensive, measures to reduce pollution emissions, this is not the case in developing countries.

A recent World Bank report states: "Motor vehicles in many developing countries are not as fuel efficient as in industrialized countries. Many of the vehicles are old and poorly maintained because of lack of spare parts and other resources. For example, in India a major portion of the vehicle fleet is older than 10 years. Two-stroke engine motocycles are also a major source of air contaminants. Moreover, the gasoline used in most developing countries still has a high percentage of lead."[25]

In Mexico City the number of automobiles rose from 680,000 in 1970 to 2.6 million in 1989, and the Mexican government estimates that fewer than half the vehicles are fitted with even modest pollution control devices.[26] "Virtually none are equipped with state-of-the-art exhaust treatment systems. Only recently has unleaded gasoline become available. The lead content of leaded gasoline was lowered during 1986 and 1987, but there are indications that it has increased since then. . . . In addition, more than 40 percent of the cars are more than 12 years old, and of these, most have engines in need of major repairs."[27] It is estimated that motor vehicles are responsible for more than 80 percent of all air pollution in Mexico City, about 75 percent of all air pollution in Sao Paulo, about 70 percent of all air pollution in Tunis, and no doubt similar levels in cities in most other developing countries.[28]

Similarly, poor vehicle maintenance and a large number of two-stroke motorcycles are shown to contribute to high air-pollution levels in Indonesia, and in the Philippines poor-quality fuel (notably with high sulphur and lead content) is singled out as a principal cause of high urban air pollution.[29] In Bangkok the costs of switching to less lead- and sulphur-intensive fuels, together with the administrative difficulties of monitoring compliance with more stringent standards in a situation in which vehicle numbers have risen rapidly, have been quoted as additional obstacles to any substantial reduction in pollution from motor vehicles.

Poverty and Non-Sustainability

In addition to the generally favorable relationship between higher incomes and the environment, particularly as regards water supply and sanitation, as well as air quality, there are, of course, numerous particular instances of the way that low incomes cause environmental degradation. Mention has already been made of one of the most common instances: namely, the poverty-deforestation-poverty cycle, as in the case of Thailand described in Box 2.3.

BOX 2.3 - DEFORESTATION AND POVERTY IN
THAILAND

According to one authoritative report, in Thailand, "Poverty and deforestation are locked in a vicious circle of mutual reinforcement."[30] A typical sequence is where poverty and lack of any other employment alternative drives people to cut down trees and cultivate the land, often with damaging longer-term effects on either soil productivity or water supplies, or both. It is also reported that "Landless and small-scale farmers, among others, encroach on forest reserves in search of a better livelihood. They either clear the land themselves usually following legal or illegal loggers, or they purchase the land from influential persons who claim control over large areas of forest reserves. During the first few years after encroachment, crop yields are relatively high because of the nutrients in the slashed-and-burned forestland. Once these nutrients are exhausted yields begin to drop. . . . Except in areas where off-farm employment is abundant, farmers sooner or later are forced by declining productivity to move deeper into the forest in search of new, more productive land."[31] The harmful effects of deforestation in Thailand had become so serious by 1989 that the Thai government banned commercial logging activities, though it is reported that the ban is difficult to enforce.[32]

As in Thailand, and some other countries, deforestation in Brazil is partly caused by "push" from landless peasants, for whom "migration is basically motivated by the possibility of accumulating wealth (and, with luck, becoming a landowner) through the clearing of lands in a frontier area where property rights are still undefined."[33] But it also has been partly exacerbated by government policies, such as road construction, tax exemptions, fiscal and credit subsidies for investment programs, and so on. This was probably the main force behind the rapid pace of "frontier settlement" and its associated deforestation.

Poverty does not contribute to deforestation only in rural areas, or only as a result of the search for short-term cultivatable land. Deforestation also can be caused by the consumption of biomass fuels in low-income situations, even in urban areas. Furthermore, the inverse relationship between income levels and the use of biomass for fuels is apparently reversible, and consumers have switched from modern fuels back to biomass when incomes fell. "For example, in sub-Saharan Africa, woodfuel demand grew by 3.1 percent per capita annually from 1975–85 while real gross domestic product (GDP) per person fell by 1.8 percent each year."[34]

Deforestation, then, is caused partly, if not largely, by poverty—aggravated in some cases by policies. Then, in turn, it can make poverty even worse. In the longer run it destroys a valuable source of income from timber, or leads to soil erosion and/or reduction in local water supplies. For example, in the Philippines it is reported that "A major external or indirect consequence of forest degradation on sloping lands is an increase in soil erosion.... The costs of soil erosion include upstream (on-farm) and downstream components. The former can be measured as the decline in the productivity of the soil as nutrients are lost and structural properties such as moisture retention are degraded. The latter includes the future reductions in agricultural and industrial production...."[35]

And the role of deforestation in the poverty-environmental degradation-poverty cycle is not confined to direct effects of this nature. It also can take the form of reducing easy access to water supplies with consequent increase in the time taken—invariably by the women in the community—to fetch water for domestic purposes. This then, in turn, reduces such time as they have available for alternative activities, whether marketable or not, or domestic activities that help sustain the health of their families. For example, in a study of Nepal it was reported that as a result of "rampant environmental degradation including deforestation, in areas where growth is stagnant . . . in the long run, water from forest streams becomes more scarce and is replaced by water from more distant or contaminated rivers and ponds."[36]

Numerous studies have reported the long periods that women in rural communities in developing countries often have to spend fetching water, with consequent aggravation of their poverty if their water supply is threatened by environmental degradation, as well as by other causes of a breakdown in their main water supply systems.[37]

Another such poverty-environment-poverty cycle is often found in coastal areas, such as those in the Philippines where "Like the uplands, coastal and near-shore fisheries are a public resource, the open-access nature of which has attracted the most impoverished elements from adjacent agricultural and coastal areas and induced them to use nonsustainable extraction techniques. Destruction of coastal mangrove forests opens interior areas to increased typhoon damage, creating a backward linkage." A similar vicious circle in the Philippines is reported to affect the million or so poor people employed in the fishing industry, who tend to fish beyond the sustainable yield. This is needed in order to reduce pressure to clear forests, especially in upland areas, or to overfish limited water resources.

In short, a principal cause of many forms of environmental degradation is the combination of rising population with a lack of ways of making a living other than those that degrade the environment. Most developing countries share the problem of, say, the Philippines, of which it is reported that "Improved management of natural resources requires an attack on underlying causes of degradation and depletion, specifically excessive population growth and poverty, which are the main sources of migratory 'push' into the uplands and coastal areas. . . . A strong program to reduce population growth rates . . . and measures to create jobs for unemployed and underemployed rural residents . . . will be crucial to the long-run prospects for reducing the rate of environmental degradation."[38]

This emphasis on population growth raises important questions concerning the mix of population and incomes per head in determining environmental pressures. Slower population growth usually permits both (a) less burden on environmental resources and (b) a faster growth of incomes per head. Insofar as the latter appears in the longer run to lead to improvements in the environment, slower population growth makes a double contribution to reduction in the danger of environmental degradation. However, the whole population-environment nexus lies outside the scope of this book.

Conclusions

The conclusion from the above is, first, that in developing countries there is no conflict between growth and the "quality of life." Economic growth is essential in order to preserve life and to remedy some of the worst features of the environment from which these countries suffer. In the next chapter I shall show that the favorable and positive relationship between income levels and the most important features of the environment as far as most of the world's population is concerned holds more generally over time and space.

But, even if there were a conflict between growth and the environment, there is no reason why poor countries should choose between them in the same way as rich countries. The "tradeoff" between the two is likely to be very different in countries where economic output is much smaller than in more affluent countries. Rational choice depends not only on one's basic preferences between goods and services of the conventional kind, on the one hand, and environmental quality, on the other; it depends also on how much of each one has.

Poorer people will naturally have a greater incentive to give priority to more goods and services rather than to the environment in general. In the same way poor countries, in which a large proportion of the population may be constantly preoccupied with the problem of obtaining enough to eat, would be foolish to make heavy sacrifices of economic progress in the longer-term interests even of their own environment, let alone of the world in general. A man who is not sure how to provide the next meal for his family is hardly likely to worry much about the problems of posterity. In fact the notion that the developing nations would be well advised to benefit from the lessons of the advanced countries, and be chary of putting economic growth before the preservation of the environment, displays an appalling degree of insensitivity to the real problems of these countries.

Finally, it should not be thought that the developed countries ought to grow more slowly in order to leave resources available for the growth of the developing countries. Growth of the former is essential to provide the expanding markets for the products of the latter. Nothing has done more harm to the exports of the primary producers, for example, than the marked slowing down of the pace of economic growth in the industrialized countries of the world since the early 1970s.

For various reasons, therefore, the concern for the developing countries that takes the form of advising them not to make the mistake of pursuing the vain illusion of raising welfare by means of economic growth, particularly when this may even damage their environment, is a concern that the developing countries can do without. Of all the forms of bad advice on development that the poorer countries have had to put up with over the last 30 years or more, this is about the worst. It is just as well that nobody would have taken any notice of it anyway.

3. Income Levels and the Environment

Introduction

Nobody can deny that human activity had been imposing a strain on the environment even before the industrial revolution. The local environment was often severely damaged by overgrazing or destruction of tree cover in many parts of the world. But the scale of environmental damage was negligible compared with what followed from the expansion of the world population and the accompanying growth of economic activity.

Nevertheless this does not mean that rising income levels are inevitably and at all times and in all circumstances associated with a deterioration in the environment. For society has a capacity to react to events. For example, when the sanitary conditions in English cities became intolerable during the middle of the nineteenth century, pressures built up to do something about them and these pressures led to a substantial improvement over the subsequent decades. Or when, in the early 1950s, some British cities were afflicted with terrible smogs leading to the deaths of thousands of people (not to mention the closing down of a famous opera house for a few days because the singers could only be seen in the front few rows!) public opinion forced the government to take effective action.

And during the last two decades most of the advanced economies in the world have implemented policies—some less effectively than others—to deal with their local pollution problems. There even have been successful conclusions of international agreements to deal with certain forms of international pollution, such as oil "spillages" at sea, or the phasing-out of emissions of the chlorofluorocarbons (CFCs) that are believed to damage the ozone layer.[1] It is all a matter of what policies are adopted, and the evidence suggests that increasing affluence is the best route to the adoption of policies that protect the environment.

This chapter will therefore begin with an attempt to put the environmental conditions experienced in advanced countries today into some sort of long-term historical perspective. This will be followed by a brief survey of the relationship between income levels and the three specific environmental media—clean drinking water, sanitation, and urban air quality—which, as shown in the last chapter, are among the most important components of human welfare in the 75 percent of the world's population that live in developing countries. It will be shown that when we focus on these particular features of the environment it remains true that increasing economic prosperity is still the best route to an improvement in these components of human welfare.

The Environment in Historical Perspective

One of the reasons for the currently popular view that economic growth has been accompanied by a decline in welfare is the lack of historical perspective. It is true that in the absence of appropriate policies of environmental protection economic growth may bring with it environmental damage of one kind or another. People are very conscious, for example, of the noise from motorways or jet planes, or how beaches are fouled as a result of inadequate sewage discharges or oil spillages at sea, or of landscape blight caused by industrial development in one way or another, and so on. And no doubt tougher policies to protect the environment in all forms should be implemented. For reasons well known to economists, there is a presumption that, on the whole, the environment will be "used up" more than is socially desirable, in the absence of special policies, so that there is no cause for complacency. Nevertheless, few people realize how bad the environment was in the past in what are now advanced countries and how great an improvement in the environment has taken place.

For example, it is fashionable nowadays to complain about air pollution caused by automobiles in congested urban areas, such as in Central London or New York. But when Chateaubriand was taking up his post at the French Embassy in London in 1822 he wrote: "At Blackheath, a common frequented by highwaymen, I found a newly built village. Soon I saw before me the immense skullcap of smoke which covers the city of London. Plunging into the gulf of black mist, as if into one of the mouths of Tartarus, and crossing the whole town, whose streets I recognized, I arrived at the Embassy in Portland Place."[2] A few decades later it was reported:

"The space bounded by Oxford Street, Portland Place, New Road, Tottenham Court Road, is one vast cesspool, the sewers being so imperfectly constructed that their contents are almost always stagnant.... Now when the reader reflects that thousands of working men are closely confined, for perhaps 14 or 15 hours out of the 24, in a room in which the offensive effluvium of some cesspool is mingling with the atmosphere ... he will cease to wonder at the amount of disease...."[3]

More generally, the conditions in London in the mid-nineteenth century have been described in all their horrifying detail in the classic works of Dr. Hector Gavin, notably in his *Sanitary Ramblings* (in which he described the environmental conditions in every street in Bethnal Green, as typical of the condition of the metropolis and other large towns). Almost any page of this work contains descriptions such as the following: "Pleasant Row ... Immediately facing Pleasant Row is a ditch, filled with slimy mud and putrefying filth, which extends 100 feet. The space between Pleasant Row and the central square, is beyond description, filthy; dung-heaps and putrefying garbage, refuse, and manure, fill up the horrid place, which is covered with slimy fetid mud. The east end has likewise its horrid filthy fetid gutter reeking with pestilential effluvia; the southern alley is likewise abominably filthy.... I entered one of these houses on the southern side, and found that every individual in a family of seven had been attacked with fever ... the privy of this house is close to it, and is full and overflowing, covering the yard with its putrescent filth."[4]

It is hardly surprising that deaths from typhus alone in England in the mid-nineteenth century were nearly 20,000 a year, and that 60,000 deaths a year were attributed to tuberculosis, not to mention high death rates from numerous other diseases associated with unhealthy living conditions.[5] Nor were conditions in London by any means unique. Inquiries carried out by the Health of Towns Association into the sanitary conditions in the other main cities and towns produced a more or less uniform picture: "Bolton—very bad indeed; Bristol—decidedly bad; the mortality is very great; Hull—some parts as bad as can be conceived; many districts very filthy; with a few exceptions, the town and coast drainage extremely bad; great overcrowding, and want of ventilation generally."[6] The only places today where such conditions can be found are in the poorer districts of many large cities in relatively low-income countries, such as Calcutta, Manila, Mexico City, and Sao Paulo.

Income Levels and Environmental Quality Today

The General Relationship

The main reason for expecting economic growth to be good for the environment, in the longer run, as well as bad for it in specific instances and particular time periods, hardly needs elaboration. It is the only possible interpretation of the evidence. A casual glance at the state of the environment in the principal towns and cities of the world shows that the environment that matters most to human beings—notably access to water and sanitation, housing, social infrastructure and absence of the more traditional types of air pollution such as sulfur dioxide (SO_2) and smoke—is much better in the richer countries than in the poorer. And although the data are more fragmentary, the disparity between the environments in developed and developing countries is even greater in rural areas.

The reason is obvious. As people get richer their priorities change and the environment moves up in the hierarchy of human needs. When their basic needs for food, water, clothing, and shelter are satisfied they can begin to attach importance to other ingredients in total welfare, including, eventually, the environment. As public perceptions and concerns move in the environmental direction, so communities will be more willing to allocate resources to this purpose. And this shift in expenditure priorities is easier insofar as richer countries will be more able to afford them.

For example, United States public and private expenditures on pollution abatement and control (PAC) represent nearly 2 percent of the gross national product (GNP), which is a higher share than for any other country for which comparative data are available. And the share is still rising.[7] These expenditures rose in the United States at an average annual rate of 3.2 percent over the period 1972–1987, when total real GNP rose by 2.6 percent.[8] The only other country for which comparable data are available for any length of time is Germany, where, too, total private and public PAC expenditures rose (at constant prices) at an annual average rate of 3.4 percent during the period 1975–1985, raising the share of these expenditures in GNP from 1.37 percent to 1.52 percent. In Japan, data are available for a long run of years for pollution control expenditures only in the public sector, and these show an average annual rise (at constant prices) from 1975 through 1986 of 6.1 percent, which outstripped even Japan's fast rate of growth and so raised the share of these expenditures in GNP from 0.95 percent to 1.17 percent.

These increases in expenditures have done more than just keep pace with the increasing burden that, in principle, higher levels of economic activity can impose on the environment. This is partly because the pattern of output in advanced countries has been changing in a direction that tends to impose less of a burden on the environment than was the case at earlier stages of their development. At higher levels of income industry accounts for a smaller share of gross domestic product (GDP), whereas services—which are relatively nonpolluting—account for an increasing share. Even within industry there has tended to be a shift away from the highly polluting heavy industries, such as metallurgy and heavy engineering, toward high-tech, high value-added industries employing large amounts of very skilled human capital and with smaller inputs of energy or raw materials.[9] In addition, policies to combat pollution have, of course, been introduced mainly in richer countries, because they have the resources to implement their shift in priorities. As a result—as is shown in detail in the next three sections of this chapter— higher incomes are clearly associated with improvements in the environment as far as the most important traditional and ubiquitous pollutants are concerned (which are, of course, those for which there are comparable statistics).

Water and Income Levels

I have shown in the last chapter that, in developing countries, which are conventionally defined in such a way that they incorporate 75 percent of the world's population, by far the most urgent environmental problem is water—access to clean drinking water in particular. And there is clear evidence that access to clean drinking water in different countries is closely related to average income levels.

Figure 3.1 shows the percentage of the population with access to safe drinking water in countries with different income levels in 1975 and 1985.[10] Countries have been ranked in order of their incomes per head, and those containing the 20 percent of the population with the lowest income per head have been put at the left, with successive groups to the right representing countries with higher

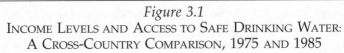

Figure 3.1
INCOME LEVELS AND ACCESS TO SAFE DRINKING WATER:
A CROSS-COUNTRY COMPARISON, 1975 AND 1985

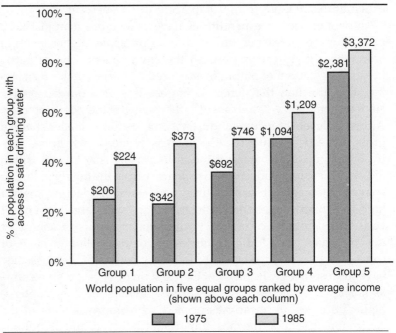

Source: W. Beckerman, *Economic Development and the Environment*

incomes per head. The average income in each group is shown at the top of the column for each group. The height of the column represents the percentage of the population that had access to safe drinking water.

As can be seen, in 1975 the bottom 20 percent of the world's population had an average income of $206. Only about a fifth had access to safe drinking water. At the other end of the scale, among the top 20 percent of the population, who had an average income of $2,381 per annum in 1975, almost 80 percent had access to safe drinking water. In short, as we should expect, higher incomes tend to be associated with a higher proportion of the population having access to safe drinking water. There has also been some progress in almost all countries over the period 1975–1985, in spite of the rapid growth of the population of most developing countries during this

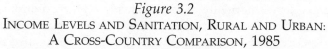

Figure 3.2
INCOME LEVELS AND SANITATION, RURAL AND URBAN:
A CROSS-COUNTRY COMPARISON, 1985

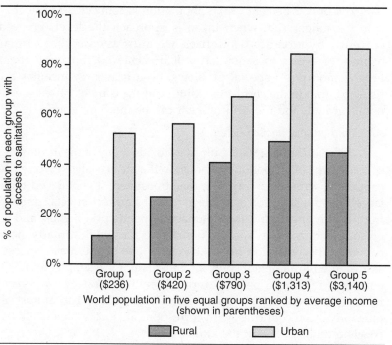

Source: W. Beckerman, *Economic Development and the Environment*

period. The relationship between income levels and access to safe drinking water is unambiguous. If you want to increase the proportion of the population with access to clean drinking water, get richer.

Although satisfactory sewerage and sanitation arrangements are more difficult to define and, hence, to represent in a simple number, *Figure 3.2* also confirms what we should expect, namely that an increase in incomes is the best way of increasing access to the sanitation facilities that most people in advanced countries would take for granted as normal attributes of a minimum standard of living. Of course in many countries the pace of urbanization has meant that sanitation and waste disposal arrangements have been totally unable to cope with the additional demands and bring the services up to the levels normally associated with even medium-income-level countries. For example, even in Thailand, where the growth of prosperity has been remarkably sustained, it is estimated that in Bangkok only 2 percent of the population is connected to sewers.

In the longer run, when incomes approach the levels enjoyed currently by advanced countries, we must assume that similar degrees of access to sanitation will be achieved. But very rapid urbanization poses special problems, even if average incomes are rising, so that in the short-to-medium run the conflict between economic growth and the environment can be more pronounced.

Air Pollution and Income Levels

(i) *Sulphur Dioxide (SO$_2$).* Sulphur dioxide is one of the most widespread forms of air pollution known in the industrialized world. By combining with water vapor in the atmosphere it is believed to be largely responsible for a whole range of harmful effects, ranging from health effects and local damage to paintwork, metals, and so on to acid rain and suspected damage to forests. But in advanced countries the reduction in SO$_2$ has been one of the major success stories in environmental control.[11] In Britain, for example, total SO$_2$ emissions fell by 25 percent during the 1970s, and by 40 percent relative to GNP. Similar results have been obtained in almost all other advanced countries, with corresponding improvements in the concentrations of SO$_2$ in the atmosphere.

Indeed if the major cities of the world are put into three groups according to the income levels of the countries in which they are located—low-income, medium-income, and high-income—we find a clear change over the last decade or so in the way their income levels are related to their concentrations of SO$_2$. Around the late 1970s the SO$_2$ levels were higher in the higher-income countries, reflecting their greater degree of industrialization. But about 10 years later the position had been reversed. This corresponded to a decline in SO$_2$ concentrations of about 8.9 percent per annum in the high-income countries and a rise of about 3.7 percent in the low-income countries. Taking all the 33 cities covered in the data on SO$_2$ ambient air quality produced by the UN Global Environmental Monitoring Service (GEMS) "27 have downward (at least 3 percent per year) or stationary trends and 6 have upward trends (at least 3 percent per year) with most improvements noted in cities of developed countries."[12]

48

(ii) SPM or Smoke. A similar story is found in the trends of suspended particulate matter (SPM) and smoke. Of the 37 cities covered in the GEMS data, the concentrations of SPMs and smoke in the air were following downward trends in 19, were more or less stationary in 12, and showed upward trends in only 6. But it is in the richer countries that SPM concentrations have fallen.[13] And, for those cities for which adequate data are available it is also clear that cities in low-income countries had ambient concentrations of SPM or smoke that were much higher than in the richer countries. Furthermore, measured by the number of days on which the World Health Office guidelines for SPM or smoke were exceeded during the course of the year, the preponderance of cities in developing countries is overwhelming.[14]

(iii) NO_x and CO. The picture is slightly more confused when we turn to two other pollutants, carbon monoxide (CO) and nitrous oxides (NO_xs), because emissions of these, particularly CO, are heavily influenced by the automobile—both the number of automobiles and the speeds at which they are able to circulate.[15] Furthermore, the limitations on intercity comparability of measures of these pollutants are particularly severe. Hence, in terms of ambient air concentrations of, say, NO_xs, "cities of the developing and developed countries are found at both ends of the concentration range . . . some of the lowest NO_2 values are reported from the two Indian cities Bombay and New Delhi, presumably because traffic levels are relatively low."[16]

Nevertheless, some overall difference can be observed between cities in poor and rich countries. For example, although there are some exceptions—notably London, Frankfurt, and Amsterdam—trends in ambient NO_2 concentrations in most other cities in developed countries are now stable or declining, in spite of sustained increases in automobile numbers. By contrast, the trends are generally rising in cities in developing countries.[17] The picture is roughly the same for CO ambient concentrations. Data are only available for cities in eleven countries, and CO concentrations are declining in all of them. With one exception—Santiago—the cities are all in high-income countries. By contrast, fragmentary data for a few individual cities in developing countries confirm the rise in concentrations of these pollutants.

(iv) Lead. Another highly publicized pollutant is lead in gasoline. In recent years almost all industrialized countries have taken effective measures of one kind or another to reduce lead emissions from automobiles, often with striking results. For example, the total quantity of lead used in gasoline in the United States was cut from 170,000 tons in 1975 to 40,000 tons in 1984, and Japan has made even greater progress. By contrast, "Few developing countries have yet made significant reductions in petrol lead content. . . ."[18] There have been no falls, or negligible falls, in lead levels in petrol in Africa and South and Central America and the Caribbean, whereas there has been a big fall in Europe and North America, and quite a big fall in Asia, even without taking account of the consumption of unleaded petrol in these countries.[19]

In general, therefore, although we cannot say precisely how overall "air quality" should be defined, or at exactly what level further increases in incomes lead to improvements in air quality, it is fairly clear that it does so sooner or later. How much sooner or later—that is, at what point in time or level of income—urban air conditions reach a state when effective policies are introduced will depend on a host of variables, including technical, social and political variables. It is not surprising, therefore, that the record of individual countries shows a reversal in the trend in the traditional pollutants (SO_2 and SPM or smoke) at very different stages in their history. In Britain, for which country data on these two basic pollutants go back several decades, a considerable improvement began in the late 1950s.[20]

In the United States the reversal of trends in emissions of the main pollutants, which were closely followed by trends in concentrations, took place in the early 1970s. One exception to this was SPMs, emissions of which reached a peak in about 1950 and fell off rapidly in the following two decades, largely as a result of rising incomes combined with changes in technology that led to a major switch from the use of coal for residential heating. Thus, the controls introduced in the early 1970s greatly accelerated an existing downward trend.

The Role of Policy

This last point illustrates the role of policy in shaping the precise relationship between economic growth and environmental pollution. In the longer run higher incomes are clearly associated with improved environments, but the transition period may be a long and painful one, during which the environment can seriously deteriorate. How long and painful the transition period is, depends largely on the policies pursued by governments, but partly on other variables. Changes in the pattern of output, or in the technical relationships between specific economic activities and their environmental impacts, have played a major part. But changes in social structures, political pressures, public awareness and, above all, the resulting policies adopted by the authorities have also been important.

However, policies do not emerge in a vacuum independently of accompanying economic and social conditions. The former are often very dependent on the latter. The stringent air pollution controls probably would not have been introduced in Britain in the 1950s, even after the notorious "killer" smog of 1952 in London, had not other factors led to a shift to more efficient forms of heating in many homes and to the virtual disappearance of cheap domestic service.[21] In the same way, the absence of democracy in the Soviet bloc was no doubt largely responsible for the failure of the authorities to worry much about the environment. What mattered was the achievement of the planned production targets. The welfare of the citizens was of minor importance.

At the same time, the above data show that a country's environmental priorities depend largely on its income level. In the past, when income levels were much lower than they are today, developing countries did not worry much about pollution. In the early 1970s, for example, countries such as Brazil and Algeria were in the forefront of the opposition to the then newly emerging shift of emphasis—in the richer countries—away from economic growth in favor of more care for its environmental effects. At the World Environment Conference in Stockholm in 1972 Brazil made it clear that it intended to continue to industrialize without concern for environmental problems. But conditions in cities such as Sao Paulo were already becoming almost intolerable, and within a few years there was a major shift in policy in the direction of environmental protection.[22] By the mid-1980s, even though industrial production and vehicle numbers were still rising in the Sao Paulo area, the main air pollutants were falling.[23] A similar position was adopted by Algeria at the 1972 conference, and Algeria was late in signing various international treaties designed to reduce pollution of the

Mediterranean Sea. Algeria, too, soon began to show more concern with the environment, but not until the late 1970s.[24]

Air pollution from road transport provides a striking example of the way policies determine the incidence of any particular form of pollution. The severity of this problem in the fast-growing cities of developing countries has been mentioned already. By contrast, the largest reductions in automotive pollutants have been achieved in Japan, Germany, and the United States as a result of their relatively early introduction of stringent controls on motor vehicles. There has been a move in this direction in most Western European countries, although in some cases the policies adopted so far seem to have been offset by increases in the number of vehicles.[25] Similar regulatory measures also have been introduced recently in some developing countries, but so far, with one or two exceptions, not with much effect, and, as discussed earlier, this is largely the result of their generally lower ability to afford, or monitor, the required policy changes.[26]

Differences in policy priorities would not matter quite so much, of course, if environmental policy were purely a national or local concern. But some policy issues have international implications, notably those designed to deal with threats to "the global commons." This phenomenon is not entirely new, because international action to tackle transnational environmental problems goes back many decades (if not centuries, if action to combat the spread of cholera is included). And even if the developing countries themselves do not see climate change as posing a sufficient threat in the medium run to justify their devoting large resources to reducing their emissions of "greenhouse gases," the greatest potential for reducing the otherwise inevitable increase in greenhouse gas emissions that will take place in the future lies in the developing countries. This is because of their future population growth and their current low levels of per capita energy consumption compared with those of the developed countries. By contrast the developed countries have the resources to take effective action to moderate global warming, but less incentive to do so. This is chiefly because of the relatively small impact of global warming on their economies, given the small share of agriculture in their national products. It will be extremely difficult, therefore, to reach international agreement on measures to deal with such global issues.[27] This is all the more reason not to divert vast resources of time and energy in an attempt to cobble together some hastily contrived agreement until the alleged threat of climate change is more thoroughly considered. Chapters 6 and 7 of this book sketch out some of the major questions that have to be raised in any discussion of the global warming threat.

4. The Problem of Finite Resources, or How We Managed without Beckermonium

The Fallacy of "Finite" Resources

Resources are either finite or they are not. If they are, the only way to ensure they last forever is to stop using them. Stopping economic growth is not enough. Levels of consumption would have to be reduced to infinitesimal levels if finite resources were to be made to last forever. But of course even the most fanatical proponents of "sustainability" would hardly go that far. They would soon sell a critical pass by confessing that, maybe, after due reflection, taking everything into account—etc., etc., etc., blah, blah, blah—the human race eventually would find ways of coping with the changes in the balance between demand and supply of resources that take place.

In other words, we cannot have it both ways. Either resources are finite in some meaningful sense, in which case even zero growth will fail to save us in the long run, or resources are not really finite in any meaningful sense, in which case the argument for slowing down growth collapses. In *The Limits to Growth* this dilemma was avoided by cutting off the computer printout at the year it becomes clear that even their proposed stationary state still would be untenable on account of exhaustion of what they assume to be a finite supply of resources.

But suppose, for the sake of the argument, we take leave of our senses and, in spite of the evidence produced in the rest of this chapter, we still believe that, one day, economic activity will stop growing and start shrinking on account of a limitation on resources. What are the implications? Do we decide that it would be better to give up some output now in order to have more in the distant future—which is what the eco-doomsters urge us to do? There are at least three reasons why this is not obviously the right choice to make.

First, which is preferable—that 10 million families should be better off over the next 100 years, or that 100 families should be better off over the next 10 million years? How much of the former are we prepared to sacrifice for an uncertain chance of the latter? And why stop at zero growth now? Why not cut output? After all, what is so special about the figure "zero"? Why not slow down growth to 1 percent per annum, or to minus 2.2 percent? The more you cut output the longer the finite resources will last. Does the figure "zero" have some mystical attraction for the eco-doomsters?

Second, the choice also depends on the *probability* that failure to slow down growth will lead to an exhaustion of resources in the future. If we could be *certain* that maintenance of current growth rates would lead to a sudden and general exhaustion of resources, then it might be reasonable for society to sacrifice some rise in living standards for generations alive today in order to spare future generations a sudden and catastrophic fall in their living standards. But if the risk of such an eventuality is very low, it would be irrational for society to do so. In the rest of this chapter I show why the risks are in fact negligible, and probably nonexistent.

Third, much depends on exactly when the catastrophe is expected to occur. There is little point in saying that the increasing use of resources must, *someday*, come up against finite supplies unless we know roughly when this will happen. How useful is a forecast that it is going to rain "someday"? In other words, if we believed that there was a serious risk of running up against resource limitations in the lifetime of our children or grandchildren, then we might be worried and prepared to do something about it. But if the limit is to be reached in 100 million years, we might not feel personally involved in the problems of the people alive at that time, and we might well assume that some way out of the difficulty would have been found by then. After all, when we ponder on the fantastic technological progress that has been made in the last 20 or 50 years, the mind boggles at the progress that will be made over the next 100 million years. Tautologies about finite resources, therefore, although they are apt to be triumphantly repeated over and over again by eco-doomsters, are really not much help in the decisionmaking process.

Of course, the eco-doomsters have always maintained that resources are being used up so fast that the day when their scarcity will be a serious constraint on economic activity is not far off. This is usually demonstrated by comparing existing "known" reserves of most mineral resources with the rate at which they are being used up. But predictions based on this method are nothing new and they always prove to have been unfounded. As I show in this chapter, they are based on a total misunderstanding of the statistics on reserves of resources and of the economic mechanisms that are set in motion when any resource becomes scarce.

How Fast, If at All, Are Finite Resources Being Used Up?

The Recent Past

Back in 1972, one of the pioneering critics of economic growth, Ed Mishan, wrote: "And though in the constructs of economists there are always substitute resources waiting to be used whenever the price of an existing resource begins to rise, there is no knowing yet what, if anything, will substitute for a range of such apparently essential metals—lead, mercury, zinc, silver, gold, platinum, copper, tungsten—that will become increasingly scarce before the end of the century."[1] The same theme—namely, that the models and assumptions made by economists fail to take account of lack of substitutes for nonrenewable resources—is still often echoed by eco-doomsters.

One of the latest "finite resources" fairy tales is the story of photosynthesis. Lester Brown, who is president of the environmentalist Worldwatch Institute in Washington, D.C., and who warned us about the imminent world food shortages about 20 years ago—before the accumulation of food surpluses had begun to create serious problems for international trade—has recently warned us: "The photosynthetic product of the planet has been declining slowly for some time now, although probably at an accelerating rate." And he goes on to say: "Question: Can the economic product of the planet continue to rise if the photosynthetic product continues to decline? The answer: No. If the photosynthetic product continues to decline, eventually there will not be enough biochemical energy to support even the life of this room. That is not a debatable point."[2] In a recent lecture Sir Crispin Tickell, chairman of a newly created panel to advise the British government on sustainable development, echoed this fear when he said that "few realize the extent to which we have been appropriating the resources of the earth for our own purposes. Already we use—or abuse—some 40 percent of total photosynthetic production on land. Even so most economists (not so much dismal as half-witted) still work in concepts which take little or no account of these factors."[3]

Now, half-witted we economists well may be, but nobody can accuse us of being dismal pessimists, at least as far as photosynthesis is concerned, or as far as I, for one, am concerned. As explained in Box 4.1, the photosynthesis scare story is so absurd that when, just to make sure, I rather shyly consulted one of my eminent scientist colleagues in Oxford about it he burst out laughing and expressed surprise that I had bothered even to take notice of such an idea.

As for the more common fear that we shall run out of non-renewable mineral resources, Dr. Mishan's 1972 warning that we might approach exhaustion of some key materials by the end of the century was apparently backed up by the famous 1972 report to the Club of Rome, *The Limits to Growth*. This study, which contained an impressive display of computer printouts and diagrams to give an air of scientific precision and authenticity, dazzled many people who ought to have known better.[4] For example, it inspired the Bishop of Kingston to publish an article in one of the quality Sunday newspapers in which he said, "The computer is adding precision to what used to be regarded as mere prophecy by cranky ecologists."[5] Why a bishop should have so little respect for "mere prophecy" is an interesting question, particularly in this context. After all, in addition to his other achievements, it was the prophet Elisha who cleared up one of the earliest recorded instances of pollution, namely the polluted waters of the city of Jericho, some 3,000 years ago.[6]

A major conclusion of this study is that, at current rates of consumption, the world would shortly run out of supplies of many key minerals. As can be seen in Box 4.2, the predictions of that study, like those of Dr. Mishan, have been decisively refuted. The table in Box 4.2 compares the 1970 estimates of reserves of key metals and primary fuels as given in *The Limits to Growth* with the 1989 figures and the estimates of how much of the metals in question had been consumed in the 19 years that had elapsed.[7] It can be seen that the 1989 reserves are much greater than those reported in 1970, for all the items covered, in spite of the fact that cumulative consumption

BOX 4.1 - THE PHOTOSYNTHESIS FAIRY TALE

Photosynthesis is the process by which plants absorb carbon from the carbon dioxide (CO_2) in the atmosphere as part of the mechanism by which they grow. The amount of photosynthesis taking place, therefore, depends on how much vegetation there is and how much CO_2 there is in the atmosphere. If there is less vegetation—for example, because land that had been covered by carbon-absorbing vegetation has been converted for other purposes, such as for building cities or motorways—then there will be less photosynthesis. But this just would have reflected a fall in the "demand" for it from vegetation. Insofar as some, or most, of the vegetation that has been destroyed to make way for other uses of land had not been used for human consumption in one way or another, it must of course be true that the proportion of total photosynthetic product that was "appropriated for our own purposes" will have risen. But this is no cause for concern. It simply means that a lot of the photosynthetic product that previously had been produced was of no use to us. It was, in effect, wasted. Now there is less of it. So what? Would it be better if 99 percent of the total photosynthetic product had been of no use to the human race, as was the case a few centuries ago?

If the decline in the total amount of photosynthesis taking place had been caused by a shortage of carbon in the atmosphere, implying an increasing constraint on future plant growth, there might be cause for concern. But this is not the case. The concentration of carbon dioxide in the atmosphere is increasing. Indeed this increase is the basis for one of the most widespread eco-doomster scare stories: namely, that it will lead to catastrophic climate change. The real constraint on the growth of food from plants has been availability of good soil, irrigation, good agricultural techniques, civil wars, and so on. To argue that the slow decline in global synthetic product signals some sort of threat to our future is like arguing that because my energy use declines when I am on holiday I ought to worry about whether I shall come up against an energy constraint later on.

BOX 4.2 - HOW WE USED UP ALL THE RESOURCES
THAT WE HAD AND STILL FINISHED UP WITH MORE
THAN WE STARTED WITH[8]

| | Reserves (mn. metric tons unless otherwise stated) | | Cumulative consumption |
	1970	1989	1970–89[9]
Aluminum	1,170	4,918	232
Copper	308	560	176
Lead	91	125	99
Nickel	67	109	14
Zinc	123	295	118
Oil[10]	550	900	600
Natural Gas	250	900	250

For two of the items listed above, namely lead and oil, more was consumed in the period 1970–1989 than had been recorded in "known reserves" in 1970, so we ought to have run out of supplies already. Consumption of natural gas and zinc during the period 1970–1989 was also just about as great as the initial level of known reserves of these products, so as I am writing these lines we must be dipping into the last few grams of each. But surprise, surprise! For all these products we have more now in known reserves than we had when we started. Clearly, there must be something fishy about the definition of "known reserves" and some major flaws in the whole finite resources argument.

during the intervening years has been large relative to initial 1970 reserves.

There are other crushing refutations of the more recent predictions of the imminent exhaustion of nonrenewable resources. For example, in 1980, Paul Ehrlich, another of the more famous eco-doomsters, took on a well-publicized $1,000 bet with the economist Julian Simon that, by the end of the decade, five products of Ehrlich's choosing would have higher prices (reflecting increasing shortages). The five products chosen by Ehrlich were copper, chrome, tin, nickel, and tungsten. In the event, by the end of the decade the prices of all five products had fallen.[11] Some people may believe that Ehrlich was just unwise in his product selection. But, as Stephen Moore has shown, he would have lost the bet more or less whichever set of five products he had selected. Moore examined 33 major natural resources and found that, by the end of the 1980s, 33 showed a "real" (i.e., adjusted for general inflation) decline in price, and only two showed a rise. For 11 of the products the price fell by more than 50 percent.

As for the predictions of the other great anti-growth guru, E. F. Schumacher, they fare no better. In *Small Is Beautiful*, published in 1973, Schumacher argued that new oil discoveries and exploration could not keep pace with the rise in demand for oil, and that to maintain a ratio of reserves to annual consumption of only 20:1, which would be far less than the 40:1 ratio in the past, would require enough new discoveries to raise proved reserves to about 80 billion tons by 1980, an outcome that he described as looking "pretty fantastic."[12] In the event, the 1980 reserves were 88 billion tons, and by 1989 they had risen to 136 billion tons. Furthermore, far from falling from 40:1 to 20:1, the ratio of reserves to annual consumption figure had risen to 44:1![13]

The Longer-Run History

As Nobel Laureate Robert Solow put it, "The world has been exhausting its exhaustible resources since the first cave man chipped a flint, and I imagine the process will go on for a long, long time."[14] Nevertheless, prophecies of impending doom on account of the approaching exhaustion of raw materials have been common throughout the ages and go back at least as far as ancient Greece.[15] Imminent catastrophe unless we renounce our wicked ways has always been a popular theme. More than 100 years ago the great economist Stanley Jevons predicted an inevitable shortage of coal within a short space of time.[16] But, although coal demand has since increased far more than Jevons anticipated, known reserves of solid fuels are now estimated to be sufficient for at least another 400 years.[17] And how many people believe that in 400 years' time the world will still be using such a dirty and polluting fuel?

A study carried out in 1929 concluded that ". . . assuming a continuity of present techniques and a London price of 3 cents per pound, it is clear that the world's resources [of lead] cannot meet present demands." Sixty years later nobody is worried about lead shortage. In fact people are more worried that too much of it is around. The same 1929 report concluded that "the known resources of tin . . . do not seem to satisfy the ever increasing demand of the industrial nations for more than 10 years."[18] But more than 40 years later the authors of *The Limits to Growth* were worried because existing "known" reserves of tin were only enough to last for another 15 years. Still, that was better than in 1929 when they were only supposed to be enough to last us for 10 years. At this rate we shall have to wait millions of years before we have identified enough tin reserves to last us forever. Meanwhile we shall just have to go on using up that 10 years' supply that was all we had back in 1929.

Soon after the war the famous *Paley Report* was prepared in response to a fear in the United States concerning increasing scarcity of domestic mineral supplies. This report confirmed that domestic supplies would be inadequate, so that rising demand for increasingly scarce imported supplies would raise their prices in relation to the prices of manufactured goods and move the "terms of trade" against the industrial nations of the world. In the end, of course, nothing of the sort has happened; indeed, one of the main (justified) complaints of the underdeveloped countries has been that much of the aid they have received has been offset by a deterioration in their terms of trade.

The Meaning of "Known Reserves"

There are several reasons why the fear that growth will be brought to a fairly sudden halt on account of raw-material shortages is unfounded. One is that it is usually based on a misinterpretation of the published estimates of available reserves. Another is that it fails to recognize the many favorable feedback mechanisms in society for adjusting to changes in the supply and demand for materials; another is that it simply takes no account of the way these adjustment mechanisms have operated in the past.

As regards the former point, the usual estimates of known reserves of raw materials (namely those published by the U.S. Bureau of Mines) are conservative contingency forecasts by the exploration companies, and they are related to a certain price: if the price is higher, more resources can be exploited commercially. In other words, the known reserves represent the reserves that have been worth finding, given the price and the prospects of demand and the costs of exploration. Again, as I have pointed out already elsewhere, "the existence of only 50 years' supply of material X at current rates of utilization or 70 years' supply of some other material is no cause for concern, for the simple reason that there is rarely any point in companies' employing geologists to prospect for supplies to last mankind to the end of eternity. For example, is it seriously imagined that, if there were already 20,000 years of known reserves of copper, any geologist would be employed in looking for new copper supplies?"[19]

In the past, as existing reserves were gradually drawn on, it became profitable to seek for new ones and to develop techniques to exploit them. At no point is it worth prospecting for enough to last to the end of eternity, or even for some compromise period, such as 100 million years, or even 1,000 years. New reserves are found, on the whole, as they are needed, and, for reasons set out below, needs do not always rise exponentially at past rates. In fact, given the natural concentrations of the key metals in the earth's crust, as indicated by a large number of random samples, the total natural occurrence of most metals in the top mile of the earth's crust has been estimated to be about a million times as great as present known reserves.[20] Since the latter amount to about 100 years' supply this means we have enough to last about 100 million years. Even though it may be impossible at present to mine to a depth of one mile at every point in the earth's crust, by the time we reach the year AD 100,000,000 I am sure we will think up something.

And, as a matter of straight fact, it has usually been the case in the past that, however fast demand expanded and for however long, new mineral reserves were found (or some other painless corrective mechanism came into operation). And it is no answer to say that those of us who refuse to be alarmed have "overlooked" the fact that growth is "faster" than in the past, or that world demand is on a "much higher level" altogether, or to bandy about some other vague adjective. Even when true, which is not always the case, such propositions are irrelevant since they tell us only about the relation between the growth rate of some entity now and its growth rate in the past. They still tell us nothing about what we want to know, namely the relationship between the growth of demand for the product in question in the future and the growth of supply of it, also in the future.

The same sort of irrelevant proposition has been true in the past anyway, without being followed by exhaustion of supplies. For example, copper consumption rose about 40 times during the 19th century, and demand for copper was accelerating at the turn of the century from an annual growth rate of about 3.3 percent per annum, taking the average of the 19th century as a whole, to about 6.4 percent per annum during the period 1890–1910. Annual consumption had been about 16,000 tons in the first decade of the 19th century, and was over 700,000 tons in the first decade of the 20th. Given the rapid growth of consumption the "known" reserves of copper at almost any time in the 19th century would have been exhausted many times over by subsequent consumption if there had been no new discoveries. But at the end of the 19th century known reserves were bigger than at the beginning.[21]

And even in the postwar world, with what are believed to be unprecedented rates of economic growth, the story is the same. From the supply point of view, faster rates of economic growth have taken place precisely because of faster rates of growth of technical progress of all kinds and faster development of the basic resources required. Resources have still increased to match demand. For example, in 1945, estimated known copper reserves were 100 million metric tons. During the following 25 years of unprecedentedly fast economic growth 93 million metric tons were mined; so, if we accepted the eco-doomsters' sort of analysis, there should have been almost no copper left by the end of the period. But no, reserves were over 300 million tons, that is, three times what they were at the outset. The same applied to zinc, known reserves of which were 63 million tons in 1949; so it should all have been used up given that production of zinc during the fast-growth years up to 1970 amounted to 75 million tons. Instead, as shown in Box 4.2, reserves in 1970 were 123 million tons. Similarly, iron-ore reserves rose fivefold during the 1960s, and bauxite reserves rose sevenfold in the fast-growing 1950s and 1960s.

Favorable Feedback Effects of Material Shortages

One of the main flaws in the argument that economic growth should be slowed down or brought to a halt, because otherwise the

---

BOX 4.3 - TRENDS IN COSTS OF ALTERNATIVE
ENERGY SUPPLIES

The World Bank's *World Development Report 1992* states that
''. . . developments in renewable energy in the 1970s and
1980s—in solar, wind, and biomass energy, in particular—
have led to remarkable cost reductions in these technologies.''[22]
It goes on to show that the main obstacles to greater exploitation
of solar energy in the past—namely, their cost and the amount
of land required—are both declining in importance. Conver-
sion efficiencies have greatly increased and have reached a
point where, even if there were no further progress, less than
0.1 percent of these (developing) countries' land area would
be required to meet, in theory, the whole of their primary
energy requirements. Of particular interest is the dramatic fall
in the costs of photovoltaics, since this technology constitutes
a means by which solar energy can be stored and hence used
when wanted and not just when, or soon after, the sun has been
shining! The World Bank data show that the cost of electricity
generation from photovoltaics has fallen from nearly $10 per
kilowatt in 1970 to about 20 cents per kilowatt in 1990, and is
likely to fall to about 6 cents per kilowatt by the year 2020, at
which point, like other sources of electricity from solar energy,
it would be about the same cost as electricity produced from
natural gas or coal.[23]

---

limits to raw materials would be reached suddenly and with drastic
consequences, is that it fails to allow for the various feedback mechanisms at work in the economy. These have always tended to ensure
that supplies and demands are matched one way or another. This
may not always be achieved by finding new supplies, of course.
Sometimes a rise in price will act to slow down the growth of
demand, in which case there will also be a growth of substitutes
and economies in the use of the material in question. Oil may well
turn out to be a major example of this process.

Although there are enormous possibilities of finding new oil
reserves under the sea bed, or in vast unexplored areas of Russia

and the Far East, not to mention the enormous possibilities in the extraction of oil from tar sands (and shale)—and a single deposit (in Alberta) has been estimated to contain more oil than the whole of the oil reserves figure given in *The Limits to Growth*—there appears to be a fair measure of agreement among the experts that, *at present prices*, supplies would not increase to match demand much beyond the early part of the next century. But what are the implications of this? They are the same as for any product, material or otherwise, the supply of which at the initial price cannot keep pace with the rise in demand: *the price rises*. As this happens, the growth in world demand for oil will of course slow down. Less oil would be used for many purposes, such as heating and the production of electric power, for which there are increasingly economic substitutes, and there would be a stimulus to further development of alternative sources of energy supplies.

As I have written elsewhere: "It is true that if tomorrow the world were suddenly to wake up and find that there was no more oil or iron ore, as in some science fiction story in which some bug from outer space feeds on minerals or destroys all the vegetation and so on, we would be in a mess. But this sort of thing happens only in science fiction."[24] This is mainly because of the favorable economic feedback mechanisms—that is, the incentives to new exploration, recycling and use of substitutes—that would all be occurring gradually as the increasing scarcity of any product led to an upward trend in its price.

It is true that a cutback in demand in response to a rise in price will also correspond to a rise in the real costs to society of producing the material in question. That means that, other things being equal, economic growth would slow down. This situation has existed in the past. For example, over the ages, economic growth has often been limited by the exhaustion of timber resources in what, in the distant past, were the more developed parts of the world. But on the whole the "other things" do not remain equal, particularly in an era in which technological progress proceeds on such a wide front. And one of the favorable feedbacks in the economic system has been technical progress of the kind just described in connection with energy. Sometimes technical progress takes the form of progress in mining or exploration, so that new reserves have been found when needed, or lower-grade ores prove to be economically useful.

But it also often takes the form of the development of completely new materials, or new uses for old materials.[25]

As Professor Beckmann has pointed out, it is important not to confuse "nonrenewable" resources with "nonreplaceable" ones.[26] In particular the development of synthetic products and major technological breakthroughs of one kind or another have rendered obsolete some of the classic uses of many basic materials. Synthetic rubber is one of the best examples: it was produced in response to urgent needs, during the Second World War, as a substitute for natural rubber; for almost all purposes it is as good as natural rubber and for some purposes it is better. Synthetic materials such as plastics are even replacing many metals.

Of course, as Professor Beckmann rightly adds, if the attention of the average eco-doomster is drawn to the way that synthetic materials have vastly added to society's range of resources, he will usually complain that such synthetics only add to pollution since they are indestructible. "If it is nonrenewable, don't use it, use something indestructible instead, [but] if it is indestructible, don't use it either. Nothing is feasible except the two possibilities he has set his heart on: a return to the caves or doomsday."[27]

In other cases, technical progress means that many materials may hardly be wanted at all within the next few decades. For example, the tungsten that appeared on Dr. Mishan's 1967 list, which is used in most electric light bulbs today, will probably never be synthesised economically in the foreseeable future. But the light bulbs currently in use will probably be used far less by the end of the century, since they are extremely inefficient in electrical engineering terms compared with fluorescent strip-lighting, which needs no tungsten. The same applies to certain uses of other metals, such as copper and aluminum in telephone lines. As Professor Beckmann correctly predicted in 1973, the telephone lines of the future would not need the electrical conductivity of these materials at all, because they would be made of glass fibers acting as wave-guides for laser beams.

Another form of technical progress has been in the means of producing materials from raw materials that are abundant. An example is aluminum, which was a precious metal until well into the 19th century, so that only the rich could afford aluminum cooking utensils. But the discovery of methods of extracting aluminum from bauxite, reserves of which are astronomical, has made aluminum so cheap that it is now used for hundreds of miscellaneous products that are thrown away after little use. And there are innumerable other examples of radical change in techniques of extracting or refining materials from ore that have enabled lower and lower grades of ores to be handled economically, such as the enormous reduction that has taken place over the decades in the lowest grade of copper that could be handled economically.

Thus a gross error in the extreme environmentalist school of thought is the assumption that it would be catastrophic if the world ran out of some useful resource. It might be if it happened overnight, but not—as it would inevitably be—if it happened over the course of the centuries. After all, as I have written elsewhere already, "economic growth has managed to keep going up to now without any supplies at all of Beckermonium, a product named after my grandfather who failed to discover it in the 19th century. In fact we manage very well without an infinite number of products that have never been discovered. . . . In other words, is it really likely that if, say, nickel had never been discovered, modern civilization as we know it would not have emerged?"[28]

The fact is that the concept of resources itself is a dynamic one; many things become resources over time. Each century has seen new resources emerge. The expansion of the last hundred years could not have been sustained without the newly discovered resources of petroleum, aluminum, and energy. What about the possibilities of tomorrow—solar energy, sea-bed resources, and what else?

Technological progress of the many kinds that have helped to increase resources *pari passu* with demand has, in fact, proceeded exponentially throughout the past. Since knowledge of the past must provide the basis for predictions of the future, the best prediction of the future would be that this technological progress would continue exponentially in the future as well. Exponentiality is a double-edged sword that the eco-doomsters should be wary of using. For if technical progress were, for example, to reduce the rate of use of some mineral from 4 percent per annum to only 1.5 percent, this would have an effect equivalent to that of lengthening the life of the mineral fivefold.

Second, if economic growth does slow down significantly in the distant future, what of it? Society still has to face a choice problem:

namely, to what extent is it desirable to slow down growth deliber-
ately now in order to postpone an eventual slowdown that might
otherwise be needed on account of the remote possibility that,
against all the evidence, we might run out of some materials. In
other words, if we let economic growth continue, and if the more
pessimistic forecasts turned out to be correct, this merely means that
one day economic growth will be more difficult, and hence slower,
than it would otherwise be. Materials will become less easily accessi-
ble. More and more resources of labor and capital will have to be
devoted to extracting them, and so we shall be able to devote less
and less to further increases in output per head through investment
in ordinary equipment or in research and technological progress.
As long as we accept that it will not happen suddenly, and will not
happen to all materials simultaneously, economic growth will just
gradually slow down. This has happened before in human history,
sometimes for centuries. And if exhaustion of all raw materials is
inevitable—that is, if we really have to face the implications of so-
called "finite" resources in a time-horizon that is relevant from the
point of view of taking present-day decisions—then why should
zero growth now be of any help in the long run?

"Sustainability" and the Stock of Natural Capital

The implication of the last few pages is that attempts to adjust
GNP for changes in natural capital and the using up of resources
may well be a useful exercise in some small developing countries
that are heavily dependent on a limited resource base. But for large
industrial countries, let alone for the world as a whole, it is a waste of
time. For clearly, on a world scale and with a long-time perspective,
conventional depreciation is just not a very useful way of looking
at long-term changes in stocks of resources. There are many physical
elements in the world which are of absolutely no use at all given
present costs of exploration and utilization, present techniques for
using them, and the present demand for the products in which
they might conceivably be used. But tomorrow all these things may
change. What a "resource" is, depends on the economic conditions
determining the usefulness of the materials in question.

If economically worthwhile, unused land can be turned into a
usable resource by irrigation, drainage of swamps, clearing of forests,
and so on.[29] A hitherto useless mineral, such as the bauxite mentioned

previously, is transformed into a useful resource by the development of techniques for converting it into aluminum. Seawater contains unlimited supplies of uranium for use in nuclear-power production, and already it is thought to be possible to extract the uranium from seawater at a not astronomical cost. Seawater has been estimated to contain about a billion years' supply of sodium chloride and magnesium; 100 million years' supply of sulphur, borax, and potassium chloride; more than a million years' supply of molybdenum, uranium, tin, and cobalt; and so on. Yet who would have thought of including seawater in the list of resources available to us 30 years ago? This sort of process of adding to the resources available to society has been going on throughout history. There could hardly be a greater conflict between the lip service paid by many eco-doomsters to the need for imaginative, forward-looking vision and the static, unimaginative nature of their concept of resources, with its failure to take account of the vast increases in resources over the past.

And technological change, or changes in patterns of output or in people's preferences that indirectly feed back onto the usefulness of different elements, and hence on what is to be counted as a useful resource and at what price, are not the only causes of increases in estimated resources in the longer run. There is also the more direct impact of constant exploration, improved mining, extraction, refining, and processing techniques, mentioned above as part of the economic feedback mechanism in response to any increase in the price of resources. And for some resources, notably forests, there is also constant natural growth. Thus if we were to adjust GNP estimates to allow for new discoveries as well as for resources used up, the result might be an upward adjustment, not a downward adjustment as is claimed by the environmentalists who clamor for more money to be spent on making estimates of "sustainable" GNP.

As shown above, the world's stock of key minerals has actually risen over the last 20 years in spite of having "used up" during that period more than had been in the stock at the outset. The same applies to many resources in individual countries. For example, in Britain the total area of forest cover has more than doubled since the beginning of the century.[30] In 1991 known reserves of natural gas were about 20 percent higher than in 1981, in spite of the fact that the accumulated consumption during the decade amounted to almost half of the initial stock.[31]

Is Food an Exception?

Food is the only commodity the supplies of which are often not enough to meet "demand," at least locally. For as far as food is concerned the neat market-equilibrating mechanism outlined above, namely, the rise in the price and all the favorable feedbacks that this induces—does not help much; it only makes the poor even poorer. And there is no close substitute for food in total. Some eco-doomsters therefore frighten people with visions of starving hordes rampaging over the world, or of people standing 10 per square yard as a result of exponential growth of population. How serious are these fears? And what are the implications for economic growth as an objective of policy?

Population Growth

Rising population in many parts of the world is certainly one of the most urgent and serious problems to be faced by the world as a whole. In many countries a fast-rising population is the greatest obstacle to a rapid increase in its standards of living. It is also one of the major causes of environmental degradation in many countries, as I explained in Chapter 2. It is imperative therefore that current efforts to help poor countries reduce their birth rates should be given high priority.

At the same time we must put the food/population balance into perspective. In the first place, the phase of rapidly rising population that the underdeveloped countries are now experiencing corresponds to a similar phase that the developed world passed through at various stages over the last 50 years or more. To begin with, advances in incomes lead to a fall in death rates and an extension in the average length of life. Hence, with birth rates unchanged, there will obviously be rapid increases in population. But this is then followed by a phase in which the higher incomes are accompanied by higher standards of literacy and education, and different economic and social motivations, which all lead to a fall in birth rates, so that eventually the rates of increase in population slow down. We should not forget that, for very poor people in many parts of the world, a large number of children is the only available form of old-age insurance, particularly when the infant mortality rate is high. When this rate is reduced, there is less economic incentive to have such large families. This is only one of the many ways that rising incomes—

that is, continued economic growth—will help to reduce the rates of increase of population in these countries.

Trends in Food Output

As for the output of food, here we have another clear example of the failure of earlier eco-doomster predictions to be fulfilled. For example, Lester Brown, whose warnings about photosynthesis have been dismissed above, warned us, in the early 1980s, that the period of food security was over, and that "As the demand for food continues to press against the supply, inevitably real food prices will rise. The question no longer seems to be whether they will rise, but by how much."[32] In fact, among the products covered in the Stephen Moore survey mentioned previously were agricultural products. Moore showed that on average food prices declined by more than 30 percent in the 1980s, even more than the average decline in the price of minerals (20 percent), energy (15 percent), and forest products (15 percent). This is not surprising given that, taking the world as a whole, the last 10 years or more have been characterized by food surpluses, not shortages.

And this applies even in the longer term. In spite of much talk about the damage to soil, water supplies, forest cover, and so on, world food output has been rising faster than population, so that world food output per head rose by 0.5 percent per annum compound over the last 20 years (the same figure as for the less developed countries [LDCs] taken as a group, though it fell in African and Oceanic LDCs). One analyst of longer-term trends concludes, "More people enjoyed adequate nutrition in 1990 than ever before in the world's history. Per capita crop production continued to increase, with important gains in such countries as India and China. . . . Given the increase in food production and the breadth of the gains in a wide variety of countries and basic food staples, there is little doubt that a higher proportion of the world's population had more adequate food than ever before."[33] Of course, there have been terrible famines in many parts of the world. But these have been caused mainly by local wars—as in the Sudan, Somalia, and Bosnia. A paper presented recently at a conference of the British Royal Philosophical Society on environmental problems stated that increasing food scarcity could lead to local wars. So far it has been local wars that have led to food scarcity.

It may well be that the eco-doomsters are right about the negative aspects of potential food output—loss of topsoil, water shortages, and so on. But the above data suggest that the negative trends are not gaining on the positive ones—such as improved technology, irrigation, and so on. And because, in the future, the rate of population growth will gradually slow down, the prospects for the balance between food output and population look even more favorable. And this is so in spite of new scare stories about the effects of global warming on food output, which are discussed in the next chapter.

Conclusion

The "finite resources" argument is flawed in every respect. It is logically absurd and obviously at variance with the whole of historical experience, and it takes no account of the way that societies adapt to change in the demands and supplies of materials. It is based on a concept of resources that is static and unimaginative, and an underestimate of the human capacity to make technological progress and adapt to changing conditions. It reflects a petty, defeatist view of human resourcefulness.

5. Biodiversity and the Extinction of Species

Good and Bad Reasons for Species Preservation

It is widely believed that we must give high priority to preventing the massive current extinction of species of plants and animals. Failure to do so, one might think, would demonstrate a lack of compassion for living creatures or inadequate respect for their "rights," or, if we adopt a purely anthropocentric view of the world, it would, in the longer run, harm the interests of the human race in many ways. As the philosopher Mary Midgley puts it, "There simply is no lifeboat option by which human beings can save themselves alone, either as a whole or in particular areas ... the interests of different species coincide so often that really enlightened self-interest would not dictate seriously different policies from species-altruism."[1]

There is probably more than a grain of truth in these propositions. Few people can be so insensitive as to fail to be moved by the beauties of nature and to be awed by the incredible variety and complexity of the natural world and its constituent ecological systems. And in spite of great uncertainties as regards the facts, there is good reason to believe that some of this diversity is under serious threat as a result of human activity—chiefly activity that reduces the habitat for most of the species that currently exist. Furthermore, as the eminent ecologist Norman Myers has put it, unlike other forms of environmental damage, including acid rain, soil erosion and desertification, the depletion of water stocks, and so on, "Extinction of species is different. When a single species is gone, it is gone for good."[2]

Nevertheless the issue is not as simple and straightforward as might at first sight be supposed. The complexities of the problem lie outside the scope of this book, but three types of difficulty have to be mentioned here. The first relates to the motivations of our concern with species and biodiversity. The second relates to the uncertainties about the facts. And the third relates to the implications of the preceding points for policy.

First, as regards our motivations, a little reflection suggests that the species-extinction problem has little to do with either our compassion for animals or our respect for animal rights. Consider the "compassion" argument. Most of us would agree, I hope, that inflicting suffering or death on any living creature is a terrible thing. But it surely makes no difference to any individual creature faced, say, with the danger of imminent death at the hands of some hunter, or of somebody destroying his usual habitat, whether he is almost the last surviving member of some species or whether, in fact, there are countless millions of fellow members of the same species roaming the Earth. I doubt, for example, whether a cockroach being pursued by somebody trying to hit him on the head with a bedroom slipper is rather relaxed about the whole thing because he knows that there are millions more of his kind ready to replace him, or that—by contrast—a member of an endangered species of parrots in Central America would be saying to himself, if cornered by a hunter, "Oh my God! How awful! If he gets me there will be hardly any more of my species left!"

The same applies to the "animal rights" argument. Whether or not animals can be said to have "rights" is a deep philosophical issue. I suspect that most philosophers would agree with John Passmore's view: "To suggest . . . that animals, plants, landscapes have a 'right to exist' is to create confusion. The idea of 'rights' is simply not applicable to what is non-human."[3] But, as Passmore points out, we do not need to confer 'rights' on animals to believe that human beings do not have a right to treat animals without due concern for their interests. In his view the historical trend toward "the condemnation of cruelty to animals does not depend on the presumption that men and animals—let alone men, animals, plants, soil—form a single moral community. It has been a movement of sensibility, a movement based on the growing recognition that not only a positive delight in suffering—so much moralists have always admitted— but even callousness, an insensibility to suffering, is a moral defect in a human being. It is one thing to say that it is wrong to treat animals cruelly, quite another to say that animals have rights."

The same appeal to what is simply our interpretation of the way a decent human being ought to behave also could justify our concern with inanimate, nonsentient components of nature, such as plants. The grounds for this concern would of course be different. It would have nothing to do with any "interests" of the plants, for example. Only sentient beings that have a capacity for suffering (and enjoyment) can have "interests" in any meaningful sense. As Peter Singer puts it, "It would be nonsense to say that it was not in the interests of a stone to be kicked along the road by a schoolboy."[4] At the same time, there is a moral force in the Western tradition of hostility to vandalism, including the destruction of nature. We despise Marcello, in Moravia's *The Conformist*, when, as a boy, he enjoyed cutting off the heads of flowers in his garden, not for any suffering inflicted on the flowers but for his lack of moral sensibility, of which he himself was aware and ashamed. We suspect, rightly, that he is going to turn out, later in the book, to be a nasty piece of work. Lack of respect for nonsentient nature demonstrates a lack of moral sensibility that can easily merge into lack of concern with the suffering of sentient nonhuman animals and finish up in a lack of concern with the suffering of other human beings.

But suppose we adopt the "animal rights" position—as many people do. This would still provide little justification for the preservation of biodiversity and concern with species extinction. For why should the right of any particular animal to be spared unnecessary suffering or death depend on whether or not it is the member of some rare and endangered species? If one was about to destroy a member of the rare species of Oregon silverspot butterfly, would it have some moral right to say, "No, no; don't touch me! Kill that cat over there instead! There are lots of them around!" The cat might not share that view.

If we were to make moral distinctions between the rights of different species of animals—for example, preserve the "glamour species," such as nice cuddly-looking pandas, or wonderful elephants or whales, but not bother about cockroaches and other creepie-crawlies, not to mention bacteria and viruses—we would be embarking on a slippery slope that would finish up by permitting us to distinguish between the rights of other animals and the particular animal known as the human being. Surely distinctions between the basic rights to life of different types of human beings would be totally abhorrent. So how could we justify giving greater rights to members of an animal species that is nearly extinct than to members of some other animal species that may be thriving?

Thus if we are concerned about species loss, it cannot be on account of their interests or their rights, if any. The perfectly legitimate desire to minimize suffering and death of animals or the destruction of nonsentient nature should go far beyond the question of species extinction. It should influence our behavior even if there were no threat whatsoever to biodiversity. We do not recoil from the idea of hurting some pet animal for fear that its species is endangered. So, to begin with, there is no case for adopting a high moral posture over species extinction, as though a willingness to accept the disappearance of some species were a sign of insensitivity to animal suffering.

On the contrary, a concern only with the extinction of species must reflect only a concern with the interests of human beings. If we are to be concerned with species extinction—as distinct from harm to *any* living creature—we must face the fact that it must be on account of the loss of welfare by humans, not by the threatened species. The attribution of so-called "intrinsic value" to nonhuman animals and nonsentient forms of nature may well imply more measures to protect both, but it does not call for any particular concern with species extinction.

In what ways would species extinction lead to a loss of human welfare? What is biodiversity's "instrumental value" (by contrast with its "intrinsic value," if any)? In what ways does it contribute to human welfare? They are, of course, many and varied. Some are relatively materialist, such as the way biodiversity contributes to human welfare through providing food supplies, or having medicinal properties, and so on. According to the eminent biologist Edward Wilson, the loss of species would mean that "New sources of scientific information will be lost. Vast potential biological wealth will be destroyed. Still undeveloped medicines, crops, pharmaceuticals, timber, fibers, pulp . . . petroleum substitutes, and other products and amenities will never come to light."[5]

For example, about 25 percent of all U.S. prescription drugs are based on some plant or other.[6] And about three quarters of the plants involved have been shown to have been used already for medicinal purposes by indigenous populations.[7] There are well-known cases of plants helping in the treatment of serious, and often fatal, illnesses, though most environmentalists seem always to quote the same two examples. These, as almost everybody in the environmental area knows, are the rosy periwinkle (Catharanthus roseus), which has been found to provide substances that are effective in the treatment of Hodgkin's disease and childhood leukemia, and the bark of the Pacific yew tree (Taxus brevifolia), which has been shown to help in the treatment of ovarian cancer.

In addition to these specific well-known cases, tropical forests provide the habitat for innumerable insects, animals, and birds, some of which are the natural enemies of plant-damaging pests. They also provide the source of genetic material for many modern food crops. And cross-breeding with some of the wild varieties of crops that are found only in areas that are not currently under cultivation happens to be essential in many cases for resisting plant disease. Norman Myers has suggested, for example, that it is precisely this cross-breeding that has prevented major damage being done to sugarcane, bananas, and cocoa crops.[8]

In addition to these relatively "material" contributions made by species diversity to human welfare, these services "cannot form the whole foundation of an enduring environmental ethic."[9] As Professor Wilson says, "What makes us people and not computers is emotion. . . . Signals abound that the loss of life's diversity endangers not just the body but the spirit . . . it does not matter whether species have independent rights or, conversely, that moral reasoning is uniquely a human concern. Defenders of both premises seem destined to gravitate toward the same position on conservation."[10]

But how far do such arguments take us? After surveying the main defenses of preservationism—the value of species "as sources of genetic diversity, of scientific understanding, of moral renewal, of recreational enjoyment, of aesthetic pleasure" and so on—Professor Passmore concludes that "they are none of them 'knock-down' arguments; they all allow that economic considerations, in a broad sense of that phrase, might under certain circumstances outweigh the case for preservation. Scientific discoveries—for example, a method of constructing 'seed-banks' so that species could always be reconstituted—or changes in tastes, could wholly undermine them."[11] And, in addition to these uncertainties surrounding more material advantages of biodiversity, how can we place a value on the spiritual benefits that we may derive from the existence of a wide variety of species?

Before coming to these questions, however, we must consider the second difficulty mentioned above: namely, how well do we know the rate at which species extinction is proceeding? For here too the issue is far from simple.

How Fast Are Species Being Extinguished?

The answer is probably "very fast," but there is not yet any basis for even a good guess as to the likely order of magnitude. Some of the predictions to the effect that half the existing species may become extinct within the next two or three decades are based on highly speculative projections from very fragmentary hard data. For example, Professor Julian Simon of the University of Maryland has demonstrated the lack of correspondence between the alarming estimates of species extinction contained in influential documents produced in the late 1970s and early 1980s and such limited data for the past, which were anyway no more than wild guesses to begin with.[12] He compared, for example, an estimate of Norman Myers, based largely on an extrapolation made by Thomas Lovejoy of the World Wildlife Fund (in turn based on Myers's data), of possibly 40,000 extinctions per year during the last decade or two of this century with the only two estimates available for the past. These were of only one species extinction every four years, on average, between 1600 and 1900, one per year from 1900 to 1980, and a guess of 100 per year by 1980. According to Simon: "Given the two historical rates provided by Myers . . . one could extrapolate almost any rate for the year 2000. Lovejoy's extrapolation has no better claim to belief than a rate, say, one-hundredth as large."[13]

Extrapolation from a couple of estimates for the past, however, is by no means the only, or even the main, basis for aggregative estimates of the rates of species extinction. Other estimates of area-species relationships are based on extrapolations from a number of studies of individual habitats. These studies estimated the rate of extinction of species in specific localities and where the cause—usually loss of habitat—is unmistakable. Comparisons between such cases can then be used, as indeed they are, to draw more general conclusions concerning the factors that determine the impact of the reduction in the size of habitats on the survival of the species therein. Allowance is made, for example, for the absolute size of the remaining habitats and their proximity to other habitats, as well as the character of the fauna and flora in question. Such comparisons can then be used to make rough estimates of the relationship between species and the area of their habitats (particularly rain forests)—known, not unreasonably, as the "area-species" relationship. An estimate is then made of the rate of destruction of the habitats. Applying the former to the latter provides an estimate of the number of species that will be destroyed if habitat destruction continues at any specified rate.

The difficulty with this method is that the two components of the estimation method are both very shaky, in spite of outstanding scientific research carried out with great dedication, ingenuity, and persistence by many ecologists, biologists, and others. As regards the "area-species" relationship, for example, there are in fact very few benchmark estimates of species extinctions in the past that can be used to obtain a check on assumptions made about how far the results observed in specific localities can be accurately translated into aggregative relationships that would apply to the world as a whole.

Of course it would be absurd to expect precision in this field. Species that were thought to have been made extinct have a habit of reappearing. And in any case, as Edward Wilson puts it: "Extinction is the most obscure and local of all biological processes. We don't see the last butterfly of its species snatched from the air by a bird or the last orchid of a certain kind killed by the collapse of its supporting tree in some distant mountain forest. . . . So biologists agree that it is not possible to give the exact number of species going extinct; we usually turn palm up and say the number is very large." Nevertheless, Professor Wilson is apparently prepared to hazard a guess that, on the basis of what he argues are very conservative assumptions, "the number of species doomed each year is 27,000."[14] On the other hand, if the total number of species in existence is as large as 100 million, which it may well be according to Professor Wilson, and if the species loss estimate were not to be adjusted upward accordingly, this would represent an annual rate of loss of only 0.027 percent, which would, after 30 years, amount to a total loss of less than 1 percent.

The uncertainty about the order of magnitude of species loss has continued during the last few years in spite of the greatly increased attention paid to it as a result of the alarming predictions made 10 to 15 years ago. One product of the great concern with the threat of mass extinction of species was that the International Union for

Conservation of Nature and Natural Resources (IUCN, also known as the World Conservation Union) commissioned a survey of the state of knowledge concerning species extinctions. All the contributors to this survey (edited by Whitmore and Sayer) were biologists specializing in this topic, and all expressed concern at the dramatic rate of species extinction that was taking place. At the same time, they all stressed the vast deficiencies in the available estimates.[15]

For example, one of the contributors was Daniel Simberloff, a distinguished professor of ecology who with Edward Wilson carried out many years ago the famous Florida Keys experiment into the speed with which various small organisms repopulated isolated areas from which the total fauna had been eliminated. In his contribution to the Whitmore and Sayer report he pointed out: "Forests of the eastern United States were reduced over two centuries to fragments totaling 1–2% of their original extent . . . during this destruction, only three forest birds went extinct. . . . Why, then, would one predict massive extinction from similar destruction of tropical forest?"[16] Two other contributors wrote that "the IUCN, together with the World Conservation Monitoring Centre, has amassed large volumes of data from specialists around the world relating to species decline, and it would seem sensible to compare these more empirical data with the global extinction estimates. In fact, these and other data indicate that the number of recorded extinctions for both plants and animals is very small."[17]

The same authors stated that, on certain reasonable assumptions based on available data, "the annual rate of extinction would be some 2,300 species per year. This is a very significant and disturbing number, but it is much less than most estimates given over the last decade." They added, "It is impossible to estimate even approximately how many unrecorded species may have become extinct. . . . Despite extensive inquiries we have been unable to obtain conclusive evidence to support the suggestion that massive extinctions have taken place in recent times as Myers and other have suggested. On the contrary, work on projects such as Flora Meso-Americana has, at least in some cases, revealed an increase in abundance in many species." And, more specifically, "There are many reasons why recorded extinctions do not match the predictions and extrapolations that are frequently published."

Two other contributors stated, "Closer examination of the existing data on both well- and little-known groups, however, supports the affirmation that little or no species extinction has yet occurred (though some may be in very fragile persistence) in the Atlantic forests. Indeed, an appreciable number of species considered extinct 20 years ago, including several birds and six butterflies, have been rediscovered recently."[18] They concluded, "The foregoing discussion should suffice to demonstrate that the prediction of extinction rates is an almost impossible task. Many previous attempts to estimate global extinction rates have involved a 'guesstimate' at the total number of species in the world, an implied assumption that birds and mammals are in general representative of all species (inherently unlikely), an assumption that species communities in tropical forests are similar the world over, a failure to address the issue of species adaptability to secondary habitats, no mention of the effects of conservation action, and the use of species-area curves for purposes for which they were never intended. Because of these and other reasons outlined above, we feel that we cannot attach any great degree of confidence to any predictions of species extinction rates."[19]

Another contributor wrote, "Although the loss of species may rank among the most significant environmental problems of our time, relatively few attempts have been made to rigorously assess its likely magnitude. . . . While better knowledge of extinction rates clearly can improve the design of public policies, it is equally apparent that estimates of global extinction rates are fraught with imprecision. We do not yet know how many species exist, even to within an order of magnitude."[20]

The second element in the estimates of species extinction is, as indicated above, an estimate of the rate of destruction of habitats, which refers mainly—but by no means exclusively—to deforestations. But here, too, the estimates are by no means firm. Professor Simon has pointed out that various authoritative estimates have thrown doubt on the estimates of deforestation that underlie the usual estimates of massive rates of species extinction. These include estimates of total world forest area by the UN Food and Agriculture Organization and estimates by Marion Clawson (for many decades the preeminent student of forest economics) and Roger Sedjo that were made for Resources for the Future, a widely respected research institute that has always been particularly concerned with sustainable development and related issues. Sedjo and Clawson concluded that "there is certainly nothing in the data to suggest that the world

83

is experiencing significant net deforestation" though they do point out that "a hard look at the available data supports the view that some regions are experiencing rapid deforestation." In other words, it may well be true that, say, Brazilian rain forests are being rapidly depleted, as are those in Thailand and other countries, but they conclude that "the view that this is a pervasive phenomenon on a global level is questionable."[21]

Thus we do not yet have decent estimates of the rates of species extinction, although evidence at the micro-level of the way species become extinct—for example, the role of a minimum size of population, or proximity to other locations—helps provide the basis for reasonable guesses at the orders of magnitude. To some extent, however, that is in the nature of the case. For various reasons, such as the possibility—as in examples quoted above—of a supposedly "extinct" species turning up somewhere at a later date, we cannot be certain how many species have been wiped out in any given situation. On top of that, there is not even a really reliable estimate of how many species there are to begin with—Wilson suggests that the figure may be as great as 100 million.[22] In principle, therefore, it must be impossible to estimate what proportion one unknown number bears to another unknown number.

At the same time, there is a mass of scattered evidence concerning species extinction associated with loss of habitat in various parts of the world. If even those ecologists previously quoted who are most openly critical of the existing estimates remain persuaded that species extinction is proceeding at a rapid rate, we must give some credence to their fears. If I am asked whether it is raining heavily or lightly I am often prepared to say which it is without being able to supply precise rainfall data.

Policies to Prevent Species Extinction

If it did not cost society anything to protect existing species of plants or animals, then of course we should do so (though, personally, I could do without cockroaches). But how much has to be sacrificed in the interests of species preservation? What are the costs involved? There can be no precise answer to this question either, but it is important to recognize the question and the type and scale of the costs that may be involved. After all, we cannot have it both ways as Edward Wilson seems to want. On the one hand, he wrote, in co-authorship with Paul Ehrlich, "The indispensible strategy for saving our fellow living creatures and ourselves in the long run is ... to reduce the scale of human activity."[23] On the other hand, as quoted earlier, among the advantages of biodiversity Professor Wilson includes potential discoveries of new biological wealth, crops, pharmaceuticals, timber, pulp, petroleum substitutes, and other products and amenities. But economic activity is activity that is already devoted mainly to producing crops, timber products, pharmaceuticals, "and other products and amenities." What would be the point of reducing economic activity in order to provide a better basis for increasing it?

The costs that society would have to incur in order to do more to preserve species are of many different kinds, of course, and they affect different groups in society and different countries to varying degrees. First, there are general costs involved in preserving natural habitats in order to protect endangered species. For example, as a result of the operation, in the United States, of the Endangered Species Act of 1973 many projects of different kinds have had to be abandoned on account of their threat to the habitat of certain endangered species. "The Endangered Species Act first gained notoriety in 1978, when the Supreme Court stopped work on an almost finihed dam in Tennessee because it menaced a little-known fish. Since then the Act has reached its long fingers into many aspects of American life. The Fish and Wildlife Service has forced the cancellation of one dam in Colorado, because it put whooping cranes at risk; pushed the Bureau of Reclamation to postpone expanding another, because it jeopardized the humpbacked chub. ... None of this comes cheap."[24]

For example, the Supreme Court stopped the completion of the Tellico Dam at great cost to protect the snail darter, the existence of which had not been known until a few years before. In June 1978 the Court ruled that "the plain intent of Congress" was to stop extinction no matter what the cost. The language of the Act, the Court said, "shows clearly that Congress viewed the value of endangered species as 'incalculable' "—in practical terms, infinite. Obviously, a $100 million dam was worth less than an infinitely valuable fish. In the end congressional legislation provided exemption of the dam project from the provisions of the Act. The dam went ahead and, lo and behold, more snail darters turned up in rivers elsewhere.

The snail darter had to be reclassified from "endangered" to "threatened."

And there have been far more costly instances of bureaucratic action to protect an allegedly endangered species. For example, the Fish and Wildlife Service plans to save the northern spotted owl by halting most logging over an area of more than 8 million acres, which is estimated to cost tens of billions of dollars in locked-up timber that could have been logged without any net loss of forest cover. And in the case of the California gnat-catcher it is estimated that the cost would be even higher.[25]

In addition to this type of cost, there are specific costs, notably how far it is worth sacrificing other forms of medical research in order, say, to preserve species on the grounds that they may turn up new medicinal properties. Most major pharmaceutical manufactures are now very active in the screening of plants for their potential medicinal properties, and, where it seems desirable, they help to preserve and develop the species in question. For example, we have already mentioned the widely quoted case of the threatened Pacific yew and its properties in the treatment of ovarian cancer. But in Washington State this tree is now being propagated and grown for medicinal purposes by a company that has linked up with a major drug company, Bristol-Myers-Squibb.

At the same time, drug companies still put most of their research effort into synthetic chemistry, biotechnology, and microbiology. And the research into the causes and cures of diseases is bearing fruit. For example, there has been a huge expansion of the biotechnology industry in recent years, partly in response to the great advances made in our understanding of the genetic causes of various diseases. With the recently published map of the human genome it is now hoped that within the next 10 to 20 years the structure and function of almost all human genes will be understood. Even without this map the genetic causes of several diseases were found, and successful methods of using this information in the treatment of disease have been developed. It is now believed that "by [the year] 2010 gene doctors will have found a way of dealing with most diseases caused by a single gene defect. Over the next 50 years most common serious diseases will also succumb to gene therapy."[26]

We should not lightly sacrifice this research effort simply on the grounds that "one never knows, someday some other particular species—like some particular plant—may turn out to have medicinal properties." We must take a view of the probabilities involved. If we could identify the particular species that ought to be preserved it would be an easier task. But to use up vast resources in a vain effort to preserve all the species, most of which are likely to contribute nothing, is hardly a rational investment calculation, particularly if medical progress is a principal objective and when what is to be sacrificed includes resources that could be devoted to medical research.

None of this means that nothing should, or could, be done to slow down the pace of species extinction. For the species-rich habitats now under the greatest threat tend to be the rain forests in developing countries. And here, far from being determined by sound economic criteria—such as the prospective payoff in the expected discovery of species that have medicinal properties as against the payoff to laboratory research—the destruction of the forests is often stimulated by uneconomic incentives or the absence of property rights. At the same time, the immediate short-term development concerns of poorer countries may make it perfectly legitimate for them to destroy forests in order to provide food and employment for an increasing population that lacks alternative sources of income or employment. This may well be to the detriment of posterity's spiritual or tangible needs. But if, in order to protect these, large sacrifices have to be made by developing countries themselves—for example, by abstaining from clearing forests for one purpose or another—we can hardly expect them to make the sacrifice.

If the cost is to be borne by pharmaceutical companies who may then have to spend less on other forms of research and investment, it is probably best to leave it to the companies in question to assess the relative probabilities and chances of a successful outcome. In this way society would, in the end, be best served.[27] If, however, the richer countries simply want to provide incentives to the poorer countries to "invest" in, say, preservation of their forests, in the interests of the world's population as a whole, including future generations, it is a different proposition. What would be required would be some equitable sharing of the burden of the "investment."

The rules for such a sharing were debated at the Convention on Biodiversity signed at the 1992 Rio Conference on Environment and Development. Innumerable conflicts of interest came to the surface, such as the preservation of access by pharmaceutical countries to genetic material and the preservation of intellectual property rights while transferring technology to developing countries. These are difficult problems, and quick solutions cannot be expected.

Meanwhile there is little point in adding further confusion to an already complex situation—as many developing countries and some hard-line ecologists do—by dragging into the debate the question of the moral "debt" owed by the rich countries to the developing countries for having exploited the environment in the past. Moral responsibility implies that there was some choice. Because the present generation had no choice in their forebears' decision, say, to burn coal or chop down forests, they cannot be held morally responsible for them. Second, even if we believed in our moral responsibility for the actions of our forebears (and how far back does one go?), the issue of "reparation" for past sins should be quite separate from the issue of how much each country in the world should contribute to the provision of some public good or the prevention of some collective harm.

Conclusions

Species extinction is a complex problem, and we must avoid knee-jerk emotional reactions and simple answers. First, it is important to distinguish between different motivations, such as, on the one hand, compassion for the interests of all sentient beings and, on the other, the desire to preserve distinct species rather than just all members of any particular species. Second, there are great difficulties in putting even approximate numbers to the rate at which species are, in fact, being made extinct. Third, even if we accept that the positive contribution made by biodiversity to human welfare goes beyond its material contribution—medicinal properties, resistance to plant disease, and so on—and encompasses the spiritual benefits that we derive from the beauty and awe-inspiring complexity of nature, we still have to ask ourselves what costs we are prepared to incur to preserve species.

Here, too, no clear answer is available. Indeed, no attempt has been made, to my knowledge, to provide one. But, as with the data for species extinction, there is anecdotal evidence to the effect that the costs of species extinction may often be very great. Furthermore, they may often have to be borne nowadays by developing countries.

So, if the rest of the world takes species preservation seriously, it must be prepared to intensify its efforts to help developing countries in this field. This should not be based on any false notion of moral debt. It should be based on the long-term self-interest of the world as a whole.

At the same time, as shown in earlier chapters, the best way to help developing countries reduce their destruction of forests as a means of solving their problems of poverty and employment is to help them develop economically in other ways. Too often the emotional appeal of species conservation is used to do the opposite: to promote protectionism that damages the export potential of developing countries. This is the case, for example, when environmentalists support trade restrictions on imports from developing countries in the alleged interests of preserving dolphins, or certain hardwoods.[28] As Jagdish Bhagwati writes, "The aversion to free trade and GATT that many environmentalists display is unfounded, and it is time for them to shed it."

6. Global Warming and Scientific Uncertainty

Introduction

A Louis Harris poll in the United States a few years ago showed that most people rated the environment more important than a satisfactory sex life.[1] This may tell us something about American sex life. It may also tell us something about the impression made on many people in advanced societies by the widely proclaimed imminence of ecological disaster on account of various dramatic environmental threats, of which "global warming" is one. The public is constantly told by environmental pressure groups that governments must take immediate action to implement drastic cuts in fossil fuel consumption, in the interests of checking the accumulation of carbon dioxide (CO_2) in the atmosphere, irrespective of the cost.

Of course we have to be concerned with the impact that human beings are having, for the first time in their history, on the Earth's climate balance. For, as recent research has shown, the overall basic climate system is by no means as stable as had previously been believed. But how much climate change would result from the upward trend in carbon dioxide emissions and what the economic consequences would be are unresolved questions, and in this and the following chapter I try to put some of the other side of the story by highlighting the uncertainties involved.

For the one thing that is certain about the global warming issue is that an immediate significant cut in fossil fuel consumption means a drastic cut in world energy consumption and hence in standards of living. And the social and political upheavals to which this would lead would also be catastrophic. Furthermore, as earlier chapters have shown, a rise in income levels is the only way that the urgent environmental problems facing the 75 percent of the world's population that live in developing countries can be overcome. Hence, no attempt should be made to reduce present living standards and their prospective future increase without a more balanced appraisal of the global warming threat than is generally presented to the public. The alarmist story already gets an extensive hearing. Apart from the obvious media interest in publicizing apocalyptic scenarios, many other groups in society have an interest in promoting the global warming scare. Many scientists see it as a means of obtaining finance for hungry research budgets, and given the importance and complexity of the problem I would be the last person to begrudge them their money. But other organizations and individuals parade the global warming scare for less worthy reasons—political popularity, personal ego-trips, parading their moral sensibilities, or financing pseudo-scientific activities.

As a recent article in *Nature* put it, "In Britain, for example, separate groups pursuing commercial interests, foreign policy goals, and domestic politics each discovered their own uses for the warming hypothesis. For some, the opportunities included the pursuit of global scientific research agendas, for others, the enhancement of bureaucratic power at home. . . . Calls for environmental regulation were generally attractive to environmental bureaucracies . . . beleaguered national politicians gained a world stage on which to indulge in global green rhetoric without, as yet, having to face issues of domestic implementation."[2] The commercial and industrial interests include, as the author points out, the natural gas and nuclear energy industries, because they provide, respectively, sources of energy that produce far less carbon than conventional fossil fuels or none at all. Hence, by emphasising the global warming threat, they strengthen the case for public support.

Not being a scientist—or even a rock star, a politician, a diplomat, or related to any royal family—it might be thought that I am not qualified to express any view about global warming. But I would hate word to get around among my colleagues at Oxford that I was reluctant to write about a subject simply because I did not know much about it. And, fortunately, one does not need to know much about it in order to learn that the really top scientists in the climatology field are acutely aware of the gaps in their understanding of the process of climate change.[3]

The Limits on the Scientific Consensus—Such As It Is

There is no doubt that a massive increase in carbon concentrations in the atmosphere, which results from the rapid increase in fossil fuels as a source of energy, would lead to a rise in temperature, *other things being equal*. But there is considerable doubt as to how far other things do remain equal, and how great the rise in temperature will be. For although the basic physical laws are beyond dispute, the determination of the world's climate is so incredibly complex that it is not yet possible to model it with much confidence.

In the first place, it should be appreciated that human activity is not the only source of greenhouse gases (GHGs), of which carbon dioxide is the most important. Indeed, the anthropogenic (i.e., human) contribution is relatively very small. As has been shown in recent research described in Box 6.1, the natural changes in carbon concentrations have been very great. Of course, the natural influences on the climate are very long-run, and there is not much one can do about them anyway. And if a complex system—such as the human body or the Earth's climate—is in equilibrium it can often

---

BOX 6.1 - NATURAL CHANGES IN CARBON
CONCENTRATIONS

Records from air bubbles trapped in ice cores revealed in the Vostok ice core experiment show enormous variations in CO_2 concentrations over the last 150,000 years, long before humans were having any impact.[4] And more recent evidence from drillings carried out by the U.S. Greenland Ice Sheet Project II have shown that drastic and rapid climate changes took place in the distant past long before human activity was responsible.[5] Indeed, although it is sometimes asserted that the apparent rough correlation between the CO_2 concentrations and the estimated temperatures over the last 150,000 years proves how CO_2 concentrations affect temperature, the direction of causality is generally believed to be the other way round. The decline in temperature over the period in question was probably the result of a small change in the Earth's orbital characteristics, which would have led to a fall in the CO_2 concentration because cooler oceans absorb more CO_2.

be seriously disturbed by a relatively small change in one of its components. So the real issue is how far the climate balance, such as it is, is likely to be affected over the next century or so by human activities. In the interests of comparability between various predictions of the effects on climate of the increase in carbon concentrations in the atmosphere, most of the estimates refer to the impact on climate of a doubling of the CO_2 concentration. This base-line increase in the carbon concentration is generally expected to occur, in the so-called "business as usual" scenario (i.e., the absence of specific policies designed to reduce the rate of increase of CO_2 emissions), sometime toward the end of the next century, though some experts would put it much earlier.

How much would this affect climate? The Intergovernmental Panel on Climate Change (IPCC) which many—but not all—climatologists would accept as representing the general consensus in this field reported in 1992 that its ". . . best estimate, based on model results and taking into account the observed climate record" was that a doubling of the carbon concentrations would lead to a temperature increase of 2.5°C, but with a range around that estimate of one or two degrees on either side.[6] And the IPCC's "best estimate" of the relationship between the carbon concentration and the resulting rise in temperature yields a rise in temperature in 50 years' time of between 0.8°C and 1.5°C.[7]

But the extent to which there is a consensus close to these estimates is disputed by some eminent experts. For example, Richard Lindzen, Sloan Professor of Meteorology at MIT, member of the National Academy of Sciences and a prominent contributor to current climatological research in top scientific journals, has publicly deplored the extent to which the lack of a consensus in this field is generally concealed.[8] His own predictions are of far less warming than those of the IPCC report, and he has objected to the declaration by the National Academy of Sciences to the effect that there is a general consensus over the degree of warming that one might expect. Similarly, a recent report written by Frederick Seitz, a past president of the (U.S.) National Academy of Sciences; Robert Jastrow, founder of the Goddard Institute for Space Studies; and William Nierenberg, director emeritus of the Scripps Institute of Oceanography at San Diego, none of whom can be regarded as an irresponsible teenage scribbler, argued that global climate modeling was still so unsatisfactory that any number of other hypotheses would explain such global

94

warming as has been observed over the last century just as well as the CO_2 hypothesis.

Of course, if asked whether a continuation in the upward trend in CO_2 emissions, *other things remaining equal*, would lead to some global warming, all scientists would answer "Yes." But this is like asking scientists whether they all agree that the world is round. What really matters is (i) how far will other things remain equal— for example, how far will the direct warming impact of the increased carbon in the atmosphere be modified by increased cloud cover resulting from a tendency toward greater warming, or increased sulphate aerosol accumulations in the atmosphere, or a greater rate of absorption of carbon in the oceans and hence (ii) *by how much* the global climate is expected to change, after allowing for these and other complications?[9] To such questions the degree of consensus among the answers is apparently very much lower. According to Professor Lindzen, global warming ". . . is the only subject in atmospheric science where a consensus view has been declared before the research has hardly begun."[10]

The Climate Change Uncertainties

It is true that the main models of the earth's climate that have been built up represent an intellectual achievement of the first order. But the climate system is of mind-boggling complexity and all reputable scientists seem to agree that there are still major gaps in the understanding of the global warming phenomenon.

The basic global warming story is that global warming will take place on account of the accumulation in the atmosphere of certain "greenhouse gases" (GHGs), of which carbon dioxide is the most important for practical purposes. This, as indicated above, is produced by burning fossil fuels (as well as other means, some of them natural). These gases do not block much of the incoming energy from the sun, which is the way that the earth warms up. But they do block some of the outgoing long-wave radiation reflected back from the earth (including the oceans). And this outgoing radiation is one of the ways that the earth cools down. Normally, the system would be more or less in balance and the incoming warming would be matched by the outgoing cooling processes. But if the greenhouse gases accumulate, the latter will be checked more than the former, so that the temperature of the earth might well rise. Nevertheless, even abstracting from major natural changes such as solar activity and so on, the climate system is far more complex than this basic story might suggest, and many of its workings are still only dimly understood.

The average layman watching the usual TV pictures of arrows representing energy entering the atmosphere from the sun and the arrows representing energy escaping back from the atmosphere gets the impression that it is the outgoing radiation that explains most of the cooling of the surface of the earth. But, in fact, the most important cooling process is evaporation, with the evaporated moisture being carried upward by convection. And it is not yet possible to model accurately the behavior of water vapor and cloud cover, or the interaction between the atmosphere and the oceans, or the way that water mixes at different depths and at different temperatures, or even whether, on balance, clouds have a cooling effect or add to warming, and how far their effect depends on other complex scientific characteristics of clouds. And it is generally agreed that better modeling of the increased evaporation and convection that would occur as a result of warming could indicate negative feedback effects that moderate the increase in warming that would otherwise take place.[11] For example, in 1989 some improvements made to the modeling of cloud cover in the British Meteorological Office model reduced the estimates of the temperature increase associated with a doubling of the CO_2 concentrations from 5.2 degrees to 1.9 degrees.[12]

Another mistaken but widely encouraged belief is that the climate models' predictions have been confirmed by temperature changes over the past century. But, in fact, it is now generally conceded that there was a large upward bias in the temperature trend indicated by earlier data (e.g., reflecting the growth of urban areas). And this has been confirmed by recent satellite observations, some of which show no global warming over the last 10 to 15 years.

Nor is it true that the failure of the main climate models to match past temperature trends can now be explained away by appealing to the cooling effect of the increase in sulfate emissions from the burning of fossil fuels. The story here is that one of the effects of increased emissions of sulfur particles is to reduce the size of water vapor droplets in clouds and hence increase the extent to which clouds will reflect back incoming energy from the sun. But, as one of the leading experts in this field, Tom Wigley, makes clear, "In reality, these processes are complicated and it is still not possible to quantify this indirect effect reliably."[13] It is generally agreed now that earlier 1987 estimates of this effect were probably many times greater than it is now believed to be. In any case, world sulfate emissions have been declining in recent years.

Furthermore, other changes, notably the decline in stratospheric dust, should have added to the temperature, so that the amount of the observed rise that should be attributed to CO_2 (or to unknown natural causes) should be reduced. Some estimates that take account of these various influences suggest that the residual trend increase in temperature over the course of the last century would be only about 0.3°C, as compared with the more widespread belief that it has increased by about 0.5°C.[14]

Even if one accepted the usual estimate that there has been an upward trend in temperature of as much as 0.5°C over the last century it is difficult to match it with the geographical or time pattern that the global warming models would predict. This is because (i) most of the trend rise occurred between 1900 and 1940, when CO_2 concentrations were increasing by only about 0.1 percent per annum compared with 0.5 percent per annum now; (ii) there was a fall in temperature between 1940 and the early 1970s; (iii) the models predict that more warming would take place at higher latitudes than near the equator, whereas the opposite has occurred. Hence, as Sir John Mason concludes, "The timing of the fluctuations in the temperature record, and the fact that any significant greenhouse warming is likely to be delayed for several decades because of the thermal inertia of the oceans, strongly suggest that these are natural climatic fluctuations."[15]

For the natural influences on the climate include some relatively short-term natural variations such as changes in the angle at which the equatorial plane is inclined to its orbital plane (about 23°). There has also been a slight long-run upward trend in global temperature since the end of the "Little Ice Age" that began around the 13th century and ended toward the end of the 18th century. So a rise in average temperature since then could well be the continuation of a recovery from this Little Ice Age.[16]

Furthermore, even if one accepted that there has been a trend increase of about 0.5°C over the last century or so, and that this is related to the actual increase in the CO_2 in the atmosphere, the relationship between the two variables implies a "climate sensitivity"—that is, the effect of the CO_2 on temperature—that is less than that implied in the latest IPCC estimates. In fact, recent research suggests that if one used the relationship between the rise in CO_2 and the increase in temperature induced by the change in greenhouse gases since 1765, the doubling of the CO_2 concentration that might be expected to occur around the latter half of the next century would only raise the global temperature by 1.2°C, by comparison with the IPCC's range of between 1.5°C and 4.5°C.[17]

One thing that the various models do agree on is that the climate change resulting from global warming would not be spread evenly over the globe. But the effects on local climates are, at present, impossible to predict with any acceptable degree of accuracy. Most of the models agree that there will be more rainfall—as one would expect, because higher temperatures will mean more evaporation of water vapor, which will come down as more rain. Nevertheless, where exactly the predicted increase in rainfall will take place is impossible, so far, to predict with any accuracy.

The fact is that the models do not tell us where it will rain more as a result of global warming. If all the extra rain falls in Ireland, or even in England, it will do no good at all, whereas if it all comes down in Central Africa it would be immensely beneficial. It is true that it is more likely to be the former. This is not because of the usual operation of "Murphy's Law" but because there are sound meteorological reasons why, in general, rainfall will decrease in large continental areas far removed from the seas and increase in areas bordering on the seas. However, although these factors are, of course, incorporated in the models, they have conspicuously failed to explain observed regional differences in climate change. It is for this reason that some predictions that have been made to the effect that climate change will put hundreds of millions of people at risk of starvation must be treated with great skepticism—quite apart from their failure to allow adequately for the scope for international trade in food to remedy regional variations in food demands and supplies, as it has done for centuries.

The good news, however, is that where the predictions of the models have been consistent with the evidence of the last 50 years or more, the changes have been favorable from the point of view of food output. In particular, the predicted overall increases in rainfall

---

BOX 6.2 - THE FALLIBILITY OF REGIONAL
CLIMATE PREDICTIONS

One example of the impossibility, in the present state of knowledge, of making anything like accurate predictions of climate change in specific regions, is the fact that the Northern Hemisphere has warmed less than the Southern Hemisphere, which is quite contrary to the predictions of the climate models. This cannot be attributed to the greater production of sulfate aerosols in the Northern Hemisphere, because the climatic effects of these are distributed unevenly across the globe.[18] In any case, this would not help explain why the Arctic region—not noted for its industrial output—has shown some cooling over the past 50 years when, according to the models, it should have shown the most warming. And, most important of all perhaps, the predictions that there would be increasing drought in the central states of the United States have not been born out. Indeed, "Of the nine states with the largest change toward increasing soil moisture, six—Colorado, Iowa, Kansas, Missouri, Nebraska, and Oklahoma—are located in this agricultural heartland."[19] It is not surprising, therefore, that a detailed recent study concluded that "The . . . uncertainties in model-based predictions of regional climate changes are large. For instance, the seasonal and spatial details of current precipitation patterns are generally not well simulated, and the predictions of greenhouse gas-induced changes in precipitation vary greatly from one model to another."[20]

---

and in cloud cover (which tends to reduce afternoon temperatures) do seem to be taking place. There is also confirmation of the prediction that temperatures would rise most at night where it would usually be welcome and where it would add least to evaporation rates so that soil moisture is more likely to increase than to fall. This would be good for plant growth, as is also the increase in CO_2 concentrations. "These global patterns are internally consistent with one another, they are consistent with climate changes observed during a time when equivalent CO_2 increased by 40 percent, and they are consistent generally with the predictions of the numerical models. We already are watching the greenhouse effect unfold before our eyes, and the observational evidence is not pointing to disaster."[21]

Uncertainty and the "Precautionary Principle"

This, however, is not a book about science. What matters here is what policy implications follow from the predicted climate change. It is mainly in this connection that appeal is sometimes made to the so-called "precautionary principle." It is asserted that faced with a possibility, however remote, of some catastrophic development, prudent policy demands that whatever action that is required to prevent it be taken. It is sometimes suggested, in a vague and knowing way designed to blind people with science, that this corresponds to some concept in game theory known as the "minimax" strategy. This is one in which players in some game adopt the strategy that will lead to the least damaging outcome in the event that their opponent is adopting the most harmful strategy. But this particular game theory setup has no bearing on the global warming problem. For it assumes that players are able to assign definite known values to the net damage arising under different strategies.

But with the global-warming problem, society is faced with the choice between (i) accepting some remote and unquantifiable possibility of sharp climatic change in the longer run with possibly severe economic effects and (ii) certain economic and social catastrophe if draconian policies are adopted to avoid it.[22] For the economic, and hence social, costs of taking action designed to avoid all conceivable possibility of catastrophe would be astronomic. On this point there is no uncertainty at all. And nobody would dream of always adopting a policy designed to avoid the worst catastrophe that could possibly happen irrespective of the certain costs of doing so. If people acted in that way nobody would ever leave their homes for fear of being run over or mugged.

In the global warming case, therefore, society is faced with a choice between options that are incommensurable. How to choose in such a situation is a fascinating philosophical problem and lies outside the scope of this book.[23] It seems that the usual rules of cost-benefit analysis are not much help, nor are other rational choice decision rules including those found in game theory. In that case choice has to be made on the basis of temperament, taste, social preference, and so on. I suspect that most people's choices would be heavily influenced by the certainty of the disastrous impact that the adoption of measures to prevent all chance of severe climate change would certainly have on the population of the whole world, and particularly in the Third World where economic growth is so badly needed. But I would not try to argue that it would be illogical for somebody to make a choice that is much more risk-averse, more concerned with the interests of distant generations, and less concerned with the suffering that the policies they advocate would inflict on people alive today.

7. Global Warming and the "Precautionary Principle"

How to Sell Economic Predictions

In his wonderful book *A Connecticut Yankee in King Arthur's Court*, the great American humorist Mark Twain describes an incident in which a charlatan "magician" is impressing a large crowd of people by spectacular demonstrations of his magical powers. His method is to tell the multitude exactly what various distant kings and emperors are doing at that precise moment, although they are hundreds or thousands of miles away. Because the crowd did not know any better they were very impressed. It may be difficult for us today to believe it, but the fact is that, in the Middle Ages, people were almost as gullible and credulous as are many people now when confronted, for example, with predictions of catastrophe in 100 years' time. Anyway, the Yankee decides to perform a simple test of the magician's powers that could be checked immediately by the audience. Facing the magician and with his back to the crowd, he puts his hands behind his back and challenges the magician to say what he is doing with his right hand. Of course, the magician has no idea, and his limitations are immediately exposed.

This illustrates the state of affairs in long-range predictions of the economic effects of global warming, or of any particular economic measures to check it, such as carbon taxes. The chief thing is to make the predictions for a period of 50 or 100 years in the future. Nobody then will ever bother to check whether they were correct, or even know about them. And even if some strange research student in 50 or 100 years' time digs up old predictions and exposes their errors, the authors will long be dead. Or if they are not dead—for who knows what advances there may be in medical science, Heaven forbid, to keep them alive?—they probably will have passed retirement age and no longer will be fighting for promotion or fat research grants.

The first principle of economic forecasting then—if you don't want to be caught out—is not to make forecasts for next year or the year after. For, as we have seen in the last decade or so, all short-run economic predictions have been ludicrously wrong. During the last two or three years economists have failed to predict the Japanese recession, the solidity of the American recovery, the scale of the collapse in the German economy, and the turmoil in the European exchange rate mechanism. As a result, short-range economic prediction is now rightly regarded by the public with great suspicion, if not with open derision. So if you want to impress customers, stick to predicting something really simple, like the precise global composition of output in 100 years' time, the way each country's production is distributed among different sectors, the technical progress in energy use and the relative prices of different sources of energy, and, finally, the amount of energy that will be consumed in the world and how much of it will be in different forms of carbon intensity. Nobody in 100 years' time will know if you got it wrong, and nobody—least of all yourself—will care.

But of course there is more to it than that. For any old fool could present some long-range predictions. You still have to convince the authorities that hand out research grants, as well as your peers in the profession, that you are able to do a solid professional job. In the old days, magicians could get away with a bit of mumbo-jumbo, make a few flames, and dance around some totem pole. Nowadays you have to be more sophisticated. So the second principle of getting grants for predicting the economic effects of climate change over the next 100 years is to promise to construct an elaborate computerized model. Therefore the best-known and most highly respected predictions of the economic damage that will be done by increased carbon emissions over the next century are extremely complex computerized models, embodying perhaps hundreds of equations. Otherwise, why should any grant-giving body hand out large sums to support the research? If you ask for a million dollars, say, to produce a dynamic optimization multisector international model of the economy, you stand a good chance of getting it. For an extra million dollars you might offer to make the model inter-planetary, or even intergalactic, while you're at it. You never know, some charity or government foundation might support it.

After all, the basis of the second principle is that the bureaucracies that staff most large grant-giving institutions measure their output by their input—that is, by how much money they have been able to disburse in grants. To get promotion inside such organizations it is necessary to sponsor really big projects. Otherwise how can you justify a bigger staff, a bigger office, more travel to discuss the project and monitor its progress, and so on? If somebody like me were to apply to such a body for, say, £500 to pay me for the half day's work that would be necessary to write out on a couple of sheets of paper what can be safely predicted about the economic effects of climate change it would cause great hilarity in such an organization. One can imagine the official who received my request running excitedly around the office saying "Hey! Look at this! Here's some poor schlemiel called Beckerman who is asking for £500 for some project!"

As a result of these two principles of getting grants for long-range modeling of climate change, there are several very complicated computerized models on the market for making the requisite predictions. But in fact none of them is necessary. It can all be done on the back of an envelope, or even in one's head.

The Economic Impact of Global Warming

My Back-of-the-Envelope Estimate

The fact that alarm over the predicted effects of global warming is vastly exaggerated can be demonstrated by one simple piece of evidence. This does not require gigantic systems analysis or computerized models of the world's climate or economy, and hence vast research grants; but it easily refutes the widespread notion that the human race is some tender plant that can only survive in a narrow band of plus or minus 3°C. This is the present dispersion of the world's population over widely different temperature zones. For example, taking the average temperatures in the coldest month in the countries concerned, 32.3 percent of the world's population live in a band of 0°C to 3°C, whereas 18.8 percent live in the band 12°C to 15°C, and 14.6 percent in a band 24°C to 27°C! The same wide dispersion exists if we take average summer temperatures. Furthermore, across countries as a whole there is no correlation at all between average temperatures and income levels (even excluding Middle Eastern oil states).

Of course it will be argued that such cross-country comparisons cannot adequately take account of the speed of temperature change over time. In principle there is some truth in this. But, as Thomas

Schelling has pointed out, "most people will not undergo in the next 100 years changes in their local climates more drastic than the changes in climate that people have undergone during the past 100 years. No climate changes are forecast that compare with moving from Boston to Irvine, Calif., or even perhaps from Irvine to Los Angeles. The Goths and the Vandals, the Romans and the Vikings, the Tartars and the Huns migrated through more drastic changes than any currently anticipated; Europeans who migrated to North and South America similarly underwent drastic climate changes. In this country in 1860 barely 2 percent of the population lived outside the humid continental or subtropical climates; in 1980 the percentages outside these zones had increased from 2 percent to 22 percent. Furthermore, the microclimates of urbanized Tokyo, Mexico City, and Los Angeles have not deterred their population growth; the microclimates of London and Pittsburgh changed dramatically during the century before 1950 and have changed again almost as dramatically since then."[1] Some of the U.S. internal migration over the last few decades to which Schelling refers relates of course to the millions of United States citizens who have moved south or west in order to live in the warmer climates of California or Florida. Global warming could mean that future generations would not have to go to all the trouble!

Agriculture

Simple back-of-the-envelope calculations also suffice to show that, for the United States at least, global warming hardly could have a significant impact on national income. For the sector most likely to be affected is agriculture, which constitutes only about 3 percent of U.S. GNP. Other sectors of economic activity are hardly likely to be affected at all and some, such as construction, will probably be favorably affected. So, even if the net output of agriculture fell by 50 percent by the end of the next century this is only a 1.5 percent cut in GNP.

In any case, as shown in Box 7.1, the net effect of climate change on U.S. agricultural output is likely to be negligible. Of course, in some countries the effects on agriculture will be different. In some, notably Canada, the former USSR, and China, the net effects will be favorable as the production regions move northward and growing

---

BOX 7.1 - GLOBAL WARMING AND U.S. AGRICULTURE

In the northern states of the United States global warming would mean longer growing periods and less disruption through frosts. And the higher carbon dioxide concentration is actually good for plant growth, which means that plant growth could be just as great with less water.[2] In fact, for the United States alone estimates by the Environmental Protection Agency show that the net effect on U.S. agriculture is uncertain in direction, with the possible range of effect lying between a net gain of $10 billion and a net loss of $10 billion.[3] Even if the outcome is at the worst extreme end of this range, namely minus $10 billion, this is a trivial sum compared with U.S. GNP of about $6 trillion. Even a cut of 50 percent in net agricultural output by the year 2090 as a result of global warming, which nobody would suggest is likely, would merely mean that the American population will have to wait until 2091 to achieve the level of income that they would otherwise have achieved in 2090. I am sure that they would find ways of adapting to this disappointment over the course of the next century.

---

periods are extended.[4] Professor Nordhaus of Yale University has surveyed estimates for other countries and reported, "Detailed studies for the Netherlands and Australia found that the overall impact of a CO_2 equivalent doubling will be small and probably difficult to detect over a half-century or more. The Coolfont Workshop (in which teams of experts gathered on a very short-term basis) estimated the impact of climate change upon six large regions—the United States, Europe, Brazil, China, Australia, and the former USSR. This report found the impact of climate change to be generally favorable."[5]

Furthermore, all this leaves out of account the probable, indeed inevitable, contribution that will be made by the continued rapid improvements in agriculture and plant technology as a result of genetic engineering and other technological innovations. Even if, on balance, global warming did raise the real costs of achieving given agricultural output by, say, 10 to 20 percent by the middle of the next century, these are likely to be covered many times by savings from continued increase in control over plants, possible production of new proteins, technological progress in water conservation and irrigation, and so on. Furthermore, over the last four decades food production has been rising faster than demand, so that some barely noticeable cut in the rate of growth of agricultural production—if any—does not spell mass starvation. Famines, as we now know, have been more the result of wars, appalling policies, civil strife, and ethnic discrimination than of acute physical food shortages in any given area.[6]

Sea Level Rise

The predicted rise in sea levels has been greatly reduced in recent years. In 1980 it was predicted that the sea level would rise by as much as 8 meters. In early 1989 it was predicted that it would rise by only 1 meter; in early 1990 (as in the IPCC report) the predicted rise by the end of the next century was down to about 65 cm, and current authoritative estimates now put it as low as 30 cm by the end of next century, assuming a 4°C rise in average temperature by then. If we were to extrapolate trends in these estimates, the sea level would be predicted to fall, with consequences for many seaside resorts that might be as serious as sea level rises! Indeed this scenario is perfectly possible for good scientific reasons explained in Box 7.2.

BOX 7.2 - SEA LEVELS AND THE MELTING OF THE POLAR ICE CAPS

One of the most widespread myths about climate change is that it would lead to calamitous flooding as a result of the melting of the polar ice caps. But this has recently been totally debunked by a team of experts who have suggested that the world's largest ice sheet remained stable during more than 14 million years of dramatic natural fluctuations in temperature! They have even stated that global warming might reduce sea levels on account of the increased evaporation and precipitation leading to more snow falling on the ice caps.[7] For if water is, in effect, removed from the sea and deposited on the ice caps in the form of snow, the sea level must clearly fall.

But suppose sea levels did rise appreciably, what would be the economic effects? A few years ago, when it was still predicted that the sea level would rise by as much as 1 meter, the United States Environmental Protection Agency estimated that it would cost about $100 billion to protect U.S. cities by sea walls. Applying a 1.5 percent per annum compound growth rate to the present U.S. GNP of about $6 trillion would give a GNP by the year 2090 of about $27 trillion, so that as a fraction of GNP in the year 2090 the once-for-all capital cost of sea walls would be about 0.4 percent! As a fraction of cumulative U.S. GNP over the whole of the next 100 years—the time during which the work would have to be carried out—the amounts involved are of course totally trivial.

What about the rest of the world? Estimates by William Cline of the Institute for International Economics, also assuming that the sea level would rise by 1 meter and that the costs of sea walls for other threatened coastal cities are comparable to those of the United States, arrived at costs of adaption, plus valuing the land lost in Bangladesh, of about $2 trillion.[8] What would this be as a proportion of world income? As pointed out in Chapter 1, there are good reasons for believing that the rate of growth of output per head in the world as a whole will be no slower than over the past few decades and probably even faster. As shown there, if we make the rather conservative assumption that output per head will rise by only, say, 1.5 percent per annum over the next century, output per head toward the end of the next century would be about 4.4 times as great as it is now. And by that time world population will almost have certainly stabilized at, say, about twice the present level, so that world GNP would be roughly $200 trillion.

This means that the $2 trillion capital cost of adaptation to the rise in the sea level would still be only about 1 percent of a year's GNP, so that as a fraction of cumulative world GNP over the whole period it would still be negligible. And given (a) that the latest predictions of the rise in the sea level are about half those assumed in these estimates, and (b) that a given reduction in the estimated sea level rise implies a more than proportionate reduction in the costs of adaptation or the damage done through land loss, the costs of adaptation and land loss for the world as a whole would be negligible, even allowing for a generous margin of error in the estimates.

Now that may be all very well for the world as a whole but it is not much consolation for the people of Bangladesh, where 20 percent of the land could be lost under the sea with a 1 meter sea level rise. But, leaving aside the falling trend in the estimates of the sea level rise, suppose, purely for the sake of illustrating the logic of the choices to be made, that measures to prevent the climate change and the consequent sea level rise would cost the world community $20 trillion—that is, 10 times as much as the cost of protection against the rising sea level. It clearly would be in everybody's interests, including the Bangladeshis', to make some sort of deal such as not incurring the $20 trillion costs that would be needed to prevent the sea level from rising and handing over, say, a fifth of the resulting economy—namely $4 trillion—to the people who would suffer from the sea level rise. The latter then gain—$4 trillion to carry out work costing only $2 trillion—and the rest of the world still has a net gain of $16 trillion.

In other words, the alternative course of action that is being urged on all sides, namely to prevent the sea level rising at any cost, would mean that the world is being asked, in effect, to incur costs of $20 trillion—or whatever the cost would be—to prevent the Bangladeshis from suffering the effects of the sea level arise when there would be a very much cheaper way of sparing them these effects. The alternatives would include measures that could raise their overall income levels substantially, such as helping them to diversify their economies by facilitating their trade possibilities, or other means. And if the rest of the world is so concerned about Bangladesh that it is prepared to incur drastic cuts in today's living standards in order to prevent global warming, it also would be much cheaper just to make it easier for Bangladeshis to come and live in the Western world. Of course, they might not want to emigrate to the Netherlands, where over half the population already live quite happily below sea level and where most of Amsterdam is several meters below!

If the estimates of the costs of significant reductions of CO_2 emissions referred to below are anywhere near reality, it is clear that the world and the Bangladeshis would be far better off if adaptive policies were taken, rather than drastic action to prevent the threatened rise in sea levels. Anyway, because it is suspected that far more land is being lost every year as a result of soil erosion than is likely to be lost through climate change, if the world is seriously concerned about land loss there are policies that could be adopted to reduce it without drastic reductions in world CO_2 emissions.

Other Effects of Climate Change

Estimates have been made for other effects of climate change, such as a greater need for air conditioning (which would, however, be offset by less need for space heating), forest loss, and the sheer disutility for some people of living in a warmer climate (but not for all those people who would like to do so but cannot afford to or are tied to their present locations by other factors). However, these effects are even more uncertain than those referred to above, and are likely anyway to be less significant.

For example, one particular scare story is that global warming will lead to a great increase in the frequency of storms. But in fact very few hard results have been produced concerning this effect of global warming, and for a very good reason. On the one hand, it is true that insofar as the seas become warmer the area over which hurricanes "breed" will expand. On the other hand, storms are correlated with temperature "gradients"—that is, the transition between high and low temperatures—so that insofar as the temperature increase is predicted to be greatest in high latitudes, where it is generally colder, the worldwide temperature gradient will diminish. To calculate the incidence of storms would, therefore, require a far more accurate breakdown by small geographic area of the effects of the climate change than is feasible given current modeling.

In fact, storms, like heatwaves or incidence of rainfall, depend very much on more local conditions than can be encompassed in the present state of the art of climate prediction. For example, a major study recently carried out on the impact of climate change on the UK concluded: "Given the scenarios of UK climate change noted above, it is likely that the occurrence of hot, dry summers would increase while the chances of extreme cold winters would decrease" (a prospect devoutly to be wished by most residents of the UK!). It went on: "For other extremes, such as severe storms, the scientific 'state-of-the-art' precludes even reasoned speculation."[9] This is consistent with the conclusion of the IPCC scientific working group, that "climate models give no consistent indication whether tropical storms will increase or decrease in frequency or intensity as climate changes; neither is there any evidence that this has occurred over the past few decades."[10]

The Overall Effect

Hence it seems impossible to escape the conclusion that, even under pessimistic assumptions, the annual cost to the world as a whole of global warming associated with a doubling of CO_2 concentrations is likely to be almost negligible by comparison with the value of world output over the period in question. Such estimates as have been made of the overall effect on the world economy of a doubling of the CO_2 concentration suggest that world output or income would be reduced by about 1 or 2 percent.[11]

Suppose these estimates are much too conservative. Suppose the real impact is that world output would be reduced by 10 times as much—that is, by 10 percent by the end of the next century below what it would otherwise be. Then, instead of average world income per head being 4.4 times as great as it is now, it would be only 3.96 times as great. Would this be so great a disaster? Would it justify rushing in now in a vain effort to achieve international agreement on draconian measures to restrict carbon emissions? Would it justify immediate action rather than waiting until further progress has been made in understanding climate change? Would it justify running the risk of imposing heavy costs on the present generation rather than devoting more time, effort, and resources to helping the developing countries to overcome the environmental problems that they are facing today, not to mention many environmental problems in the richer countries?

The Costs of Preventing Climate Change

But what would it cost to implement drastic action to cut CO_2 emissions by the most economical means, namely imposing a carbon tax or a system of internationally tradable permits in carbon dioxide emissions? Here the uncertainties are as great as, if not greater than, those embodied in the scientific models used to predict climate change. Nobody can predict with much accuracy the future pattern of economic growth over the next century in a manner that enables us to identify how much fossil fuel would be burned and hence what needs to be done to reduce fossil fuel consumption by any given amount. Nor can anyone say with any degree of reliability how sensitive the consumption of fossil fuels is to different levels of carbon taxes. It may well be that the estimates of how far fossil fuel consumption would fall if carbon taxes were to be imposed, *given the present prices of substitutes*, are well below what the impact of carbon taxes would be in the more distant future when technological progress will have led to further rapid reductions in the prices of renewable fuels and in energy-saving technologies.

Finally, insofar as any taxes raised by imposing charges on carbon-intensive fuels ought to be refunded to the economy somehow or other—so that they merely change the pattern of fuel use rather than exert a deflationary impact on the economy as a whole—the effect could be favorable. If taxes on other economic activities were to be reduced, there would be efficiency gains that might well outweigh the "efficiency" losses caused by the carbon taxes.[12] On the other hand, a tax on a basic input into the economy, which is what carbon taxes or energy taxes would mean, could have a more serious impact than other taxes such as those that are levied on different items of consumer expenditure.

Vast computerized models tend to blind people with science and impress grant-giving institutions. But the estimates that they churn out of the cost of measures designed to cut CO_2 emissions significantly are highly uncertain. The estimates also differ with respect to the amount of reduction in emissions that they assume for purposes of calculating the costs. It is inevitable, therefore, that different models lead to widely different estimates. But for what they are worth it seems that the order of magnitude of the costs would be somewhere in the region of 5 percent of output for the world as a whole (which probably implies twice this amount for North America and Western Europe, where per capita carbon emissions are relatively very high). This is not surprising because—again without the aid of a sophisticated computerized model—it is obvious that, if carried out quickly, a drastic cut in the use of fossil fuels in any modern industrialized economy could cause severe economic disruption.

And the above estimates of the cost of measures to reduce global warming are likely to be underestimates, because they assume that the cuts in emissions are achieved by the most economical means, notably the imposition of some carbon tax. But the chances of this are remote, since it is most likely that, if any international agreement to reduce carbon emissions is ever negotiated, it would be rather along the lines of existing agreements to reduce CFC emissions in order to protect the ozone layer. These agreements, notably the Montreal Convention, are in terms of quantitative limits on national emissions, which are far more costly than some price mechanism solution, such as the carbon tax solution used in most estimates of the cost of reducing CO_2 emissions.

The Very Long-Term Effects of Climate Change

Most eco-doomsters say that we cannot wait another decade or so to clear up the major uncertainties surrounding the predictions of climate change and its effects. The above discussion of the damage that might be done by a doubling of present concentrations of carbon in the atmosphere neglects the fact that, in the even longer run, the continued accumulation of GHGs changes climate and raises global temperatures to the point that it can no longer be so lightly dismissed. William Cline of the Institute for International Economics, for example, has projected the effects of climate change over the following three centuries.[13] He argues that, given the well-known time lags in the climate change process, although global temperatures may rise by only 3°C by the end of the next century (under the "business as usual" scenario), there is a further unavoidable rise in the pipeline of several more degrees.

Of course, because the predictions of climate change and its effects over the next century are terribly shaky to begin with, their extrapolation over another century or two would require outstanding intellectual courage were it not for the fact that the author will not be alive at the time the predictions are tested. After all, there have been vast technological changes in energy use in the last hundred years. And these will probably be dwarfed by the changes that will take place over the next century, let alone the following century, during which an incomparably greater number of people will be engaged in technological and scientific research all over the world. Nobody can suppose that the world of the late 22nd century will bear much resemblance to the world that we know today and that energy will still be produced on a large scale by dirty and polluting substances such as coal.

For example, who could have predicted that the overall efficiency of modern, gas-fired, combined-cycle power plants would have about 10 times the efficiency of power stations built at the beginning of this century, or that the thermal efficiency of steam engines would be now about 40 times as great as that of the earliest engines, or that the most advanced fluorescent lights have an efficiency about 900 times as great as the original kerosene lamps? And progress is now being made in developing economically viable forms of renewable sources of energy that emit no carbon at all.[14]

Even without, as yet, any significant recourse to the many forms of renewable energy under investigation—hydropower, wind, solar thermal, photovoltaics, ocean thermal, and so on—there have been major reductions in the ratio of both energy use and carbon emissions to GNP. For example, over the period 1950–1985 carbon emissions per unit of GNP in the United States have fallen at an average rate of 1.3 percent per annum. Cline does not declare his assumption about this trend. But, from his predictions of GNP growth and CO_2 emissions, we can work out what assumption is implied in his predictions. And it appears that he is asssuming that the carbon emissions per unit of GNP will fall by only about 0.7 percent per annum in the latter half of the 21st century—that is, only about half of the annual fall between 1950 and 1985. Moreover his estimates appear to imply that the ratio of carbon emissions to GNP will fall even less thereafter, and will actually rise during the last 75 years of the period covered in his predictions!

Furthermore, more climate change would induce specific innovations to deal with it. That has been the pattern of technical innovation throughout the ages, ever since humans began to make fires and wear animal skins to keep warm. In earlier periods much of the planet was totally uninhabitable for climatic reasons. But with current technology all that has changed, and humans can live comfortably in almost any climate on Earth. And in the more recent past the pace of technological innovation that reduces the significance of climate has been incomparably faster. As one writer has put it, "Technological inventions and innovations that have had roles in human ability to adapt to climate over the last 100 years or so range widely: food preservatives (1873) to overcome problems of seasonal food production; light bulbs (1879) to make work safe and effective indoors; aluminum (1887) and other structural materials to resist environmental deterioration; refrigeration (1895) and air conditioning (1902, 1906) to facilitate activity in hot seasons and locations;

115

automobiles (1890s) to provide personal transportation that is much less sensitive to climate than horses or pedal bicycles"—and so on and so forth.[15]

So What's the Hurry?

One of the most frequent arguments in favor of early action in environmental matters is the so-called "precautionary principle." But this is just a pompous way of saying that, as in many human activities, we should bear in mind the case for taking out some sort of insurance against unpleasant events or make investments designed to prevent the event ever taking place. It is argued, in fact, that even if we cannot be certain that serious damage will follow from global warming it is worth incurring costs now to reduce future global warming just in case the damage otherwise turns out to be serious.

Expenditures designed to reduce the risk of global warming are not of course the same as taking out an insurance policy. With an insurance policy we pay a premium now in the expectation that if the event against which we are insuring actually takes place—the house is burned down or burgled, or the car is stolen, and so on— the insurance company will compensate us for the damage. In other words, we will be no worse off when the unfortunate event occurs; only the insurance company will lose. The policy constitutes a way of redistributing the losses involved. But in the global warming case, heavy expenditure now to reduce global warming is designed to reduce the chances of the unfortunate event ever taking place. It is much more like an investment in smoke alarms, burglar alarms, better locks on doors and cars, and so on. The calculation, therefore, is how far such an investment seems worthwhile. For nobody in their senses is prepared to invest any amount, irrespective of the probabilities, on the grounds of some "precautionary principle."

And the above survey indicates several reasons why hasty action is undesirable and why it is better to wait until we have more information about the likely severity of climate change.

(i) First, we have seen that even if we adopt warming scenarios that are at the top of the range of possibilities indicated in the latest IPCC report, the economic effects are not likely to be catastrophic. And, as shown above, on balance it looks much more likely that any global warming that takes place will anyway be very much smaller than this—of the order of 1 to 2 degrees with a doubling of CO_2—and that the effects may be beneficial rather than harmful.

(ii) Second, delaying action by several years makes a negligible difference. Schlesinger and Jiang, for example, show that a 10-year delay and switching over from the IPCC's "business as usual" scenario (i.e., no action taken to reduce global warming) to a tough anti-global-warming scenario would only reduce the increase in temperature by the year 2100 by between 0.1°C and 0.3°C, according to whether one adopts the bottom or the top of the IPCC's range of global warming predictions. They conclude, "This indicates that the penalty is small for a 10-year delay in initiating the transition to a regime in which greenhouse-gas emissions are reduced."[16] So if we delay action by 10 years the extra warming that would occur by the year 2100 would be only about 0.2°C. We would all have plenty of time to change into lighter shirts. Of course, as the authors go on to say, we should continue research into climate change "so that we do not squander the time that nature has given us to obtain a realistic understanding of the climate response to increasing concentrations of greenhouse gases."

These estimates match those of other climate change experts. For example, Balling shows that since the "actual" rise in temperature over the last century is only about half what the models used in the IPCC report would predict, and since about half the "actual" rise can probably be explained by non-CO_2 factors (notably the decline in stratospheric aerosols), the actual rise over the next century could be only a quarter of the IPCC's predictions. On this basis a delay of 10 years in the switch from "business as usual" to a policy of reducing carbon emissions would add only 0.05°C to global temperature by the time that CO_2 concentrations have doubled (i.e., some time in the latter half of the next century).[17] At the same time there has been an explosion of research into climate change during the last few years, so that we can expect major improvements in our knowledge of this phenomenon during the course of the next few years.

(iii) Furthermore, there is a very large momentum behind research into global warming now. We can expect substantial advances in the scientific understanding of it during the next decade. So it is much more sensible to support this research than to rush to conclusions that could prove to be very expensive. This is particularly so in the light of the following economic considerations.

117

(iv) In Chapter 4 it was argued that a reduction in the supply of some material relative to the demand would not matter as long as there was time for the economy to adapt. Incentives would be set up to find substitutes and to economize in its use. But if the change were to be dramatic—if the world were to wake up tomorrow and find that it had suddenly run out of supplies of some basic raw material—the effect could be extremely expensive, and possibly catastrophic. The same applies to drastic action to curtail energy consumption. If, in the light of further scientific progress, it is found necessary to carry out any significant cut in energy use, it is far less expensive to bring it about gradually, thereby giving the world time to invest in substitutes, in technological progress to economize in energy, and gradually to switch patterns of production and consumption into less energy-intensive forms. Drastic, large-scale action is a recipe for economic disaster and tilts the balance of costs and benefits heavily on the wrong side.

(v) Furthermore, as we have already shown, even without any special measures to curb energy consumption—indeed even with a decline in the "real" price of most energy sources over the last decade or so—there has already been considerable technological progress in the exploitation of renewable energy resources or in methods of economizing in energy in general. A continued reduction in the costs of energy-economizing investment or in the use of non-polluting renewable energy would mean that the cost of measures to cut energy use would be further reduced. It would be absurd, therefore, to press for rapid early cuts in energy consumption before taking advantage of cheaper methods of reducing this consumption that can be anticipated over the next decade or so.

(vi) Finally, because there is little point in any individual country trying to reduce global warming by itself, effective action to reduce it depends on international agreement. It will be immensely difficult to reach effective international agreement to reduce carbon emissions, if only because of the vast differences between countries in how far they lose or gain from any action. This does not mean, however, that it is impossible to reach agreement. But it means that hastily contrived agreement is hardly likely to be the most efficient. It is more likely to be some form of agreement that imposes quantitative limits on the carbon emissions of different countries than agreement embodying least-cost market mechanisms. Given more time, there is at least some chance that the international community could agree on some sort of economic mechanism for allocating carbon-emission reductions among countries that (i) minimized the total burden on the world economy and (ii) ensured an equitable compensation for those countries—especially the developing countries—who will be least able to bear the costs.

In such a situation, is it really worth making expensive investments in measures to enforce rapid reductions in CO_2 emissions if the penalty for waiting is so small? What the "precautionary principle" slogan seems to imply, therefore, at least in this context, is "Take action now when it is very expensive rather than wait a few years when technical progress will have made it much cheaper and we shall have a much better idea of whether it is necessary anyway."

At the same time there is little doubt that there are market failures in energy use. In particular, large subsidies are paid in many countries to the production and use of coal, which is among the "dirtiest" forms of fossil fuel from the point of view of its carbon emissions. Road transport, which is usually unduly favored on account of a failure to impose full social costs on it, is a principal source of increased GHG emissions in advanced countries. In developing countries old-fashioned production techniques are far more energy-intensive and polluting than those that are available today in advanced countries. But what is more inexcusable is the degree of economic support given to uneconomic industrial activities and the destruction of tropical forests (though this makes relatively little difference to global warming). In all countries there are market failures that prevent the optimal implementation of measures to economize on energy use, though environmentalist estimates of the significance of such market failures are often exaggerated.[18] Thus action taken now to reduce the various subsidies to excessive energy use, deforestation, and carbon emissions would be not merely costless: it would actually reduce costs.

Conclusions

Global warming has to be taken seriously, but is no cause for alarm or drastic action. There is plenty of time to improve our understanding of the science, and to take measures to cut out uneconomic uses of fossil fuels, and to remedy market failures that lead to inadequate research into alternative sources of energy. It does

119

not justify diverting vast amounts of people's time, energies, and funds from more urgent environmental problems, particularly those in developing countries. We are not on the edge of an abyss, and the human race is not facing destruction on account of the accumulation of greenhouse gases. Global warming is far more glamorous and telegenic of course than building better lavatories in the Third World, or ensuring a stock of the gene pool of endangered species, or tackling air pollution or bad housing in many cities in advanced countries. But it is to these environmental issues that people who are genuinely concerned with the welfare of their fellow creatures— both those who are alive today and those who will be alive in 100 years' time—should pay attention.

Although we should give high priority to improving our scientific understanding of the climate change phenomenon, how society should strike a balance between the apparently relatively minor damage that global warming would impose on future generations on the one hand and the burden that the present generation should bear in order to take drastic action to prevent global warming on the other is not a matter that can be decided purely on scientific grounds. Nor is it a matter to be decided by pressures from semi-hysterical eco-doomsters. Scientists may often have their own axes to grind, but science is a field of human activity in which, in the end, truth will prevail and error will be exposed. This is not the case in evangelical crusades.

PART II

GROWTH, WELFARE, AND SUSTAINABILITY

8. Growth and Welfare: Must They Conflict?

The Two Prongs in the Anti-Growth Attack

As I pointed out in Chapter 1, there have been two main themes behind the widespread view that the objective of economic growth must be abandoned.

The first is that economic growth does not make us any happier; indeed it is often argued that it makes us less happy, and that the "costs" of economic growth include a deterioration in the quality of life.

The second is that growth of the kind that we have been experiencing for decades is not "sustainable" because sooner or later it will come up against the limits set by "finite" supplies of resources or the capacity of the ecosystem to absorb harmful pollutants or the loss of biodiversity. The physical constraint on growth was the theme of the well-known report to the Club of Rome, *The Limits to Growth*, publihed in 1972,[1] and the theme has been repeated with variations ever since. One of its variants is the claim that we should abandon the emphasis on the growth of GNP, which is basically a measure of the amount the economy produces, and concentrate instead on the goal of "sustainable development." This, it is argued, takes account of the extent to which society is using up nonrenewable resources of all kinds (including its capacity to absorb CO_2 emissions and waste products).

There is some overlap between the two anti-growth themes. Those who maintain that economic growth leads to a decline in the "quality of life" do so on various grounds. One is that the quality of life is being reduced by the increase in pollution, which, it is alleged, is an inevitable by-product of economic growth. Conversely, the claim that past patterns of economic growth cannot be sustained much longer on account of the exhaustion of nonrenewable resources or

123

rising pollution also implies a reduction in the quality of life. Nevertheless, the two themes can be treated separately for they point to different conclusions even if they share some assumptions. One is saying that growth is bad for us whether we can have it or not. The other is saying that old-fashioned growth patterns are unsustainable whether we like it or not. In this book I try to show that both conclusions are false.

The late Professor Lord Robbins (Lionel Robbins) accurately described the first of the two anti-growth themes as follows: "And now there is arising a . . . school of thought which argues that . . . growth itself is something which is intrinsically undesirable; and that to recommend anything on the ground that it will promote growth is simply to reveal an essentially philistine character, an indifference to all that makes life anxious and ugly in the present age and an insensitiveness to truly civilized values."[2] For it is true that this part of the anti-growth argument generally takes the form of insisting that economic growth has involved an excessive concern with *material* output, particularly of a "vulgar" kind, that often represents the gratification of artificially created needs by the advertising in a "consumer society" devoted to promoting—in the words of a pioneering critic of economic growth—"the mushroom growth of television, automobile ownership, air travel and mass tourism,"[3] and that the growth "rat race" destroys not merely the visual amenities of town and country, but also our ability to communicate with our fellow men, our sense of aesthetic and moral values, and even our pride in our work. "All we can say in general is that the idea of work as a source of legitimate pride, as a source of gratification, forms no part of the ethos of an industrial civilization."[4]

GNP and Welfare: The Economist's Approach

The distinction frequently made by critics of economic growth between the coarse materialists who are in favor of growth and the environmentalists who perceive the sordid realities behind modern economic growth is often accompanied by the notion that—with two or three honorable exceptions—like Ed Mishan, or the late Kenneth Boulding, or the late E. F. Schumacher—all economists are in the materialist camp, and that they all worship at the shrine of GNP (which is often mistakenly believed to comprise only material output).

124

Sir Crispin Tickell in his article "What We Must Do to Save the Planet" writes: "The instruments of economic analysis are blunt and rusty. Terms such as . . . 'gross national product' have come to be misleading. They are more than ripe for redefinition."[5] Before showing that the widespread environmentalist mistrust of the concept of gross national product (GNP) is totally misplaced, one simple fact suffices to destroy their claim that it bears little relationship to what really makes life worth living. This is that there is enormous pressure from people living in countries with low GNP per head to emigrate to countries with high GNP per head. And there is not much evidence of any great desire by many people to move in the opposite direction.

Of course all economists know that, at best, GNP is simply one component of welfare: namely, that part of total welfare which, in the classic phrase of one of the greatest economists of the century, A. C. Pigou, "can be brought directly or indirectly into relation with the measuring-rod of money."[6] Indeed, in order to describe the relation between economic welfare and total welfare, Pigou went on to point out, 70 years ago, what some people today believe to be a great revelation, namely that ". . . there is no guarantee that the effects produced on the part of welfare that can be brought into relation with the measuring-rod of money may not be canceled by effects of a contrary kind brought about in other parts, or aspects, of welfare; and, if this happens, the practical usefulness of our conclusions is wholly destroyed. . . . The real objection then is, not that economic welfare is a bad index of total welfare, but that an economic cause may affect noneconomic welfare in ways that cancel its effect on economic welfare."[7]

Furthermore, in the same book Pigou actually used the now fashionable term "quality of life" in the course of his enumeration of the various ways in which a rise in *economic* welfare (which is more or less what a rise in GNP is supposed to measure) may fail to lead to a corresponding rise in *total* welfare. In particular he emphasized the fact that "non-economic welfare is liable to be modified by the manner in which income is earned. For the surroundings of work react upon the quality of life."[8] He also discussed the effect on welfare of aesthetic and ethical sensitivities, or the manner in which income is spent, and some of the other ingredients of welfare that now tend to be trumpeted by most environmentalists as constituting final proof of the irrelevance of national-product measurement for policy purposes.

The environmentalist criticism of the national product concept overlooks the fact that this concept, which embraces countless individual items that contribute to welfare, is the only substantial part of welfare that has been precisely defined and systematically and carefully measured. After all, suppose we had started out by saying, "Now, let us measure human welfare in order to see whether it is rising or falling, and under what conditions it does so, and so on." Presumably we would have tried to draw up a list of all the things that we believed contributed to "human welfare." We would then probably have felt obliged to leave aside ingredients such as people's love of their neighbors, joy of living, satisfaction from family reunions, pleasure in breathing the clear morning air, or watching birds, on the grounds that though they might be the most important things in life (to some people), no way of measuring them could be found. Then, with luck, up would speak some bright spark who would point out that, while not disputing the supremacy of the items listed, it would be a pity to drop the whole idea of trying to measure how much welfare has changed just because no quantitative estimate could be made of these particular components, so why not at least measure those components which people *did* seem to want— like food, clothing, housing, health care, educational services, travel, leisure activities, and so on—and which *could* be measured, since they were the subject of transactions in terms of some common unit, namely money? "True," he would add, "this isn't the whole of welfare, by any means, but it would at least seem to be part of it, and perhaps an important part judging by the amount of time and trouble people devote to getting more of these things, so we might at least measure that part of welfare which is measurable."

In a sense, this is more or less what happened. But, many decades after the economists embarked on their extremely difficult work of measuring national product, and many decades after they had carefully spelled out the difference between this concept and that of total welfare, the concept of national product—the only relatively unambiguous measure we have that adds together, in a meaningful way, thousands of components of welfare—has come under fire on account of its inability to do what economists never tried to do with it, namely to measure *total* welfare.

There can never be any scientific demonstration of the relationship between income levels and welfare. For the concept of "welfare" is not one that can be scientifically established; different people can hold different views as to what constitutes welfare. But, as indicated above, the best we can do is to take a balanced view of the changes that have taken place in people's living standards as a result of economic growth.

The mere fact that economic growth has no doubt been accompanied by some deterioration in certain aspects of the quality of life— at least for some groups in society—does not prove that overall welfare must have fallen, or even risen more slowly than GNP. There are also aspects of life that are not recorded in GNP and that may have improved.

For example, we might want to include the increase during this century in the amount of social capital available (libraries, schools, and so on); the substantial improvement in working conditions and hours of work and duration of holidays with pay, as well as legal protection afforded to employees; increased social security for the old, the sick, and the unemployed; the great reduction in domestic drudgery for the homemaker; and the increased freedom to travel and to discover new horizons and new lands. If our ambition is merely to remind the public and the politicians that GNP is not everything in life and to ensure that other, negative aspects of total welfare are taken into account, a more balanced and objective debate would require us to list the benefits that are excluded from GNP as well as the costs. In the next section, therefore, we discuss some of the omitted items and also the so-called "Human Development Index," which goes beyond GNP and measures some wider concept of welfare. But, of course, it would always be open to people to dissent from this concept as well and to say that, in their opinion, welfare constituted something entirely different. There would be no way of proving that they were wrong.

Economic Growth and Welfare in the Twentieth Century

It should not be thought that, once the worst features of the industrial revolution, such as those mentioned in Chapter 3, had been remedied, further economic growth led inexorably to further deterioration in the environment—albeit in less dramatic forms. As was also shown in Chapter 3, the improvement in the environment has continued throughout the 20th century in line with increased prosperity. Most of these improvements are not adequately reflected in the growth of GNP. And the continued economic growth of the last few decades has been accompanied by major improvements in many other aspects of people's lives that are not reflected in GNP estimates and that are usually ignored by those who are determined to conclude that economic growth is harmful.

Health

One major example is health, which most people would probably put at the top of their welfare concerns. And there is no doubt that this has improved steadily over the last few decades, quite apart from any health benefits obtained from the reduction in pollution. One obvious illustration of this has been the rapid rise in the average expectation of life during the century. In the postwar years data covering most countries of the world have become available and show that global life expectancy has risen over the last three decades from 53 years to 66 years. In the developing countries it has risen from 46 to 63 and in the industrialized countries from 69 to 75. In the last 15 years it has fallen in only two countries, Sierra Leone and Uganda.[9]

It is ironic that health trends illustrate one of the ways, well-known to economists, in which a rise in GNP may underestimate the rise in welfare, not overestimate it. For the rise in health expenditures included in the GNP will correspond to the costs of health care and may considerably underestimate the welfare that will be obtained. For example, when a new vaccine or drug is developed that, at low cost, virtually eliminates diseases such as polio or diphtheria or smallpox, the resulting increase in human welfare may be out of proportion to the medical expenditures actually incurred. And it is clear from the data that there have been enormous reductions in the health risks from many of the diseases that still plagued society earlier this century, long after the industrial revolution had reached a peak and the scourges of typhoid, typhus, and cholera had been eliminated from advanced societies.

For example, deaths from respiratory tuberculosis were still running at about 25,000 per annum in England and Wales as recently as the 1930s. But by 1970 they had been reduced to about 1,000 per annum. In the United States annual deaths from tuberculosis were reduced, over the same period, from a rate of more than 50 per 100,000 persons to about 3 per 100,000. Diphtheria is another fatal

128

disease that was still widespread in the 1930s but has been practically eliminated under the combined impact of medical advances and improved sanitary conditions. In England and Wales reported deaths from diphtheria appeared to be rising toward the end of the 19th century to a peak of about 8,000 per annum in the 1890s. The number had been cut to about 3,000 per annum in the interwar period in England and Wales (it was about 7,000 per annum in the United States).

In both countries there are now virtually no deaths from diphtheria. Of course the above figures relate only to deaths, the number of cases notified being over 10 times as great. In other words, during the interwar period about 50,000 to 60,000 cases of diphtheria were notified every year, year after year, in England and Wales, mainly of children, compared with only about a dozen cases per year during the 1960s. The elimination of acute anxiety and strain from hundreds of thousands of families as a result of the virtual eradication of this and other potential fatal diseases must mean an incalculable increase in their welfare. It is right that the public should be concerned by the possibility that, for example, some children may be affected by lead in the atmosphere in certain locations. But while such environmental effects should be tackled, in judging the net effect of economic growth on welfare they have to be weighed against the extent to which millions of families have been spared the terrible anxieties associated with the prevalence of diphtheria, polio, tuberculosis, whooping cough, scarlet fever, and so on. If this balance is struck, it is impossible to conclude that, on any set of value judgments, there has not been an astronomic improvement in the general health of the population during the course of the century.

The anti-growth lobby is quick to point out an alleged connection between economic growth and a relatively limited health hazard, such as the lead hazard mentioned above, but if they were serious they would presumably want to consider also the relationship between economic growth and the incomparably greater effect on welfare caused by the virtual eradication of several very widespread deadly illnesses. For the downward trend in infant mortality has continued in the past 30 years in spite of such environmental black spots as are so triumphantly publicized by many eco-doomsters. For example, in low- and middle-income countries infant mortality has fallen by about one half between 1965 and 1988, and in high-income countries the rate fell, over the same period, from 26 per

1,000 to only 9.[10] Income may not be the only thing in life, but when a life is snuffed out there isn't even the income.

In any case, much of the alleged scaremongering about the health effects of pollution is based on shoddy science. As an article in *The Times* (of London) put it, describing a book that had been published containing the usual alarmist stories about health and the environment, "This is how it works. Take an environmental medium—air, water, or food—list all the terrible chemicals that can be found in it, selectively cite a few papers on the toxic effects of acute exposure, mention—perhaps—that it is more difficult to show hazards from lower doses, but emphasize that such a possibility cannot be ruled out. Throw in a random guesstimate of how many might be affected and another potential threat to our health is notched up. There is only one antidote to this shopping list of junk science, a careful and fastidious examination of the facts."[11]

The author of this article went on to say that the book illustrated the "lamentable scientific standards of the environmental activists— and it costs us all very dear. Hundreds of millions of pounds spent minimizing nonexistent environmental hazards in the Western world is money not spent on providing clean water and family planning services to the desperately poor inhabitants of sub-Saharan Africa."

Other Components of Human Welfare

There are various other important components of welfare that are not reflected in GNP and that have been increasing over time. They include the output of public capital, such as schools, hospitals, sports facilities, libraries, parks, and other public buildings or installations. Unlike private capital or the capital equipment of nationalized industries, the "output" of these forms of the community's capital stock is not included in GNP. But it is certainly much greater in recent years than in the more distant past and incomparably greater in rich countries than in poorer countries. Again, it is ironic that the chief constraint on these items of public expenditure in the last decade or so has been the dramatic slowing down of economic growth since the first "oil shock" of the early 1970s. Until then fast economic growth had facilitated the growth of all these components of human welfare *that are not adequately reflected in conventional estimates of GNP!*

The same applies to numerous leisure activities, not to mention homemakers' services. Over the course of the century there also has been a big improvement in the conditions of work enjoyed by the working population. This is not reflected in GNP. Even leaving aside the vast improvements in the working environment, the number of fatal industrial accidents in Britain has fallen steadily to a record all-time low and is a small fraction of what it was at the beginning of the century, in spite of a large rise in the industrial workforce during this period.

Furthermore, holidays with pay have increased and hours of work have greatly fallen over the course of the century. And leisure time is a very important component of welfare. But it is not included in estimates of GNP, of course. In fact, other things being equal, a rise in leisure would reduce GNP but would raise welfare, which is quite the contrary of the bias that the critics of growth usually attribute to the GNP figures![12]

There is little point in protesting, as do the critics of economic growth, at the way that modern society has reduced the degree of communication among human beings when one of the major developments over the last few decades has been to give most working classes the time and opportunity to see more of their friends, their families, and people living far afield in foreign countries. The increase in leisure opportunities, combined with the speed of international travel, also must have made it easier for the ordinary person to extend his knowledge of the world and his familiarity with its artistic and other wonders. It may always have been perfectly feasible for a small elite to make their way slowly to Delphi or Florence overland, but for the average man-in-the-street with, at best, one week's poorly paid holiday, it was quite out of the question.

It is true that some of the components of welfare may have been getting worse over the years as a concomitant of economic growth and the absence of appropriate policies concerning the way the fruits of economic growth are used and distributed. But if one's aim is to move closer to some assessment of how far economic welfare, as distinct from measured GNP, has changed in line with economic growth, why draw attention only to those omissions from GNP that correspond to reductions in welfare? For GNP also fails to measure many components of welfare that are probably increasing. Among the most important of these are those just discussed, notably the enormous improvements in the overall health of the population, the generally vast improvement in the sanitary and hygienic conditions of towns in most advanced countries, changes in working and housing conditions, and so on.

Over the longer run there has also been a major improvement in other aspects of life that are most important for the large majority of the population, such as social security benefits, legislation preventing unfair dismissal, or the provision of redundancy pay and severance allowances. In the earlier decades of this century if a man fell out of work through sickness or for some other reason, or retired without having been able to save much, there was little for him or his family to do except starve or scrape by on workhouse charity. This constant source of anxiety for millions of people has now been reduced (thanks to unemployment benefits, free health services, and the like).

In the earlier years of this century most working people accepted that their lot was a bad one; they did not expect it to improve, and only prayed that it would not get any worse on the following day. Those who were lucky enough to have jobs usually worked in conditions that were far noisier, dirtier, more dangerous, and more insanitary than is the case today. And they came home to far worse housing conditions than are normal today. To maintain, as do some critics of economic growth, that the conditions today are more conducive to mental anxiety on account of a faster pace of technical progress exhibits either a complete ignorance of what life was really like for working people in the not too distant past or a complete lack of imagination about what such conditions must have meant to the average working man. Of course, it is very likely that most people today have little or no conception of what life was like for their grandparents at the beginning of the century and so will be unable to assess the importance of the improvements that have taken place over the course of time and to balance these against the possible deterioration that may well have taken place in other aspects of their lives.

There are undoubtedly still many black spots and distressingly large areas of poverty in modern industrial society, particularly during a deep and prolonged recession. In the last few years the emergence of prolonged mass unemployment has led to a tragic rise in unemployment-related poverty. It would be absurd to claim that affluence can cure these and other problems. In any case, the point is that the current problems of unemployment in the advanced countries have been caused by a lack of economic growth, not an excess of it! They reflect a failure of macro economic policy, and have nothing to do with either long-run economic growth in general or its environmental effects in particular.

Over the longer run economic growth has brought major improvements in human welfare, such as those enumerated above, that are too often ignored by those who constantly proclaim the conflict between, on the one hand, economic growth and, on the other, the "quality of life." And, although the current recession has made many governments cut down on social security expenditures, the welfare provisions in most rich countries are still incomparably better than they were in the more distant past. And they are also incomparably more generous than in developing countries, as is welfare in general or the state of the environment in particular. Far more people still try to emigrate from low-income countries to high-income countries than the reverse.

The Statistical Relationship between Incomes and "Welfare"

As I argued in my 1974 book, the historical evidence up to that date was that economic growth had been accompanied by improvements in the main measurable ingredients of the "quality of life," notably those relating to health, but including also the main pollutants in advanced countries.[13] During the last 20 years there have been many more systematic studies showing that incomes per head are highly correlated both with important individual ingredients of the quality of life and with so-called "composite" indexes that combine many major ingredients of welfare together.

For example, a recent Dasgupta and Weale analysis shows positive correlations between per capita national income and individual indicators, such as life expectancy at birth, the adult literacy rate, and even with indexes of political and civil liberties (though the direction of causation here is open to question).[14] A similar study by Dasgupta, covering 50 developing countries with per capita GNP of only U.S. $1,000 per annum or less, examined the relationship between these income levels and life expectancy at birth, literacy, infant mortality and indexes of political and civil liberty, in 1970 and 1980.[15] The main finding was that, with the exception of literacy rates, all these components of welfare were positively and significantly correlated with per capita income levels and their growth.

More recently sophisticated attempts have been made, under the auspices of the United Nations Development Program, to combine

133

these and other components of welfare, or of "human development," into a "composite" index, known as the "Human Development Index." This shows a strong positive correlation between incomes per head and an index that gives equal weight to incomes, life expectancy, and literacy. As the *Human Development Report 1991* says, "Human development requires economic growth—for without it, no sustained improvement in human well-being is possible," though it adds, "But while growth is necessary for human development, it is not enough. High growth rates do not automatically translate into higher levels of human development."[16] At another point it states: "The best way to promote human development is to increase the national income and to ensure a close link between economic growth and human well-being."[17]

Are We Just Satisfying "Artificial" Needs?

One of the main arguments in the anti-growth school of thought is that—to a cultivated person—economic growth represents an increase in activities that do not really add to human welfare. Many of the activities are alleged merely to satisfy needs that have been artificially stimulated in the consumer society. Others are believed to be really expenditures that are needed to meet the costs of economic growth—such as the costs of treating the victims of road accidents, or clearing up oil spillages. So one way or the other increased economic activity does not really make any net addition to welfare.

But the relationship between changes in "needs" and overall welfare is a rather complex one, for the following reasons:

(i) It may well be that some, or even most, people are happier when they experience an increase in certain needs, even if these cannot be entirely satisfied. For example, many people have a "need" to listen to music, but do not have the time or the money to go to as many concerts as they would like, so are unable fully to satisfy this need. But the fact that there is a gap between their needs and their satisfactions, does not mean that they are "worse off" than if they did not have this need. Most of them would still maintain that, even though it cannot be completely satisfied, this particular need helps them to lead a fuller and richer life.

(ii) And even if an increase in some needs did not make people "happier" it is still arguable that they raised human welfare rather than reduced it. For example, we might approve of the needs in

134

question—they might include an awakened need to do something about improving the environment. What constitutes being a rise in welfare is a value judgment that can quite well take the form of believing that what distinguishes humans from animals is precisely the multiplicity and diversity of human needs. Of course, the gap between people's needs and their satisfactions can be narrowed by reducing the needs to the level of, say, the domestic dog, which are confined to a square meal (uncooked) per day, daily walks, and a moderate display of affection by its owners. Some people may argue that this is the road to happiness, and, if combined with a dedication of one's life and thoughts to spiritual matters, is also the road to salvation. Others may maintain that human beings fulfill their nature more by acquiring new "needs," and that this is desirable. In the words of the French sociologist Henri Lefebvre, "The more needs the human being has the more he exists."[18]

(iii) A third issue is whether it matters how far certain needs are artificially induced or not. For it seems impossible to make any sharp distinction between artificially induced needs and other "natural" needs. In any case, the artificiality or otherwise of the needs seems to have little connection with whether or not they add to welfare. Satisfying an artificial need may add to welfare, whereas satisfying some natural need may be bad for it, depending on one's concept of welfare. After all, I happen to experience a desire to listen to certain kinds of music, but I certainly was not born with it. As the late Anthony Crosland reminded us in a classic work of contemporary political analysis, it is impossible to draw a sharp dividing line between those of our needs that are innate and natural and those that have been artificially developed as a result of many factors, including our whole social environment.[19]

Furthermore, even if it were possible to draw a dividing line between artificial and natural needs, what is so moral about natural needs and so immoral, or undesirable, about artificial needs? Would some people's artificially induced "need" to listen to music or to acquire knowledge be less desirable a component of welfare than some other people's rather primitive instinct to rape women? There is obviously no way of settling disputes about what needs are good or bad and how far some needs add to welfare or subtract from it. The rival views on this subject are not rival propositions about the way the world behaves; they are simply rival criteria of "good" and

135

"bad" or of "better" and "worse." As such they lie outside the field of scientific discourse.

Suppose that both needs and satisfactions are rising, but needs are rising faster than satisfactions. Some people would say that the rise in needs makes society worse off. Some would see the rise in satisfactions as making society better off. And some would say that society is worse off because the satisfactions are rising less than the needs. There is no scientific way of saying which group is right. They are all just defining "better off" in different ways.

Welfare and "Keeping Up with the Joneses"

Critics of economic growth or of "consumerism" often argue that what matters more to a people in a high-consumption society is not their absolute levels of income, but their positions relative to other people. Dr. Mishan wrote that "the more truth there is in this relative income hypothesis—and one can hardly deny the increasing emphasis on status and income position in the affluent society—the more futile as a means of increasing social welfare is the official policy of economic growth."[20] A few years later the same basic point was developed at great length in *The Social Limits to Growth* by the late Fred Hirsch, who also was an economist.[21] Hirsch also mentioned that other economists had made the same point before, notably Sir Roy Harrod.

But this argument is a double-edged sword in the hands of those who are concerned about the pollution of the environment. For if a person's welfare is entirely a matter of his relative position, then extra global pollution is of no importance to society as a whole. For either we all become equally more exposed to pollution, or it is unevenly distributed, in which case although some people suffer from being more affected than others, those who suffer less presumably gain from a rise in their relative positions.

In fact, most people would probably accept that welfare depended both on one's relative position and one's absolute level of income. But in that case growth in the latter must add to welfare. In other words, there are two possibilities. Either (i) welfare depends only on one's relative position, or (ii) it depends both on this and on one's absolute position. If the latter, then the increased output of goods and services cannot be written off as if they did not contribute to welfare. And if welfare depends only on one's relative position, then there is not merely no point in growing, there is no point even in staying where we are! Why not let GNP fall and pollution rise? As long as everybody becomes worse off together it will make no difference to welfare. And if some people get poorer more quickly than others, the fall in their welfare will be offset by a rise in the welfare of those whose relative position has become better!

Economists and the Growth Objective

As shown above, many people now proclaim that maximum economic growth should *no longer* be society's objective and should be replaced by the objective of "sustainable development." The chief weakness in this attack on the economist's approach to growth is that, in fact, no professional economist would ever have advocated maximum economic growth as an objective. Maximum economic growth *per se* is simply a silly objective, as any economist would know.

Why? First, as explained, economists are well aware that economic welfare is only a part of total welfare and that an increase in economic welfare can conflict with some noneconomic components of total welfare (though it can also add to them). But for the sake of the argument here let us leave aside the noneconomic components of welfare, such as love of one's neighbors, tolerance, social peace, justice, and so on. Sticking to economic welfare for the time being, this is regarded by the economist as having two dimensions; first, the size of the economic cake, and second, the way it is shared among the population. In other words, the economist sees economic welfare as being derived from the level of *consumption* and the equality of its distribution. Note the emphasis on *consumption*; not investment, or exports, or the balance of payments, or anything else—just consumption. For that, in the end, is what we get out of the economic system in the way of goods and services that contribute directly to our economic welfare. Also, economists do not limit the definition of consumption to include only material goods. Consumption includes not only the usual goods and services, but also such spiritual and aesthetic delights as listening to chamber music or admiring Titian's paintings.

But the fact that, in the end, welfare is derived from consumption does not mean that we should no longer use any resources for investment or for research and the promotion of technical progress,

137

and should immediately switch all our productive resources to the satisfaction of today's consumption. For what about tomorrow? Or next year, and so on? A rational man tries to maximize welfare over some relevant period of time, such as his lifetime (and allowing for such bequests that he may wish to pass on to his heirs). To this end he will often be prepared to sacrifice some consumption now in order to obtain more welfare from consumption in the future.

The same applies to society. It may be perfectly rational for society to sacrifice some consumption now in order to enjoy a higher standard of living in the future. But there is a limit to how far one should go. It would be absurd to cut current consumption by, say, 80 percent, to reduce food supplies to subsistence levels, to allow people only the minimum essential clothing and heating, to send children down the mines, to introduce compulsory 12-hour working days, and so on, in order to achieve the maximum possible investment rate simply to maximize the growth rate. For this clearly does not maximize *welfare* over the time-span relevant for society's decisions. The loss of welfare from such a cut in *current* consumption would far exceed any conceivable increase in welfare in later years obtained by the higher level of investment today.[22] In other words, such an excessive switch of resources from current consumption to future consumption would not achieve a sensible objective, which would be to maximize consumption over some period of time.

How much one would be willing to sacrifice some consumption today in order to raise consumption in the future depends on various factors, including one's particular situation and prospects. For example, it would be folly for a starving man to sacrifice one loaf of bread now in order to have 10 loaves next year; he would be dead by then. Even in less extreme cases the same principle holds. For example, a young married man with a family and heavy mortgage payments to make on his house, who has not yet reached his full potential earning capacity, may not want to put a lot of money aside in order to have an even higher income when his children have grown up and the mortgage is paid off. Much will depend, therefore, on the level of consumption we enjoy at present, and the level we expect to enjoy in the future, and the uncertainty that has to be attached to the prospect of future rewards in return for abstinence now.

The essential point is that it is *welfare* over some relevant time period that should be maximized, not the growth rate of consumption, let alone the growth rate of output. If those who sneer at the economist's proposed objective disagree with it, they should say exactly in what way they disagree with it and what they would put in its place. The economist's proposed objective rules out maximizing welfare now, but equally it rules out trying to achieve maximum growth. What society should aim at is the growth rate that maximizes welfare over the whole time period in which it is interested. This growth rate is called the *optimal* growth rate. It will be that growth rate at which the sacrifice of present welfare is just offset by the extra future welfare that this faster growth will permit. This depends partly on society's relative valuation of present as compared with future consumption, which must be a subjective matter and is not one on which economists have any special claim to pontificate. It must depend also on a purely technical, factual consideration, namely how much current consumption actually has to be sacrificed in order to have more consumption later. Even our struggling young man might be prepared to put aside some of his income for investment if he were offered a really attractive proposition, yielding, say, 25 percent per annum. Given these two considerations—one a matter of subjective judgment and the other technical—there will be an "optimum" growth rate that will achieve the objective of maximizing welfare over the time period in question.

In the same way that economists do not have any special ax to grind as to what constitutes the socially optimal rate of growth, they do not have any special ax to grind as to how society should allocate its output at any point of time between competing uses. There is no special economist's view, for example, as to how far society should allocate its total output between food, clothing, consumer durables, education, health, or the environment or any other particular use of resources. All economists try to do is to set out clearly the criteria by which society should allocate its resources *given society's preferences* and the constraints and opportunities open to society, if society is seeking to maximize its welfare.

How much society should allocate to the environment at any particular moment is simply another dimension of choice. And it is essential not to confuse the issue of how resources should be used at any particular moment with the issue of how consumption should be spread over time, which is the growth issue. But it is a common confusion. For example, many people believe that the existence of excessive traffic congestion or pollution provides arguments against economic growth. But in reality it only provides arguments for the view that resources may not be allocated optimally now.

For example, Professor J. K. Galbraith, who ought to know better, associates the case against growth with the lack of public amenities (such as better public transport) and environmental nuisances such as the noise of jet planes. Others think that growth must be stopped or slowed down on account of the excessive pollution that can be seen around us or read about in the newspapers. But this is nothing to do with growth. This is a question of the misallocation of resources; in one case as between the private and the public sector, and in the other as between the protection of the environment and other uses. Zero growth would not prevent this sort of resource misallocation; the private cars would not disappear to be replaced by adequate and prosperous public rail and road services. If anything, slower growth will merely make it more difficult for governments to achieve the desired switch in the way our national products are used. In Chapters 2 and 3 I gave numerous instances of the way that poverty and the absence of economic growth contribute to the environmental problems of developed countries.

Given that economists are very much concerned with the problem of what is the optimal growth rate for society, they are of course under obligation to consider how far, if at all, economic growth does conflict with due concern for the environment. Indeed, as pointed out earlier, economists have been in the forefront of the demonstration that, in the absence of appropriate policies, society will, as a rule, make excessive use of environmental facilities. Economists are thus as much concerned with the environment as anyone. For they are as much concerned with the environment as they are with any specific component of human welfare, be it climate change in 50 years' time, traffic congestion in cities today, health care, adequate housing, decent working conditions, and so on. The problem is to find the right balance between these different components of welfare, particularly when the supply of some may conflict with the supply of others. To begin with, we need to see how great is this conflict and, insofar as there is one, what policies can reduce it and how far we seek some compromise between the various components of welfare. But this requires some attempt to assess how far society values these competing claims on the various possible components of its welfare. To do this it is necessary to try to attach values in some common unit, such as money.

This characteristic of the economist's approach to the problem of striking a balance between competing objectives is also frequently the object of misunderstanding in many environmentalist circles. It is true that economists try to estimate where possible how much people value all the things that they do value—including the environment—in terms of prices. This is an extremely tricky operation, particularly for the environment, much of which does not pass through the market mechanism. However, a lot of hard, detailed, and intellectually demanding work goes into the attempt to ascribe values to environmental assets and services. Environmental economists pioneered research in this area about 20 years ago and many scholarly contributions have been made since then to the estimation of environmental values.[23] This work is essential for the design of effective policies to protect the environment, whether regulatory or incorporating some element of the market mechanism.

The fact that the studies in question try to attach monetary values to the environment does not represent any particularly materialistic view of the goods and services in question. The objective is simply to provide some comparable units by which the value that people attach to the environment can be traded off against the value that people attach to other goods and services that contribute to their welfare. If everything could be valued in terms of Beethoven quartets, that would be just as acceptable. But the technical problems of doing this would be insuperable.

Of course many "deep ecologists" will reject the attempt to attach any monetary values to the environment for various reasons. They prefer the obscurantism of their mystical rhetoric. But without some way of comparing alternatives rational choice seems impossible. If some people believe that there is an overriding value in preserving trees that cannot be made commensurate with other values, there is not much we can do about it. How they compare the value they get from trees with the value they attach to sitting on wooden chairs, reading books and papers made out of woodpulp, eating at wooden tables, and so on, is a mystery to me. And I happen to prefer the economist's approach to the mystical approach. Or, as David Pearce puts it, more tactfully, "I find it difficult to have to present my work in terms that are always satisfying to theologians, or people who like to talk in terms of moral absolutes. You can't argue economics with theologians."[24]

Finally, the economist's concept of *optimal* growth by no means rules out any concern with *sustainable* growth. For example, during the Second World War there was a considerable incentive for economic statisticians to estimate what the economy was producing and was hence available for the war effort.[25] This meant estimating *gross* national product, which makes no deduction for how much output needs to be put aside to maintain intact society's stock of capital, including roads, houses, schools, transport facilities, and so on. It was clearly recognized that running down these assets in the interests of the war effort could not continue indefinitely. In other words, the sort of economic growth achieved during the war was not technically sustainable. But it was certainly optimal at the time. The alternative was to lose the war.

It is true that there are also many circumstances where technical sustainability and optimality may conflict. Sustainability is certainly relevant, and it would be a foolish person who invested his savings in some project that would yield a return of, say, 25 percent without checking how long the project would last. But the technical sustainability of a project is only one aspect of its desirability and there is no justification for the overriding status of an ethical injunction that it has been given in most environmentalist discussion. However, the reasons for this are discussed fully in the next chapter.

9. The "Sustainable Development" Alternative

The "Sustainable Development" Muddle

During the last few years the fashionable concept in environmental discourse has been "sustainable development." It has spawned a vast literature and has strengthened the arm of empire builders in many research institutes, universities, national and international bureaucracies, and statistical offices. Environmental pressure groups present the concept of sustainable development as an important new contribution to the environmental debate. It is claimed that it brings new insights into the way that concern for the environment and the interests of future generations should be taken into account in policy analysis. But in fact it only muddles the issues. As two distinguished authorities in this area, Partha Dasgupta and Karl-Göran Mäler, point out, ". . . most writings on sustainable development start from scratch and some proceed to get things hopelessly wrong. It would be difficult to find another field of research endeavor in the social sciences that has displayed such intellectual regress."[1]

It seems high time, therefore, for somebody to spell out why, if the Emperor of Sustainable Development has any clothes at all, they are pretty threadbare. In this chapter I maintain that "sustainable development" has been defined in such a way as to be either morally repugnant or logically redundant. It is true that, in the past, economic policy has tended to ignore environmental issues, particularly those having very long-run consequences. It is right, therefore, that they should now be given proper place in the conduct of policy. But this can be done without elevating sustainability to the status of some overriding criterion of policy. After all I am sure that the reader can easily think of innumerable human activities that are highly desirable but, alas, not indefinitely sustainable!

In 1992, at Rio de Janeiro, the United Nations held a Conference on Environment and Development (UNCED), in which almost all the

143

countries in the world participated. At this conference the countries adopted a major document of several hundred pages, known as "Agenda 21," which set out, among other things, the agreed intentions of the countries to take account of environmental objectives in their domestic policies, to monitor their own developments from the point of view of their "sustainability," taking full account of environmental changes, and to submit regular reports on these developments to a newly established "Commission on Sustainable Development" (CSD).[2]

Agenda 21 is full of references to "sustainable development." For example, Chapter 8 states that "Governments, in cooperation, where appropriate, with international organizations, should adopt a national strategy for sustainable development. . . ." It goes on to say that countries should draw up sustainable development strategies the goals of which ". . . should be to ensure socially responsible economic development while protecting the resource base and the environment for the benefit of future generations." But what are socially responsible goals in this area, how far should we protect the resource base, whatever that means, and what are the legitimate interests of future generations that have to be protected?

All these, and many other questions arise as soon as we ask what exactly "sustainable development" means, and what is so good about it? As many writers have pointed out, there is a danger that sustainable development is treated as a "motherhood and apple-pie" objective.[3] But, as Harvey Brooks puts it, "For the concept of sustainability in the process of development to be operationally useful it must be more than just an expression of social values or political preferences disguised in scientific language. Ideally it should be defined so that one could specify a set of measurable criteria such that individuals and groups with widely differing values, political preferences, or assumptions about human nature could agree whether the criteria are being met in a concrete development program."[4]

It may well be that this is asking too much of the concept of sustainable development and that it can be of some use without being fully operational. But, as it stands, the concept is basically flawed. This is because it mixes up together the technical characteristics of a particular development path with a moral injunction to pursue it. And a definition of whether any particular development

144

path is technically sustainable does not, by itself, carry any special moral force. The definition of a straight line does not imply that there is any particular moral virtue in always walking in straight lines. But most definitions of sustainable development tend to incorporate some ethical injunction without apparently any recognition of the need to demonstrate why that particular ethical injunction is better than many others that one could think up. One obvious rival injunction would be to seek the highest welfare for society over some specified time period.

The result of the fusion of technical characteristics with moral injunctions is that the distinction between (a) positive propositions about the threat to the continuation of any development path and (b) normative propositions concerning the optimality of any particular pattern of development is hopelessly blurred.[5] Instead, a sustainable development path should be defined simply as one that can be sustained over some specified time period, and whether or not it *ought* to be followed is another matter. In other words, it should be treated as a purely technical concept—not that this necessarily makes it easy to define operationally.[6]

This is most clearly seen when we decide whether to embark on a specific project. Consider, for example, a simple mining project in a poor country. Implementing the project might be the best way for the people concerned to obtain some funds to keep alive and to build up productive facilities to enable them to survive in the future. This might include investing in some other activity—such as promoting sustainable agriculture, or investing in their education and technical training. In this case, although the project will not be technically sustainable, it ought to be carried out. In the economist's jargon it will be "optimal." And we can also imagine the opposite scenario: specific projects—such as certain forestry projects where replanting can offset the cutting—that might be sustainable but are not "optimal," perhaps because they are not worthwhile from an economic point of view and would involve the community in excessive costs of cutting and transport relative to the revenues they could earn from sale of the timber.

In other words, we immediately make the distinction between sustainability, defined as a purely technical concept, and optimality, which is a normative concept. Many economic activities that are unsustainable may be perfectly optimal, and many that are sustainable may not even be desirable, let alone optimal. As Little and

Mirrlees put it in the context of project analysis, "Sustainability has come to be used in recent years in connection with projects. . . . It has no merit. Whether a project is sustainable (forever?—or just a long time?) has nothing to do with whether it is desirable. If unsustainability were really regarded as a reason for rejecting a project, there would be no mining, and no industry. The world would be a very primitive place."[7]

Changing Fashions in "Sustainable Development"

One of the most famous definitions of sustainable development is that contained in *Our Common Future,* the 1987 report of the World Commission on the Environment and Development.[8] This report (known as the Brundtland Report after its chairperson, Mrs. Brundtland, the prime minister of Norway), defined sustainable development as "development that meets the needs of the present without compromising the ability of future generations to meet their own needs." But such a criterion is totally useless because "needs" is a subjective concept. People at different points in time, or at different income levels, or with different cultural or national backgrounds, will differ about what "needs" they regard as important. Hence, the injunction to enable future generations to meet their needs does not provide any clear guidance as to what has to be preserved in order that future generations may do so.

Over the past few years innumerable definitions of sustainable development have been proposed.[9] But we can identify a clear trend in them. At the beginning, sustainability was interpreted as a requirement to preserve intact the environment as we find it today in all its forms. The Brundtland Report, for example, stated, "The loss of plant and animal species can greatly limit the options of future generations; so sustainable development requires the conservation of plant and animal species."

But, we might ask, how far does the Brundtland Report's injunction to conserve plant and animal species really go? Are we supposed to preserve all of them? And at what price? Are we supposed to mount a large operation, at astronomical cost, to ensure the survival of every known and unknown species on the grounds that it may give pleasure to future generations, or may turn out, in 100 years' time, to have medicinal properties? About 98 percent of all the species that have ever existed are believed to have become extinct, but most people do not suffer any great sense of loss as a result. How many people lose sleep because it is no longer possible to see a live dinosaur?

Clearly such an absolutist concept of "sustainable development" is morally repugnant. Given the acute poverty and environmental degradation in which many of the world's population live, we could not justify using up vast resources in an attempt to preserve from extinction, say, every single one of the several million species of beetle that exist. The cost of such a task would be partly, if not wholly, resources which otherwise could have been devoted to more urgent environmental concerns, such as increasing access to clean drinking water or sanitation in the Third World.

When it soon became obvious that the "strong" concept of sustainable development was morally repugnant, as well as totally impracticable, many environmentalists shifted their ground. A new version was adopted, known in the literature as "weak" sustainability. This allows for some natural resources to be run down as long as adequate compensation is provided by increases in other resources, perhaps even in the form of manmade capital.[10] But what constitutes adequate compensation? How many more schools or hospitals or houses or factories or machines are required to compensate for using up some mineral resources or forests or clean atmosphere? The answer, it turned out, was that the acceptability of the substitution had to be judged by its contribution to sustaining human welfare.

This is clear from one of the latest definitions provided by David Pearce, the author of numerous works on sustainability. His definition is " 'Sustainability' therefore implies something about maintaining the level of human well-being so that it might improve but at least never declines (or, not more than temporarily, anyway). Interpreted this way, sustainable development becomes equivalent to some requirement that well-being does not decline through time."[11]

The first important feature of this definition is that it is couched in terms of maintaining "well-being," not of maintaining the level of consumption or GNP, or even of maintaining intact the overall stock of natural capital, a condition that is found in many definitions of sustainable development including one to which David Pearce had earlier subscribed (though in collaboration with two other authors who clearly had a bad influence on him).[12] This, for example, implies that sustainable development could include the replacement of natural capital by man-made capital, provided the increase in the latter compensated future generations for any fall in their welfare that might have been caused by the depletion of natural capital. In other words, it allows for substitutability between different forms of natural capital and man-made capital, provided that, on balance, there is no decline in welfare.

But this amounts to selling a crucial pass in any struggle to preserve the independent usefulness of the concept of sustainability. For if the choice between preserving natural capital and adding to (or preserving) man-made capital depends on which makes the greater contribution to welfare, the concept of sustainable development becomes redundant. In the attempt to rid the original "strong" concept of sustainable development of its most obvious weaknesses the baby has been thrown out with the bath water. For it appears now that what society should aim at is not "sustainability," but the maximization of welfare. In other words, it should pursue the old-fashioned economist's concept of "optimality."

The Individual's Choice between "Optimality" and "Sustainability"

Suppose somebody wants to choose between two possible courses of action—that is, which of two possible careers to pursue. Let us assume, for the sake of the argument, that the only difference between the two careers is the level of income he would earn in each and hence the level of consumption that he can enjoy, and that they are roughly the same as regards conditions of work, prestige, job satisfaction, life expectation, location, and everything else. We can then assume that his welfare at any point in time—his "instantaneous welfare"—is correlated with his income at that point in time.[13] Suppose now that one of the careers will ensure him a steady but very modest level of income, and hence welfare, throughout his life, and the other will ensure him an income/welfare level that is higher than in the first alternative *in every single year of his life*, but that includes a decline in income/welfare in the middle of his life, say, when it may decline for a few years (possibly followed by a further rise, though this condition is not essential to the argument). Which path will he choose? Obviously, he will choose the latter.[14] The "optimal" path is the one that gives him the greatest prospective welfare over his lifetime, which, in the economics jargon, is the one that maximizes the present value of his lifetime income. In this simplified example, the "present value" of his lifetime income must be higher in the second case than in the first.

Why should he care about a temporary decline in his income/welfare if it is by choosing the path containing it that he will maximize the present value of his total welfare over the whole of his life? Insofar as the prospect of a temporary decline in income was a worry, he would simply invest more heavily in earlier years and use the subsequent extra income to boost his income in the years when income would otherwise decline.

Of course, in this example the problem is simplified in two ways. First, it is assumed that the level of welfare expected in the non-sustainable path is greater in every year than it is in the sustainable path, in spite of the temporary decline in welfare in the former. Second, only one person is involved, so there is no need to take account of the way in which the two income paths differ with respect to their effect on the equality with which incomes are distributed among different members of the population, let alone between different generations. We shall examine these distributional considerations in the next section, when we consider welfare maximization for society as a whole.

Meanwhile, as regards the first problem, suppose our rational individual is faced with a choice between two paths of income which intersect—that is, one is higher than the other in some years but lower in others. In this case, to compare the "present values" of the two income streams he would discount future incomes at whatever rate of interest he could get on his savings and investment, or would have to pay if he borrowed money. But, again, there seems to be no reason why he should attach special importance to a temporary decline in income during his lifetime, or even a permanent one for that matter. The time path of his income stream throughout his life will be taken care of in the discounting exercise. He will be free to borrow, or lend, in such a way as to allocate his consumption over time so that it maximizes the present value of his welfare.

Optimality for Society and the Distribution of Income

The second simplification in our example was that, by concentrating on choice for a single individual, we bypassed the problem of inequalities between people, or generations, in the distribution of income or welfare. But when we are concerned with optimality for society as a whole, rather than for an individual, account has to be taken of these distributional considerations. This applies whether we are maximizing welfare of society at any point in time or maximizing welfare over some time period. Making due allowance for distributional considerations means that when we are seeking to maximize total social welfare at any point in time we should still be concerned with how equally, or justly (which is not the same thing), the total consumption of society is distributed among the population at the point in time in question. And if we are seeking to maximize welfare over time while making allowance for distributional considerations we should be concerned with the distribution of consumption over time—for example, how equally, or justly, consumption is distributed between different generations.

Both procedures fit easily into welfare economics. Environmentalists may not be aware that it has long been conventional to include distributional considerations in the concept of economic welfare— which is a component of total welfare—that one seeks to maximize. In the opinion of the great economist A. C. Pigou, who might be regarded as the father of welfare economics, "Any cause which increases the absolute share of real income in the hands of the poor, provided that it does not lead to a contraction in the size of the national dividend from any point of view, will, in general, increase economic welfare."[15]

Welfare can also be defined to include considerations of social justice and freedom, and so on. Of course, the more widely we draw the net of welfare to include such variables, the greater the difficulty in making them all commensurate with each other. True, this makes it more difficult to define exactly what is meant by the notion of "maximizing" welfare. But the same logical difficulty would apply to the assertions of environmentalists to the effect that "welfare," or "the quality of life," had declined in the past or will be harmed by economic growth.

How one should maximize the present value of society's welfare over time in a way that takes due account of the interests of future generations raises difficult, and relatively novel, problems of intergenerational justice which I discuss in the next chapter.[16] In the absence of any obvious consensus view to the contrary, we shall assume here that a unit of *welfare* accruing to some future generation should be given the same weight in arriving at the present value of the stream of welfare over time as an equal unit of welfare accruing to the present generation. In other words, we should not discriminate against future generations. We should not, therefore, discount *welfare*. This means that we do not advocate what is known in the economics jargon as "pure" time preference. We do not express a preference for consumption now, rather than later, *purely* on account of its precedence in time. There may, of course, be good reasons for doing so, such as the distinct possibility that the human race will become extinct in the not too distant future, so that investment now would be wasted.[17] Or we may simply wish to impose on the discounting operation some particular ethical views concerning the relative importance—or lack of it—of *welfare* accruing to different generations.[18]

But although we shall abstain from any such discounting of welfare, this does not mean that we should not discount *consumption*. As will be explained in more detail in Chapter 11, somebody with absolutely no preference for present over future consumption per se still would not willingly lend £1, say, in return for £1 back next year. He would know that any fool can do better than that and get some interest on his loan. For the same reason he would not pay £1 now for a £1 loaf of bread to be delivered next year. For he would be able to lend the £1 now to somebody and, next year, buy the loaf and have some money left over. At the level of society as a whole, how much is left over depends on society's rate of growth of productivity. A consequence of this growth of productivity is that goods become cheaper over time (allowing for inflation, of course). In other words, £1's worth of consumption next year is not worth as much as £1 this year. Estimates of the present value of any future stream of consumption, therefore, need to reflect whatever rate of growth of productivity we expect to be achieved over the future. This should be reflected in our choice of the discount rate.

We might even want to go further than that in our discounting procedure. We might want to make an additional allowance for the fact that, as consumption levels rise, the welfare that we can obtain from additional ("marginal") units of consumption will fall. This application of the law of diminishing marginal utility would be one particular way of taking account of distributional concerns. That is

151

to say, it would allow for the fact that higher consumption will not provide proportionally higher welfare to rich people than to poor people. Taking account of differences in the incomes accruing to different generations in this way would be the intertemporal counterpart of some conventional cost-benefit methods of allowing for the way that, say, any specific project at any moment in time may confer benefits on different income groups in society by attaching weights to their income levels. In applying this procedure to intergenerational comparisons of income and welfare levels we still would not be discounting *welfare* at all. We would simply be assuming that higher levels of consumption do not bring proportionally higher levels of welfare.

Thus the use of a discount rate does not necessarily mean, as most environmentalists—and some philosophers—appear to believe, that we attach less value to the *welfare* of future generations simply because it comes later in time.[19] On the contrary, rationing investment according to the discount rate helps to ensure that we invest now in projects that will give future generations more welfare than if we invested, instead, in projects—some of which may be environmental projects—that yield lower returns. In this way it maximizes the welfare of future generations. It is in no way "unfair" to them because we would discount future returns in the same way even if we expected to live for another two centuries and hence be among the generation that has to bear the consequences of our present decisions.[20]

Is There a Role for Sustainability?

We have argued (a) that distributional considerations can—and invariably are—included in the economist's concept of "welfare," (b) that this applies also to the intergenerational distribution of income and welfare, and (c) that one way of doing this (though not necessarily the only way) is by appropriate choice of the discount rate used to estimate the present value of welfare that society should seek to maximize. In view of this there does not appear to be any independent role left for "sustainability" as a separate objective of policy, independent of maximization of the present value of welfare. For if future generations have lower incomes as a result of any particular environmental policy this will show up—other things being equal—in a lower present value of income over whatever time period our views on intergenerational justice regard as relevant. We also might want to allow for the fact that marginal units of consumption probably add more to welfare at lower levels of consumption than at higher levels.

Nor does there seem to be any special role left to play for the particular possibility that future levels of welfare may include some temporary decline. And this is related to the second important feature of the Pearce definition of sustainability quoted above, which is that well-being must never decline, "or, not more than temporarily."[21] Apart from the qualification about a temporary decline, this is in line with most of the recent definitions of sustainable development. As John Pezzey rightly says in his survey of the various definitions used, most of them "understand sustainability to mean sustaining an improvement (or at least maintenance) in the quality of life, rather than just sustaining the existence of life." He goes on to adopt a "standard definition of sustainable development" according to which welfare per head of population must never decline (as in the latest Pearce definition mentioned above, but without the "temporary" qualification this had included).[22]

We are always free, of course, to define welfare however we wish. But it would be very curious to go out of our way to insist on the importance of widening the definition to include all sorts of environmental, distributional, social, and other considerations, but to exclude from it *changes* in the level of welfare (as distinct from the level itself). Indeed it seems self-contradictory to do so. If a decline in welfare does not affect welfare, why bother about it? And if it does affect welfare, why can't it be included in the concept of welfare that we are trying to maximize? As indicated, we might want to adopt a concept of welfare maximization that could not incorporate important, but arguably incommensurate, objectives, such as integrity, or freedom. In that case, it would be sensible to talk about maximizing welfare subject to some constraint on these other incommensurate objectives. But it seems to be logically impossible to treat *changes* in welfare itself in this way.

Furthermore, not only does it seem illogical to exclude *changes* in welfare from the concept of welfare that optimal policy should seek to maximize, it also is not clear why some special moral significance should be attached to *decreases* in the level of welfare as distinct from *increases* in it. It is no doubt true that a very rich man may

153

suffer some extra loss of welfare if he has had a bad year on the stock exchange and has had to sell his yacht. He would not miss the yacht so much if he had never had it before. But we cannot be expected to be very sorry for him. After all, how did he become rich if not as a result of a lot of *increases* in income in earlier years which, if we are to be consistent, should be given an additional value, on top of their effect in bringing him to a higher level?

On the other hand, it may be argued that this does not apply to different generations. For if some particular generation experiences a decline in its welfare we cannot assume that it was the same generation that enjoyed the previous increases. Nevertheless, if future generations experience a dip in welfare in any period, we cannot be expected to be very sorry for them *irrespective of their welfare levels*. And even if we are, there seems to be no justification for switching to a development path that yields a lower present value of welfare in order to avoid the temporary decline. For, by definition, that would imply inflicting on some other generation a loss of welfare greater than the one that was incurred by the generation that experienced the temporary decline. What sort of ethical judgment is supposed to justify such a choice? Thus, it is far from obvious that there is any moral justification for shielding future generations from any decline in income or welfare irrespective of whatever sacrifice of welfare this might inflict on other generations.

In other words, if we are to attach a separate value to *changes* in welfare, they need not be only negative. We should also include the increases in welfare—the rise that preceded the fall. Indeed, if the supposed temporary decline in welfare that is to be avoided at all costs is from a higher level of welfare than the one we enjoy now, the preceding generations must have experienced more increases in welfare than declines in welfare. On balance, therefore, the future generations that enjoyed the increases in welfare should be credited with even more welfare than the simple present value exercise would have permitted. As well as being credited with more welfare for reaching higher levels, they would be credited with even more welfare because they reached the higher levels in the only possible way, namely by experiencing more increases than declines!

Thus the exclusion of *changes* in welfare—as distinct from the *level* of welfare—from the concept of welfare the present value of which society should seek to maximize, is open to three objections. First, it appears simply to be logically self-contradictory. Second, if it is conceded that *changes* in the level of welfare can be incorporated perfectly well into the concept of welfare that we are seeking to maximize, it no longer qualifies as a separate objective of policy. Welfare maximization—that is, old-fashioned "optimality"—still rules. Third, if we want to include declines in welfare in the concept of welfare to be maximized, we should also—in the interest of consistency—include increases in welfare. That done, it is far from obvious which way the net result would affect the value of total welfare. The increases might outweigh the decreases. The man who has a stroke of luck on the stock exchange and buys a yacht may derive immense joy out of his new toy, but when, later, he is unlucky and has to sell the yacht he may not mind very much after all. He will have discovered what a nuisance it was, and how much more convenient it is just to charter one from time to time.

Of course, if the decline in living standards of future generations continued to the point that human life on this planet was no longer possible, the simple optimization rule comes up against another tricky question. This is whether it makes sense to talk about the loss of welfare caused by the extinction of the human race. As Thomas Nagel points out, "none of us existed before we were born (or conceived), but few regard that as a misfortune."[23] Would the non-existence of the human race constitute a negative item in the overall total of welfare? Perhaps the welfare of such wildlife that remained might be much higher.

Should "Sustainability" Be a Constraint?

The preceding discussion should make it obvious—if it isn't already—not only that we should stick to welfare maximization, rather than sustainability, as an overriding objective of policy, but that sustainability cannot even be regarded as a logical constraint on welfare maximization. Mimicry of the economist's use of the concept of a constraint is the latest twist in the evolution of the concept of sustainable development. It represents a further step in the retreat, under fire, by those environmentalists who have presented the "sustainable development" concept as a great breakthrough in our thinking on the subject. First they retreat from strong sustainability to weak sustainability, and then from weak sustainability as an objective of policy to weak sustainability as just a constraint. The idea now is that welfare should be maximized, but subject to the constraint that the path of development being followed be sustainable. However, this appears to represent a misinterpretation of the concept of a "constraint."

Economic theory is dominated by the notion of how to make optimal choices when faced with constraints of one kind or another. For example, it is full of the analysis of how firms may seek to maximize profits *subject to constraints,* such as the prices they can charge for the goods they sell or the wages they need pay employees. Or households are treated as maximizing utility *subject to constraints* in terms of their incomes and the prices of goods they buy, and so on. If, for example, the firm could relax the wage constraint and pay employees lower wages it could make higher profits. If a household could relax its income constraint by earning more, or by borrowing, it could increase welfare. In many other contexts, too, it might be analytically convenient to seek to maximize some objective, such as total economic welfare, subject to some constraint in terms of the other objectives, such as freedom, or justice.

But it is obvious that only if there is a conflict between the "constraint" and what it is that one is trying to maximize does it make sense to use the term "constraint." For a constraint is something that, if relaxed, enables us to obtain more of whatever it is we are trying to maximize. Where there is no conflict, however, there is no scope for a "constraint."

Sustainable development could only constitute a constraint on welfare maximization, therefore, if it conflicted with it. But, as we have seen, the "strong" sustainability criterion of policy which, in principle, could conflict with welfare maximization, has been more or less abandoned on account of its moral unacceptability. And the capital stock component of "weak" sustainability obviously cannot conflict with welfare maximization because the criterion of whether a substitution of man-made capital for natural capital is acceptable is whether it makes an adequate contribution to welfare.

For sustainability to constitute a constraint on welfare maximization, therefore, some other source of conflict between sustainability and welfare maximization had to be found. We have discussed at some length one that has been given much prominence, namely distributional considerations, particularly the intergenerational distribution of welfare. We have shown that, while it is, of course, open to anybody to define welfare in such as way as to take no account of distributional considerations, it would violate a long tradition in economics to the effect that income distribution is an integral part of welfare and that intertemporal distribution can be handled through the appropriate choice of the discount rate. We have also argued that the notion that declines in welfare—particularly temporary declines—should be given special consideration and constitute constraints on welfare maximization is also open to serious objections.

The advocates of sustainable development as a constraint, therefore, face a dilemma. Either they stick to "strong" sustainability, which is logical, but requires them to subscribe to a morally repugnant and totally impracticable objective, or they switch to some welfare-based concept of sustainability, in which case they are advocating a concept that appears to be redundant and unable to qualify as a logical constraint on welfare maximization.

Sustainability and the Measurement of National Income

As pointed out, most environmentalists, in their own concept of sustainable development, confuse the technical characteristics of a development path with its moral superiority. It is perhaps because of this confusion that they also misinterpret perfectly legitimate technical definitions that some economists have proposed, such as the definition of maintaining capital intact, or the conditions to be satisfied *if* it is required to ensure constant levels of consumption per head, as carrying with them ethical force that their originators would not necessarily attach to them at all.

For example, a famous definition of income by the late Sir John Hicks, a Nobel Laureate in Economics, is that national income is the output of a nation's economy *after maintaining capital intact*—that is, after allowing for the amount of capital used up in the course of producing the output in question. Obviously, if the capital that is gradually "used up" in the course of time through wear and tear and so on is not replaced, then, in the longer run, output will begin to decline and it will not be possible to maintain income levels. But this Hicksian definition of income, with its emphasis on the need to maintain capital intact in order to maintain income levels, is a purely technical definition of net income and has no moral connotation whatsoever.

157

More recently other economists, notably Hartwick, Weitzman, and Solow, have shown precisely how to extend the concept of net national income and maintaining capital intact to encompass the depletion of natural capital through the extraction of minerals, and precisely how much investment is required in order to compensate for using up natural capital and to maintain constant levels of consumption per head.[24] But these technical definitions of income and of sustainable consumption paths are frequently quoted by environmentalists as if they implied some moral obligation never to consume more than income so defined and hence always to maintain capital intact and follow a sustainable growth path as so defined. But the authors of these definitions usually had no intention of suggesting that they were also laying down the law as to what is morally imperative.

For example, in a much quoted article, "Intergenerational Equity and Exhaustible Resources," Nobel Laureate Robert M. Solow states that he is merely exploring the consequences of a straightforward application of the famous second principle of justice associated with the political philosopher John Rawls to the problem of optimal capital accumulation spanning several generations.[25] He states, "It will turn out to have both advantages and disadvantages as an ethical principle in this context" (page 30), and goes on to show that in normal situations "the maximin [i.e., the Rawlsian] criterion does not function very well as a principle of intergenerational equity. . . . It calls . . . for zero net saving with stationary technology, and for negative net saving with advancing technology." This is hardly a ringing endorsement of the principle of never allowing consumption per head to be lower in any time period than in any other time period. But it does not prevent many environmentalists from writing that Solow has demonstrated the desirability of the principle of maintaining a constant level of consumption per head.[26] Most of them must just be quoting each other without bothering to read Solow in the original.

Thus the fact that eminent economists have helped provide a precise basis for estimating how much investment a society would need to make, under certain highly simplified conditions, in order to compensate for any reduction in the stock of natural capital and to maintain "sustainable development" (defined as no fall in welfare levels), after taking due account of damage to the environment, does not imply that this represents some ethical injunction. It not only implies nothing at all about the optimality of sustainable growth paths, it also does not even imply that making such estimates is worthwhile in practice.

It is not even possible to estimate the depreciation of man-made capital very accurately. For it does not correspond to any actual market transactions. The flow of goods and services entering into gross national product (GNP)—such as the food consumed, the machine tools built, the services provided to consumers—are almost all the subject of two-way market transactions involving a buyer and a seller. By contrast, the depletion of the capital stock is not, as a rule, the subject of any transactions between buyers and sellers. True, firms will show estimates of depreciation in their accounts, but, for many reasons that lie outside the scope of this book, nobody in the trade would rely on these as being objective and accurate estimates of any conceptually valid true measure of capital consumption.[27] But at least the assets in question did go through the market at one time in their lives, and in some cases it may be possible to use secondhand prices to estimate the value of capital goods that have been discarded.

By contrast, most environmental assets never passed through the marketplace at all. In almost all cases there are no market observations of the value to be attached to clean air or water or beautiful landscape. True, the newly extracted supplies of minerals do pass through the market, but the known reserves are only the reserves that have been found worth identifying given prices at any point in time. As is explained in detail in Chapter 4 above, insofar as demand may exceed supply for any length of time this will lead to a rise in price which, in turn, invariably sets in motion many feedback mechanisms to restore the balance between supply and demand. These include increases in exploration and discovery of new reserves, improvements in extraction and refinement techniques, but also economies and substitution in the use of the materials in question.[28] Also, there are obvious difficulties in using prices of minerals at any point as a guide to the prices that they will fetch for the next few centuries, so that it is impossible to put any reasonable values on these resources.

Conclusions

What we have seen so far then is that

(i) "sustainability" should be interpreted purely as a technical characteristic of any project, program, or development path, not as implying any moral injunction or overriding criterion of choice;

(ii) the "optimal" choice for society is to maximize the present value of welfare over whatever time period is regarded as relevant given one's views on intergenerational justice. This can make allowance for distributional considerations, including intertemporal distribution, by attaching weights to the welfare accruing to different generations in any estimate of the present value of social welfare, as, for example, by appropriate choice of the discount rate;

(iii) anyway, because most environmentalists have now dropped "strong" sustainability and now define the "sustainability" condition in terms of how much contribution different components of the total capital stock contribute to welfare, insofar as society seeks to maximize welfare the sustainability condition becomes redundant and cannot even be treated as a "constraint."

None of the above conclusions means that we are not left with serious environmental problems when attempting to decide what is an *optimal* policy. As I have always maintained, the world is faced with real environmental problems. Economists have been well aware of the fact that, left to itself, the environment will not be managed in a socially optimal manner. There are too many market imperfections. The most important is probably the absence of well-defined property rights. But in many cases—particularly with global environmental issues, such as the preservation of biodiversity or the prevention of excessive production of greenhouse gases—it is not easy to see what economic incentives can be devised and implemented internationally in order to secure socially optimal cooperative action. These are serious issues, many of them requiring extensive scientific research and economic research into, for example, the economic evaluation of environmental assets, or the costs of pollution reduction, or the relative efficacy of alternative schemes to achieve socially optimal levels of environmental protection.

Serious research into these and related environmental problems is being carried out in various institutions all over the world.[29] It is unfortunate that so much time and effort is also being devoted to developing the implications of the sustainable development concept, including innumerable commissions and committees set up to report on it and innumerable research programs designed to measure it.[30]

10. Why Do Anything for Posterity?

The Economics-Philosophy Connection

Suppose you believed that the *total* welfare of people in, say, 100 years' time, *including the benefits they would derive from the environment*, was likely to be far greater than it is today. Would you still be worried by the possibility that the particular part of their total welfare that they derived from the environment alone was likely to be less than it is today?[1] Similarly, suppose you believed that the main burden of any major policies to protect the environment for future generations would fall on the poorer developing countries today. Would you still be willing to undertake such policies? If the answer to these questions is "Yes," then you need to consider how your ethical value system allows you to reach such apparently nonegalitarian conclusions. If the answer is "No," you are recognizing that you need to take account of factual propositions before making judgments about environmental policy issues, whatever your initial ethical value system. These examples show how impossible it is to avoid some mixture of economic and philosophical considerations when forming sensible judgments about the long-run environmental effects of economic activity. In these examples factual propositions clearly have a bearing on one's views on ethical issues.

Conversely, philosophical considerations frequently expose gaps in the conventional economist's approach to many problems.[2] Nowhere is this clearer than in environmental problems involving our obligations to future generations. As indicated in Chapter 8, the economist's answer to the question "how fast should the economy grow?" is basically an answer to the question "how should consumption be spread out over time in order to maximize social welfare?" In other words, how should society allocate resources between consumption today and consumption in the future, including future generations? But the answer to the question of how to maximize welfare over some future time period presumably depends on prior

161

value judgments, which the economist usually sweeps under the carpet.

The first of these is "how long is the time period that we ought to take into account, and how much capital should we leave intact for generations in subsequent time periods?" This is the question of intergenerational justice. It is closely related to another of the ethical issues that tend to be ignored in much economic analysis of what policies maximize social welfare (in spite of the fact—as Amartya Sen has reminded us—that economics started out life in the English-speaking world as a branch of ethics).[3]

This is that economics provides a sophisticated analysis of what is the most "efficient" allocation of resources—of land, labor, capital, and so on—*given whatever happens to be the initial distribution of assets (e.g., wealth, skills, and so on) among people*. This is usually known as a "Pareto optimal" allocation of resources. But economics has nothing much to say about how far any particular initial distribution of assets is fair or just. As Amartya Sen put it, "The concept of Pareto optimality was evolved precisely to cut out the need for distributional judgments."[4]

Since what is an "efficient" allocation of resources will depend on how assets are distributed among people to start with, it will also depend on the distribution of property rights—such as rights to own financial assets, or land, or whatever. But it is far from obvious how far future generations can have any property rights or, if they do, how they can be effectively represented in the marketplace. Hence, it is not clear how relevant is the conventional notion of optimality to the intergenerational allocation of resources.[5]

A further limitation on conventional welfare economics that happens to be relevant when we are considering very long-term issues is that the analysis is basically all about the allocation of resources among competing ends. This analysis, therefore, concentrates on the proper prices of goods and services *relative to each other*, including the proper pricing of goods and services to take account of the different point in time at which they might become available. It is not about the *overall scale* of output. And some commentators have argued that, although the price mechanism may be a fairly efficient mechanism (subject to some well-known qualifications) for optimally allocating resources among alternative uses, it cannot handle the problem of achieving the optimal *scale* of total output. This would not matter if there were no environmental limits to the total scale of world output. But some people argue that there are such limits, not just on account of finite resources such as minerals, but also on account of physical phenomena such as entropy or photosynthesis, though as I have attempted to show in Part I, such fears are groundless.[6]

Thus the question of our obligations to future generations and how we draw the boundary line in time around the society whose welfare, over time, we want to maximize, is an important one. It is probably also an intractable one, but in the rest of this chapter I shall attempt to set out the problem as I see it as simply as possible.

The Input from Philosophy

As I pointed out at the beginning of this chapter, one of the major weaknesses in the economists' concept of "optimality" is that it conceals some crucial value judgments, notably as regards *which society* we are talking about when we discuss the society whose economic welfare we are seeking to maximize. What society are we referring to when we talk about the "socially" optimal rate of discount, or the "socially" optimal rate of economic growth or rate of depletion of finite resources? Should we extend the boundaries of the society, the welfare of which we want to maximize, to include future generations? Should we treat people who are not yet born as having some moral status? And if so, what are our obligations toward them?

Of course, philosophers have studied ethics for over 2,000 years without having reached universally acceptable answers to the innumerable moral questions that arise in everyday life. And, because the problems of intergenerational justice are relatively new, it is even less likely that we can reach firm conclusions of a detailed practical nature in this area. But this is not the fault of the philosophers. It is in the very nature of the questions, which do not lend themselves to definite "answers" of the kind that we might hope to find in, say, scientific disciplines. Nevertheless, philosophers have made much progress in exposing the difficulties that need to be faced and increasing our understanding of what facts have to be taken into account in assessing the different possible decisions.

As Bernard Williams has put it in connection with environmental ethics, although philosophical considerations rarely have a direct bearing on practical policy issues, they clarify the issues and often stimulate our imaginations in a way that makes us more aware of the complexities involved. It is hoped that some discussion of them here will also make us less hasty in rushing to judgment, and more critical of much of the rhetoric that often dominates some of the contributions to this emotion-charged area.[7]

There are various possible ways in which we may approach the question of our obligations toward future generations and the environment. They do not have to be mutually exclusive. Our ethical principles may be derived from some mixture of various influences. For example, some people would find religious inspiration for the view that we have some responsibility to behave as stewards for the natural environment. This view would contrast with God's oft-quoted injunction in the Bible (Genesis 1: 28): "Be fruitful and increase, fill the earth and subdue it, rule over the fish in the sea, the birds of heaven, and every living thing that moves upon the earth."[8] However, as is persuasively argued by the economist Donald Hay, we can also find in the Bible "language which speaks of respect for nature, and an obligation to care for it."[9] But religious considerations lie well outside the scope of this book.

An alternative approach is simply to state that we feel some innate, intuitive concern for the environment that cannot be reduced to some logical deduction from some higher-level general ethical principles. This would be the position adopted by, for example, the distinguished philosopher John Passmore.[10] In a similar vein we may say that concern for the preservation of the environment and the interests of future generations is just one part of our moral intuition, and we cannot get very far in trying to systematize its origin—for example, in religion, or collective self-interest, or social convention, or socio-biological instinctive behavior in the interest of gene survival, or some other source of our usual patchwork of moral principles, the mutual consistency of which will defy any analysis. In other words, we just adopt a top-level value judgment to the effect that decent human beings ought to respect nature and the environment, and that is the end of it.

The trouble is that it cannot really be the end of it. For what is the status of such a principle? That is to say, is it an absolute principle having priority over others? Or does it have to be traded off against other principles, such as concern with maximizing the welfare of poor people today, or the principle of preserving liberty, or some other principle? As it stands it is just too vague and general to provide much guidance when difficult choices have to be made.

This is largely why many people would probably feel more comfortable if they could justify their concern for the interests of future generations by satisfying themselves that it is logically derived from some higher order and more general ethical principle. However, this is by no means a simple task, and may well be impossible.[11]

The "Identity Problem"

An example of the sorts of difficulties that are faced is the so-called "identity problem." Suppose, as a result of some particular environmental policy called (following Derek Parfit's usage) "the depletion policy," the people who will be alive in, say, 100 years' time will not be the same people as those who would have been alive had we followed instead "the conservation policy." And suppose, as a result of having adopted the depletion policy, the environment and the overall standard of living of the people who happened to be alive in 100 years' time was not as good as it would have been had the conservation policy been adopted instead. Would it make sense to say that the population alive in 100 years' time had been "harmed" by our having adopted the depletion policy? Under our starting assumption those people would not have been born had we adopted the conservation policy instead. So, as long as they find life worth living and are pleased to be alive, what do they have to complain about? If they think they are better off than if they had not been alive they must agree that they are better off than if we had followed the conservation policy.

Now it cannot be claimed that our starting assumption is unreasonable as far as any major environmental policy is concerned. For example, suppose drastic action were to be taken now to cut carbon dioxide emissions in order to slow down global warming. This would certainly involve a rapid cut in our combustion of fossil fuels—particularly coal and oil. And given the dependence of the world economy on these inputs there would be wholesale changes in the levels of economic activity and in patterns of world trade and production. Almost everybody's job in the more advanced countries would be affected, with feedback effects on the rest of the world. People would have to work in different jobs, in different localities, with different hours and under different conditions and with different colleagues.

Inevitably this would affect whom they meet, what social lives they have, and so who marries whom, and, even if they marry the same people, it would affect the precise timing and conditions of the conception of most of their children, who will, therefore, not be the same people as those who would have been born under the conservation policy. And this will affect whom the other children marry and when and where, and so on, so that by the second and third generation it is certain that almost all the people alive in 100 years' time will be different from the people who would have been alive had nothing much been done to cut consumption of fossil fuels. In short, the *identity* of the people alive in 100 years' time will not be the same as the *identity* of the people who would have been born had a different policy been pursued.

Can we say that they have been "harmed" by our having adopted the depletion policy? The answer would presumably be "No," if we subscribed to the apparently[12] compelling ethical principle that there is no harm when there are no persons harmed. As Parfit puts it: "Wrongs require victims: our choice cannot be wrong if we know that it will be worse for no one."[13] This assumption is an inherent part of a more general view about morality known as "a person-affecting view" or "an identity-specific view." According to that view, actions are morally good or bad if they are good or bad for those people whom they affect.[14]

Clearly, this line of argument, if accepted, would imply that we cannot harm future generations whatever major environmental policy we adopt. Hence, we have a free hand in the choice of such policies, and certainly need not worry about niceties such as how to compensate the victims. As it happens, Parfit himself is unwilling to accept these implications of the identity problem, but he shows that it is difficult to find an escape route. Some suggestions have been made for circumventing the identity problem, but it would be out of place to go into them here.[15]

Many people would be inclined simply to reject the basic assumption that harms (or benefits) only exist in relation to some actual people who are harmed or benefited. In daily life this might well be the approach the average person would adopt. For example, a person might prefer a scenario under which one's great-grandchildren, if there are to be any, will be better off as a result of some action one might take (such as making certain financial provisions for heirs) even though the person is persuaded that his or her action will affect the identity of the great-grandchildren. For example, according to how much money is left to the children they might marry at a different age, or to different people, and follow different careers involving different life styles and so on. Thus most people—consciously or not—would adopt a somewhat impersonal utilitarian ethic, which advocates the maximization of utility irrespective of whether the persons whose utility is to be maximized are the ones who would have been there if we had acted differently.[16] So let us consider briefly whether this utilitarian ethic is what we are looking for.

Utilitarianism

To the economist, the utilitarian ethic, according to which our moral duty is to seek to maximize "utility" for society, is the most natural ethical principle with which to begin. For it is just the philosophical counterpart of the economist's notion of maximizing utility along the lines set out in Chapter 8. And cost-benefit analysis, which is one of the basic tools of economic analysis, is fundamentally based on utilitarian value judgments.

Utilitarianism is also, perhaps, the most widespread ethical principle. Even though most people may not be conscious that they subscribe to it, they may still accept that a policy that maximizes the sum of people's utilities (defined widely) is probably morally good, or right, even though it may be unfavorable for them or for certain individuals. James Griffin has written of utilitarianism that, of the various ethical principles to which people may appeal to justify moral codes, "It may not be the most loved but it is certainly still the most discussed moral theory of our time."[17] At the same time it would not be claimed that utilitarian considerations had, or ought to have, a monopoly of moral considerations, and conceding some role to a utilitarian approach to environmental issues does not necessarily preclude other approaches.[18]

Utilitarianism may also seem to have some instant appeal to those who want to defend the interests of future generations because utilitarianism does not allow any bias in favor of present generations over future generations. A major feature of utilitarianism is that each person's interests are to be weighed equally; everyone is to

167

count for one and no one for more than one, which might, on the face of it, appear to be a very egalitarian doctrine. However, many philosophers and economists disagree about this and there is room for dispute as to what it means exactly.[19]

Furthermore, utilitarianism may not get us very far in identifying our obligations to future generations. For—like welfare economics— it leaves open the question of the time period over which the maximization of utility is to be achieved. Even if we adopt some arbitrary time period, as is often the case in economics, we are still left with the question of how much capital stock has to remain at the end of the period. But this would depend on what subsequent consumption stream later generations are believed to deserve. So this would not help us escape from the problem of whether we really want to take account of mankind to the end of its existence, or to compromise at the next 100 years or so![20]

There are, of course, other reasons why utilitarianism is not much help in answering questions about intergenerational justice. In the first place, it is not concerned really with distributive justice for its own sake at all. It is true that equality and liberty play a prominent role in the classical utilitarianism of Bentham, Mill, and others. But this was chiefly for their *"instrumental value"*—that is, the extent to which they helped maximize utility. They were not valuable objectives in their own right.[21]

Thus even if we decided that we should take account of the interests of future generations we should have to consider a further question, namely what exactly is a "just" *distribution* of welfare between different generations? It is one thing to say that we are all in favor of taking account of the interests of future generations, but it is another to say that their interests take priority over those of many of the people alive in the world today. Vague declarations to the effect that we are in favor of taking account of the interests of future generations do not get us very far. The problem is how we weigh the interests of future generations against those of the present generation. What are the tradeoffs? What are the technical relationships? How much does it cost, in other words, to provide a better environment for future generations? This is where the economics comes into the ethics.

Another limitation on utilitarian ethics in the present context is that it does not provide much guidance when the size of the population may be affected by the policy we adopt. For example, if a faster rate of population growth reduces incomes per head, is this still desirable on utilitarian grounds as long as *total* utility is maximized? Changes in population constitute a well-known challenge to utilitarianism quite independently of our concern with the environment, of course. But it is particularly relevant in environmental problems. There is little doubt, for example, that one of the major strains on the environment is the increase in population in many parts of the world, so that a policy to reduce population growth would help reduce environmental pressure. In other cases, different policies to protect the environment could affect—favorable or unfavorably— the growth of population. But once changes in population enter into the picture our moral intuitions do not usually provide very clear guidance.[22]

Suppose, for example, we want to maximize *total* utility, not *utility per head*. Now there would be less strain on the environment if the world's population were much smaller, or were to grow much less rapidly or not at all. But an addition to the world's population might well increase total utility even if, as a result, the utility enjoyed by everybody in the world was reduced so much that life was only just barely worth living.[23] This implication of "total" utilitarianism has been dubbed by Parfit "The Repugnant Conclusion."[24]

On the other hand, if we are *average utilitarians*—that is, we want to maximize utility per head—then the obvious procedure would be to cut off a lot of heads, a procedure that most people would regard as even more repugnant. Of course, if this is ruled out by some other objective, such as the sanctity of human life, we might still find that the optimal policy requires some reduction in the growth of population. But many people would view this as a serious restriction on the freedom of persons to choose their family size. This is an example of the manner in which we may find that there are conflicts between moral objectives arising out of the plurality of our ethical principles, and there may be no simple way of trading off one objective against another.

"Contractarian" Theories of Justice

If utilitarianism does not provide easy answers to the problem of the "just" distribution of welfare between generations, what about ethical theories that are specifically about distributive justice? In fact there is a distinguished line of such theories known as "contractarian theories," associated with philosophers such as Hobbes, Locke, and Rousseau. This "contractarian" approach conceives of justice as being represented in the rules that would be embodied in a contract that would be agreed on by everybody concerned as being in their mutual interest. In other words, it resembles the outcome of a bargain by the contracting parties. Concessions are made and participants sacrifice some of their interests in order to reach a contract that, in the end, they believe is in their longer-run general interest.

Unfortunately, there are obvious major snags about applying this approach to intergenerational justice. Whether the notion of a contract that spans generations makes sense has been sharply questioned, notably by Brian Barry. Certainly there cannot be any negotiation between different generations. More formally, it seems that a contract can only be useful if certain "conditions of justice," to use David Hume's phrase, are assumed to exist. These include a moderate degree of selfishness, a limitation on resources (otherwise there is no conflict of interest and so nothing to negotiate about), and a moderate degree of equality of power. As Brian Barry puts it, "Conventions to restrain the pursuit of self-interest cannot be advantageous unless all the parties can plausibly threaten to damage one another in the absence of a convention."[25] This third condition cannot apply between generations. There is no need for present generations to enter into a contract with later generations for fear that, if they do not, later generations will harm present generations. According to Brian Barry, this means that the "circumstances of justice" simply cannot apply between generations.[26] The old question, "Why do anything for posterity; posterity has never done anything for me?," should be replaced by the question, "Why do anything for posterity; posterity can never do anything *to* me?"

However, it looks at first sight as if this problem is overcome by the famous recent contribution to political philosophy made by John Rawls.[27] For a central device of Rawlsian theory was to conceive of the contract as being drawn up *not* by people who knew what their particular situation in life happened to be, but by people in some sort of prior "original position," behind a "veil of ignorance." In drawing up the contract they would not know to what particular status in life they would subsequently be called. Hence, they would not try to press for rules that favored this or that particular class of person.

170

It is like a group of people drawing up rules for playing some game without knowing in advance what particular abilities or disabilities they will have when the game begins—for example, whether they will be fleet of foot, or very heavy, or possess good hand-eye coordination, or quick thinking, or be good at mental arithmetic, or whatever. But because we have participated in drawing up the rules we cannot complain that the rules are "unfair" if, when we subsequently discover our own situation and the game commences, it turns out that the rules of the game did not favor the particular skills that we possess.

Clearly, this is not the place to embark on a detailed discussion of Rawls's theory of justice, which raises innumerable questions and which has been the object of a vast amount of attention and scrutiny and has spawned a gigantic literature. But there is one aspect of Rawlsian theory that has received relatively little attention (apart from Brian Barry) and that is very important in the present context. This is that, at first sight, his device of the "original position" promises to be a method for developing a theory of justice between generations. For one of the things that participants in the original position do not know is *to which particular generation they will belong.* As Rawls puts it, "The persons in the original position have no information as to which generation they belong.... They (the parties to the original position) must choose principles the consequences of which they are prepared to live with whatever generation they turn out to belong to."[28] Thus they have no incentive to draw up rules that would be biased in favor of later rather than earlier generations, or vice versa. So although a Rawlsian contract would not lead to a bargain in the conventional sense of being between parties that possess some power to harm each other, it could still lead to a result that is perfectly impartial and, in that sense, "fair" or "just."

Unfortunately, there are major difficulties in attempting to apply Rawls's theory too literally to intergenerational justice. One of these is that it is not clear who will be represented in the original position. For the terms of the contract drawn up in the original position can easily determine how many generations are brought into existence and how big any generation will be. For example, if earlier generations were allowed to use up all the Earth's resources the time span of the human race might be much shorter. Because the rules drawn up, therefore, will reduce the number of generations that are represented in the original position, it is illogical to view it as being a situation in which all potential generations are represented. It is difficult to see, therefore, precisely what is meant by Rawls's statement, "All generations are virtually represented in the original position. . . ."[29]

Furthermore, the rules that the parties to the original position would actually agree on as regards justice between generations turn out to be inconsistent with the principles that they would work out as regards justice within any generation. For one conclusion of Rawls's approach is that the parties to the contract want to protect themselves in general from the worst consequences that might befall them if they happened to turn out to be among the least fortunate members of society. In the jargon of economics they would be "risk averse"—that is, unwilling to face the possibility that, if they were unlucky and turned out to be in a very unfavorable situation, they would suffer greatly on that account. So they would adopt rules that provided some protection for the worst-off members of society. According to Rawls, they would agree that the only inequalities that are allowed to exist in society are those that will improve the position of the worst-off members of society.[30] This was described by Rawls as "the difference principle."

But applying this rule between generations would lead to quite unacceptable results. For example, the rule that inequalities should be permitted only insofar as they raise the welfare levels of the poorest members of the community would make it impossible for the first generation to do any savings at all. For the first generation would presumably be the poorest generation—not being endowed with any starting capital—and if it cut its own consumption in order to invest for the future it would become even poorer. Hence, application of the "difference principle" between generations would rule out economic growth from the accumulation of capital.[31] Far from being "future generation friendly," as many environmental commentators on Rawls have claimed, the strict application of Rawlsian principles would imply either (i) that future generations share the poverty of the first generation, or (ii) that if we can rely on technical progress without savings and capital accumulation, earlier generations would be justified in running down their initial endowment of natural capital.

Thus, for one reason or another, it turns out to be very difficult to extract much guidance from Rawls concerning intergenerational justice. Indeed Rawls himself says that "the question of justice between generations . . . subjects any ethical theory to severe if not impossible tests," and he goes on to say, "How the burden of capital accumulation and of raising the standard of civilization and culture is to be shared between generations seems to admit of no definite answer."[32] At the same time: "It does not follow, however, that certain bounds which impose significant ethical constraints cannot be formulated."[33]

In particular, there is something to be retained from the notion of justice as fairness that has a bearing on environmental policy, especially as regards respecting the interests of future generations when it comes to dealing with the exhaustion of finite resources. For in spite of the above objections to the application of the Rawlsian device of the original position, his basic notion of justice as fairness and as involving some respect for the role of impartiality in settling conflicts between people, has a long established and legitimate appeal. Indeed Brian Barry maintains that, in his treatment of inter-generational justice, Rawls is in fact closer than anywhere else to his basic idea of justice as fairness.[34]

The Implications of "Fairness"

In the context of environmental policy, of course, the most obvious application of the intuitive desire to be "fair" to later generations is the belief that no generation should use up an "unfair" share of the Earth's resources *simply because it happened to be there first*. In other words, it will appear to be unfair that earlier generations raised their standards of living by using up finite resources (including clean air) at the expense of later generations simply because—for no merit of their own—they happened to be able to lay their hands on these resources first. It is rather like coming across a small water supply in the middle of a desert. Suppose there is more water in it than we need for drinking. If we are prepared to use up all the water there would be enough to take frequent baths and even, if properly engineered, to build a swimming pool. But we know that, from time to time, other people will probably come across the oasis and want to find some water left in it that they can drink. It somehow seems unfair that we should use up all the water just because we happened to be there before the others.

Why we should regard this as unfair does not worry me. Perhaps it is related to some view that a "just" distribution of assets should be one that was not based on irrelevant criteria, such as whether we happened to have been careful in the choice of our parents, or to have arrived at the oasis before somebody else. I know that this criterion of a just distribution might not stand up to critical scrutiny. But, whether or not it can be defended on such egalitarian grounds, the idea that it would be unfair to take advantage of our precedence in time—whether in using up the water in the oasis or in using up the Earth's environmental resources—is one that has a lot of appeal to our moral intuitions; at least it does to mine.

But how do we apply this principle in practice? What we need to know is (i) how far there is in fact any danger of using up so-called "finite resources," and (ii) how far we can compensate future generations by investing in other sources of economic welfare. In other words, suppose it is true that the pollution of the atmosphere from, say, manmade carbon dioxide emissions does lead to some climate change, how much loss of welfare is this likely to entail by comparison with the increase in economic welfare that will probably take place over time as a result of the usual steady rate of technical progress and capital accumulation? In short, if we subscribe fully to the imperative of "fairness" are we really obliged to stop using up finite resources or polluting the atmosphere? The underlying moral imperative of fairness may be perfectly acceptable, but its operational significance in this context—indeed in any context—will still depend on some facts.

In other words, insofar as we conclude (as I do) that we do have to take seriously the problem of respecting the interests of future generations, what are the economic implications? Some of them are of a relatively abstract nature, such as the argument about discounting future harms or benefits, which is discussed fully in the next chapter. But, as the preceding discussion has already shown, others are of a much more concrete character, such as how much harm different environmental policies will really impose on future generations, how serious is the risk that we would deplete nonrenewable resources, or how far we should drop the usual convention of treating generations as homogeneous and take account of the different circumstances of different members of the present generation—notably the differences between the poorest people in the developing countries and the more affluent members of society?

Of course the economic "facts" are difficult to establish, and the most that can be done is to examine the evidence in the light of such economic analyses and data as are available. Part I of this book attempted to survey the main facts, and it was shown (i) that there is little reason to believe that conventional economic growth will harm the interests of future generations, and (ii) that the groups in society most in need of improvements in every aspect of their living standards, including their environments, are the poorer groups in developing countries today. Of course the most that the analysis of Part I was able to do was to indicate what empirical information is relevant and possibly provide some estimates. And it may have helped somewhat in clarifying the conceptual issues involved. But the conclusions to be drawn from the facts still depend on our egalitarian values, on which I have no authority to adjudicate.

11. Is Discounting the Future "Unfair" to Future Generations?[1]

Intergenerational Justice and the Discount Rate

Whatever the right view to adopt about intergenerational justice, it will not get us anywhere unless there is some way of making the benefits or costs that future generations will experience comparable with those that will be experienced by the present generation. We cannot balance, say, the benefits that a future generation will obtain from some investment in environmental protection against the benefits that the current generation may have to give up in order to carry out that investment unless there is some way of making the benefits arising in each period comparable with each other. Unless this can be done, ethical rules governing the degree of sacrifice any particular generation should make in the interests of conferring benefits (including avoiding harm) on later generations are really so much hot air. They would be totally nonoperational, and probably conceptually meaningless as well.

Intergenerational justice could remain a nice topic for articles in the learned journals and even for some kinds of dinner-party conversation. But it would be of no practical value whatsoever unless we could find a way of making comparisons between benefits accruing at different points in time. This brings us to the "discounting" problem. Technical, and probably boring, to most people. But unavoidable if we are to go beyond fine gestures and make decisions about concrete environmental problems.

Economists take for granted that future benefits (or costs) can be made comparable with present benefits (and costs) by being converted into equivalent "present values" at some discount rate. However, they are usually well aware of certain qualifications that need to be taken into account in using this technique for evaluating projects the effects of which may span generations.[2] The few philosophers who have considered the problem seem to believe that the qualifications are so great that no discounting should be used at all in evaluating long-range projects. As Partridge points out, "The concept of discounting the future is a point of fundamental contention between economists and moral philosophers. To economists the concept is virtually axiomatic and thus beyond dispute. To many philosophers, the notion is, at best, arbitrary and unproved and, at worst, absurd."[3] John Rawls specifically dismisses the rationality of "pure" time preference—that is, a preference for a present benefit over a future benefit purely on account of its location in time and not on account of other considerations, such as an expected increase in income in the future. However, he goes on to add, "As with rational prudence, the rejection of pure time preferences is not incompatible with taking uncertainties and changing circumstances into account; *nor does it rule out using an interest rate . . . to ration limited funds for investment*" (my italics).[4]

This writing down of future benefits (or costs) by some interest rate, or "discount rate," is at the heart of all comparisons of investment projects the costs and benefits of which accrue over time. A benefit that is expected to be achieved in 10 years that is expected to have a value then of, say, £1 million (abstracting from inflation) will be valued today at much less than £1 million. How much less depends on the discount rate, or interest rate, used. At 5 percent, for example, £1 million worth of extra consumption expected in 10 years' time would have a present (i.e., discounted) value of only £614,000. For £614,000 is all that we need to invest today at 5 percent compound interest in order to get back £1 million in 10 years' time. And, at the same discount rate, if the extra £1 million worth of consumption is only expected to accrue in 50 years' time its present value today would be only £87,000.

It is this sort of comparison that can easily give rise to the widespread view that the practice of discounting future costs and benefits is "unfair" to future generations. I believe, however, that this view is mistaken, for various reasons, some of them rather complex. But before developing these arguments, two simple points must be made and will, perhaps, even suffice.

The first is as follows. Suppose medical progress were suddenly to make a great leap forward and we found that we were all going to live for, say, 200 years. As will be shown below, we would still be well advised to discount the future in making our investment and consumption plans. If, in fact, we do not live for 200 years and it will be future generations, not we, who will live with the consequences of our discounting procedures, they will be no worse off than we would be if we were alive in 200 years' time instead of them. So it is impossible to say that, by following the practice of discounting, we are treating them "unfairly" or discriminating against them. We are treating them in exactly the same way as we would treat ourselves. In the event that the discounting practice was not in their interests, it would not be in ours either, so it could still not be "unfair" to them.[5]

The second main reason why the usual objections to discounting—mainly by philosophers and some environmentalists—are unfounded is that they are invariably based on a total misunderstanding of what it is exactly that economists discount. It is widely believed that economists discount the *welfare* or the *utility* that will be obtained in the future as a result of any investment. That is to say, it is widely believed that discounting implies that a unit of utility, or welfare, accruing in the future is regarded as being of less value than an equal unit of utility today. But this is not the case at all. In general economists do not advocate discounting *utility* (or welfare). A unit of utility (or of welfare) accruing to some future generation is given the same value as a unit of utility (or welfare) accruing to the present generation. What is discounted is *consumption*—or rather the flow of output (or income) that is available for consumption at a future date. It is generally assumed, however—rightly or wrongly—that a higher consumption level in the future would mean that a given unit of future *consumption* would provide less welfare than would an equal unit of consumption today. But that is another matter, to which we shall return below.

In everyday life we may well give priority to our family over neighbors, or to our neighbors over total strangers, or to the fellow citizens of our country over those of other countries. But when we discount the future costs and benefits of any project we are not discriminating between different classes of people in this way. We do not give any priority to present generations over future generations. If there is some overall limit on how much present consumption society is willing to sacrifice in order to carry out investments then, as Rawls indicated, the use of some discount rate to ration the total investment among alternative projects according to which ones will yield most over the longer run actually raises the future consumption level—*whether our own or that of whoever happens to be alive in the future.* If low, or zero-yielding, investment projects were not weeded out by this process of selection, the total income of future generations would be lower than it would otherwise be.

The Rationality of Discounting for an Individual

Individuals generally attach more value to £1 today than to £1 at some future date (even adjusted for inflation). In other words they "discount the future." There may be various reasons for this. One is that many people expect to be richer later in life, up to a point. Consequently—in accordance with the psychological assumption known in economics as "the law of diminishing marginal utility"— they will expect to obtain less utility from £1's worth of consumption in the future than they would obtain from it today. It should be emphasized that this is not really a preference for present consumption *on account of its precedence in time.* It is a preference for more consumption now if one expects to be richer later and hence have less urgent needs to satisfy. Time only enters into it incidentally. After all, many people expect to be poorer when they are older and prefer to save now—that is, to consume less now—in order to maintain future consumption levels.

A second reason why most people "discount the future" is that there are always risks attached to any investment. One of these is the danger that the use to which the savings are put may turn out to be a mistake. The firm in which the savings are invested may go bankrupt, or the bank in which the savings are deposited may default, and so on. And even if we can protect against all these risks we are all mortal, and it would be a shame if we made big sacrifices of current consumption expecting to reap the benefits in a few years' time and then the next time we went out to do some shopping we got run over by a bus and were killed.

Again, however, time only enters into this motive for discounting in an incidental manner; and, as Derek Parfit has pointed out, the risk factor does not necessarily justify discounting for time per se in a continuous and mechanical manner.[6] For it is theoretically possible, in some cases, that the passage of time is not associated with a corresponding increase in risk. But in practice it is very difficult to think of many risks that are not closely correlated with time, whether it is the risk of a leak of radioactivity from radioactive waste buried on the bed of the oceans, or the risk of having a heart attack or of being run over by a bus before living to enjoy the fruits of our savings.

A third common motive for discounting the future is that many people also prefer present to future consumption for its own sake. For example they may simply be impatient. This latter motive is known as *"pure"* time preference. While there are some exceptions, most economists (including me) would not wish to defend the rationality of "pure" time preference in general, except in the special case of expected death for an individual or extinction for the human race.[7] In fact many eminent economists have condemned "pure" time preference in one way or another on the grounds of its irrationality.[8]

But whether or not consumers are "rational" in preferring present to future consumption—other things being equal—it does not mean that they are not behaving rationally in discounting the future in the light of the rate of return they can actually earn on any savings, or the rate of interest they would have to pay on any loans they may want to incur. A crucial distinction needs to be made between the rationality of having certain types of preferences—whether it be between consumption today and consumption tomorrow, or for eating lots of apples in the belief that an apple a day keeps the doctor away—and the rationality of adjusting one's savings or borrowings, or one's expenditure on apples, to the rate of interest or the price of apples respectively.

For a person who has no time preference whatsover, rational or otherwise, would still discount the future. The reason is simple. Consider the case of a person who does not worry about risk and is not impatient to consume now rather than tomorrow. (For the sake of the argument let us also assume that he does not expect to be any richer next year than this year.) In short, other things being equal, he would expect to derive as much utility out of £1 next year as this year. But then he discovers that, on the market, it is very easy to get a rate of return on savings of, say, 5 percent. What would he do? For every £1 saved and invested this year he could consume £1.05 next year. In the jargon of economics, the *"opportunity cost"* to him of £1 of consumption today is now £1.05 of consumption next year.

If he wanted to maximize utility over the two-year period he would obviously cut this year's consumption and invest the savings at 5 percent. In this way he would finish up with higher total utility taking the two years together. For if £1 of consumption next year looks as good to him as £1 of consumption this year, why not give up £1 consumption this year in exchange for £1.05 next year? In such a situation £1.05 next year will obviously be worth only £1 this year, since this is all he needs to invest now in order to obtain £1.05 next year. In other words, whether people have time preference or not it will still be rational for them to discount the future *faced with a market rate of interest*. They will do so because they can earn a rate of interest on savings, or will have to pay a rate of interest on loans they take out. It follows that, for a person, the rationality or otherwise of time preference is irrelevant in determining the rationality of discounting the future, given that there is a positive rate of return, or rate of interest, available on the market.

Of course, as the person in this example switches from consumption today toward consumption next year the marginal utility of the remaining consumption today will rise. He will be falling back on the satisfaction of more and more basic needs. And the expected marginal utility of consumption next year will fall. So he will only switch to the point where the extra 5 percent of consumption that he will have next year just offsets the relative fall in next year's marginal utility by comparison with this year's. At that point the marginal utility he will expect to obtain from £1 of consumption next year will be 5 percent less than the marginal utility he would obtain from £1 of consumption this year.

The same reason that explains why a person would not normally give up £1 now in exchange for a refund of only £1 next year also explains why he would not pay £1 now for a £1 loaf of bread to be delivered next year. For if he invests the £1 now he would be able to cash it in next year for, say, £1.05, buy the loaf of bread and have 5 pence left over. Hence he would only be willing to pay about 95 pence this year for the promise of a £1 loaf of bread to be delivered next year. The "present" or "discounted" value to his of a £1 loaf of bread next year would be only 95 pence. And his expected marginal utility from a loaf of bread next year must also have fallen relative to this year's bread, like the marginal utility of his consumption in general (unless there is some reason to expect a rise in the relative price of bread).

In conclusion, then, it appears that the various criticisms of the validity of "time preference" are all irrelevant to the rationality of individual choice as long as we can obtain a positive rate of return on investments and savings. But does this apply to society as a whole? We shall consider this in the next section.

Discounting for Society[9]

What Is Rational for the Individual May Not Be Rational for Society

On the other hand, the justification for the rationality of discounting on account of the rate of return available on the market—that is, the "opportunity cost" argument—does not necessarily apply to society as a whole. The main reason for this has been emphasized, interestingly enough, not by any economist but by the philosopher Derek Parfit, either alone or in conjunction with Tyler Cowen. The crux of the argument in their article is that, in discussing the way the person allocated his consumption over time, we treated him as faced with a rate of interest that, as far as he was concerned, was determined by forces outside his control.[10] It was something he had to accept as given. In the jargon of economics it was "exogenous" as far as he was concerned. Rational behavior required him to adapt to the *given* rate of interest he could get on his savings.

For society as a whole, however, the interest rate is not something that is *given* to it from outside. It is determined as a result of the mutual interaction within society between, on the one hand, the terms on which people are prepared to save, and, on the other, the interest rate that firms and governments are prepared to pay in order to borrow money. This is like the way the price of apples on the market is determined by the interaction between the demand for them and the supply. It is claimed by Cowen and Parfit that, *if we reject the rationality of basic time preference*, the market interest rate produced this way is not socially optimal and ought to be zero.

Their argument is essentially that, since people *ought* not to have any basic time preference, they *ought* to be willing to save any amount at a zero rate of interest. In that case, the rate of interest determined in the market would be zero, and investments in the economy would be pushed to the point where the return on marginal investments had fallen to zero. All the above argument about the way the consumer allocated his consumption over time would still apply, but at an opportunity cost of zero.

183

In other words, Cowen and Parfit are saying that to transpose the argument about the rationality of adapting to the given rate of interest from the individual to society as a whole would be a circular argument. For, they argue, the rate of interest that is determined for society as a whole would be zero if basic time preference were to be zero. And this, according to them, is what, from an ethical point of view, it *ought* to be. They assert, "At the optimum point suggested by the moral principle of zero discounting of consumption streams, the marginal product of capital is also zero."[11] But there seem to be two objections to this assertion.

Is the Moral Status of "Pure" Time Preference Relevant?

In the first place, it is far from certain that "irrational" preferences make people more, rather than less, reluctant to save. Many people may have "irrational" preferences in favor of the future, and may save more than is justified in terms of the uncertainties attached to their future incomes. For example, some people may be excessively prudent. Also, many people may save more than they would have wished to save if only they had been able to predict exactly when they would die. As a result, instead of allocating their capital and income over their lifetime in a manner designed just to use it all up (minus such bequests as they want to make) by the end of their lives, they save too much for fear of going on living longer. So when they finally do die they leave assets to their heirs that they would probably have preferred to spend on their own comfort or entertainment during their lifetimes. Finally, many people fail to make enough allowance for their heirs' higher income levels or for the investments they have made in their children's education. Hence they may leave large bequests to their heirs as a result of influences that might be regarded as "irrational," such as sheer apathy, or exaggerated respect for custom and convention, or an undeniably irrational concern for what people may think of them after their death. All in all, therefore, it is difficult to see what sort of facts would confirm or deny that irrational preferences must always be in the direction of saving too little.

Second, even if people's "pure" time preference is irrational, it is not necessarily irrational or immoral for democratic governments to take account of such preferences in the conduct of policy. Suppose the authorities have to decide whether to preserve some apple orchard or build a motorway in its place. In weighing the costs and benefits involved should they adjust down the value of the apples produced to allow for the fact that the public's faith in the medicinal properties of eating apples is unfounded?

It is people's preferences for TV chat shows, tobacco, opera, and apples that determine their relative prices. These are the prices that should be used in any cost-benefit analysis of the desirability of investing in the production of these goods or services.[12] If we were to value them at a zero price on the grounds that some of them may reflect preferences that are "irrational," or even "immoral," we would be adopting a degree of paternalism and moral presumptuousness that most people would find unacceptable.

As regards the interest rate, while there may be room for dispute as to the rationality of people's preferences between consumption today or next year, or the way they perceive them, it is these preferences that determine the equilibrium rate of interest on the market. Thus, leaving aside issues such as divergence between private and social risk, or the possibility that we might be more willing to save if we believed other people were doing so as well, and so on, it is people's preferences that matter, rather than how and why they are what they happen to be.[13]

If we start questioning the optimality of the pattern of relative prices in the economy on the grounds that people's preferences between different ways of spending their money are not strictly rational, where do we stop? What is meant by "rational" preferences? We could easily find plausible arguments to show that almost any consumer preference we can think of is irrational or based on incorrect information. There is a large literature in economics and psychology concerning the various tests that have been made and that demonstrate how "irrational" people's preferences appear to be in the light of certain criteria, such as consistency, transitivity, and so on. It not only applies to people's preferences as regards different points of time at which they expect to obtain benefits or incur costs. If the irrationality of consumers' preferences were to justify ignoring them, democracy might as well be abolished and our fates handed over to philosopher kings, who, unfortunately, are not only fallible too but also have great difficulty in making up their minds about anything.

Is the Argument for Discounting Circular?

What about the other component of people's time preference, namely their expectations of being richer in the future, which would reduce their future marginal utilities of consumption? Here Cowen and Parfit emphasize the alleged circularity in the case for discounting. For how far any person's marginal utility of consumption is expected to decline depends on how much he adjusts his time path of consumption to the interest rate which is "given" to him. But, according to the Cowen and Parfit argument set out above, if the supply of savings were to reflect only time preference per se (which should be zero if people were "rational"), the interest rate that is "given" to him would not be positive at all to begin with. Hence optimizing consumers would not shift their consumption patterns to the point that expected future marginal utilities were lower than those of today. Hence there would be no discounting for diminishing marginal utility of consumption to be added to the (zero) "pure" time preference in arriving at the overall rate at which society should discount future consumption.

But such an outcome is not possible as long as the psychological law of diminishing marginal utility of consumption is accepted (as it is by Cowen and Parfit). For suppose that, as they suggest, the rate of interest was tending toward zero. What would be the effect? It would tend to lead to a massive switch of current output to investment instead of consumption, since there must be unlimited investment opportunities that would yield negligible rates of return, even in the British economy. But, as the pattern of output switched away from current consumption, consumption would fall and the marginal utility of current consumption would rise relative to future consumption. As a result, a point would soon be reached—presumably before they had sunk to starvation levels—at which people would refuse to save more for a zero rate of interest.

Whether or not they would see the relative rise in future consumption levels, or the risks attached to them, as perfectly correlated with time would be totally irrelevant. They would refuse to save for nothing not because they confuse differences in consumption levels with time per se. They would do so because they would not want to starve today, and today invariably comes earlier than tomorrow. They would be adjusting to their fall in current consumption by demanding that any further savings they make be rewarded by some positive rate of interest. Obviously, in making such an adjustment time has to come into the bargain. How else could they express it?

Indeed Cowen and Parfit sell a crucial pass when they concede, "It may not be possible, however, for the marginal rate of return on capital to reach zero. The economist's assumption of diminishing marginal productivity could be wrong. *Or some other constraint may prevent attainment of a zero marginal rate of return on capital"* (my italics). The "other constraint" would be that the public would not supply indefinite amounts of savings at a zero interest rate, even if we adjusted the supply price of savings for the excess of private risk over social risk.

To recapitulate, therefore, even if it is accepted (i) that society should not have "pure" time preference; (ii) that it should regard itself as a continuing entity (all the evidence of the international developments over the last few years to the contrary); (iii) that most of the risks that people take into account are private risks, not social risks; and (iv) that expected future increases in overall consumption levels should be incorporated in a separate explicit calculation—the implication is still not that society should have a zero discount rate, but that separate allowance should be made for risk (which will generally be less for society than for individuals) and for expected future changes in consumption levels adjusted by assumptions concerning the marginal utility of consumption.

And this is precisely what economists frequently do, as indicated in the section "What Discount Rate" later in the chapter. The results of these and other adjustments to market rates do indeed usually produce discount rates that are below the average rates of return on marginal investments, even in developed economies.

The Compensation Problem

Suppose we are faced with a possibility of investing £100 million today in some environmental project that is estimated to save society from incurring £1 billion of environmental damage in 100 years' time—for example, from a radiation leak or from global warming. Suppose an alternative is to invest in some other nonenvironmental project at the rate of return that can be obtained on additional (i.e., marginal) investments in the economy. In order to simplify the rest of the arithmetic, we shall assume the rate to be 3.04 percent per annum. At this rate of return the £100 million would accumulate to about £2 billion in a hundred years' time—that is, twice as much as the environmental project. It looks as if it would be better to choose the nonenvironmental project. This would maximize the consumption opportunities available to future generations. Future generations could compensate themselves for the £1 billion of environmental damage that could otherwise have been avoided and still have £1 billion left over for other purposes.

But again, it might seem that what is true for an individual is not necessarily true for society as a whole. If an individual decides to sacrifice benefits at one period of his life in order to reap greater benefits at another, there is no question but that he feels that it is in his interests to do so. In that respect, therefore, he is "better off." But if society takes decisions which mean that, in some future period, some people may lose and others gain, it is not so obvious that society as a whole is better off, at least not unless the gainers do actually compensate the losers. And one objection that has been raised to the example just given is that we cannot be sure that those of us who gain from adopting the high-return project will compensate those who lose by our not adopting the low-return environmental project. For example, it may well be impossible to identify the future victims of some environmental risks incurred as a result of actions today. As Derek Parfit points out, "This might be so, for instance, if we would not be able to identify those particular genetic deformities that our policy had caused. This removes our reason for being less concerned now about deformities in later years. If we will not pay compensation for such deformities, it becomes an irrelevant fact that, in the case of later deformities, it *would* have been cheaper to ensure now that we *could have* paid compensation."[14] He might have added that, even if the losers among future generations from certain environmental policies pursued today *could* be identified, we cannot guarantee that future societies will want to use their greater wealth to compensate the victims.[15]

This is not the place to go into all the intricacies of this argument, which will be tackled elsewhere. But there are certain counter-arguments that have to be noted:

(a) For enthusiastic environmentalists there is a serious trap in the compensation argument. This is that time runs in only one direction and future generations cannot compensate present generations for costs incurred on their behalf. Suppose society is considering a project that involves replacing some use of the environment by some other resources—human labor, or capital. For example, more labor and capital may be used in order to reduce emissions of harmful air pollutants or effluents. These other resources will then not be available for other purposes—food, clothes, houses, education, health, or all sorts of other goods and services that go to make up our standard of living. The people deprived of these goods and services will suffer accordingly. It will certainly be impossible, in practice, to know exactly who they are. And, even if we do know who they are, future generations could not compensate them. Would extreme environmentalists prefer, therefore, to abstain from all such projects? I wouldn't.

(b) But suppose we are considering the case where both gainers and losers are members of some future generation. True, we cannot be sure that future victims can be identified or that future societies will ensure that they are compensated. But this applies also to any ordinary cost-benefit analysis in which future generations play no part. If we insisted that we only carry out projects when we know that gainers from projects will in fact compensate losers (and still remain better off), there would be very few projects that society could ever undertake. Should we never build an airport or a road because it is usually impossible accurately to identify all the losers and the gainers?

For example, it was often assumed that, apart from the usual costs of building an airport, the losers would also include the people living near them who would suffer from the noise and hence incur a fall in the value of their houses. But for many people it transpired that their property rose in value on account of improved access facilities. Most of the victims may have been residents of distant communities whose own airports lost business. And the compensation argument requires that we identify not only the victims but also the beneficiaries. For if we do not extract all the compensation from them we would have to extract it from the rest of society—for example, by higher taxes—and hence create a new class of uncompensated losers. But it would be impossible to identify the beneficiaries. The airline passengers may well save time through using the new airport, but for most of them it will be their employers who will benefit, or rather the shareholders in the companies paying for their travel time. And some of the beneficiaries may have been not just the air travelers but those who gained employment in some distant aircraft factory or the workers attracted into the area to build the airport. Clearly it would be impossible to track them all down. Hence, if we took the compensation requirement seriously we could hardly carry out any public projects whatsover.

(c) The compensation issue does not really have anything to do with discounting. Even if no discount rate were used and the total amount of investment society was willing to carry out was allocated among projects in some other manner (such as drawing lots or tossing a coin?), there would still be the problem of whether or not to invest in projects that might provide a net benefit for society as a whole, but may involve some losers as well as some gainers. Are all such projects to be eliminated from consideration? If so, hardly any investment would ever be carried out because it would be almost impossible to find any project that did not impose losses on somebody or other, however indirectly, as shown.

(d) As well as this practical reason for not taking the compensation condition too seriously, there is also a more ethical reason. If the benefits of a project exceed the costs and the compensation condition is satisfied, nobody loses from the project and one or more people gain. But how far this implies an improvement in social welfare depends on ethical judgments concerning how far one is an egalitarian. For example, somebody who does not care at all about inequality but only about maximizing total incomes—a utilitarian, for example—would not necessarily worry whether the losers from a project were compensated or not as long as total incomes rose.[16] To such a person, therefore, compensation of losers by gainers is not a *necessary* condition for increasing social welfare. By contrast, somebody who is egalitarian might conclude that, even if losers were compensated by the gainers, if the remaining benefits accruing to the gainers increase the inequality of incomes, it is undesirable. Or the losers might be rich people and the gainers poor people. In that case the project would not merely increase total incomes, but would also help promote the objective of reducing income inequality *as long as no compensation were paid*. Similarly, a Rawlsian would object to any increase in the prosperity of the rich, even if it were not at the expense of the poor, insofar as it did not lead to any improvement in the welfare of the poorest groups in society.[17]

Contemporary civilized societies help all sorts of groups in need—for example, the sick or the unemployed or the poor—without wanting to establish whether they have to be compensated for being the victims of anybody else's actions (past or present) because this is regarded as morally irrelevant information. Quite often all that matters is their *need*. If a person found a drowning man whose life he could save by pulling him out of the water, Parfit would presumably not first ask him whether somebody had pushed him in! This would be morally irrelevant information. Certainly we do not try now to identify victims of environmental decisions made in the past. Should we not give aid to starving children in Somalia until we have made sure that we have given priority to all the victims today of past decisions in all areas?

In short, the principle that, at any point in time, society should give some special status to the compensation criterion in deciding its allocation of aid to people is a highly debatable moral principle. At any point in time society should allocate resources between people according to various criteria, such as some principles of justice that may, for example, take account of need, merit, legal legitimacy and entitlement, or contractual obligation, and possibly also to the extent to which they have been unfortunate victims of environmental circumstances beyond their control. But there seems no moral reason for attaching special status to this last principle. In other words, when faced with the conclusion that a certain project may fail to satisfy the compensation condition, we usually have to reply, "Well that's just too bad for the compensation condition!"

Furthermore, we could take the view that we have to go for growth and let future society make its own mistakes about how use it—that is we should not *want* to preempt future societies' decisions about who gets compensated for what. Why only compensate future groups who have lost as a result of *our* environmental policies? Why not also expect them to compensate future groups for disadvantages imposed on them as a result of the possibly fortuitous advantages possessed by other future groups in society—for example, those that enabled these other groups to be richer or more powerful or something—or by nonenvironmental decisions taken today that will almost certainly be against the interests of some future group (one could think of dozens of examples). Instead we should accept that, if we get more overall growth, future society will have more choice, and it is not for us to deprive it of this opportunity on the grounds that it might not choose wisely or justly. This would constitute a very narrow, paternalistic, and timid view of human destiny. There seem to be few grounds therefore for believing that it would be desirable, or even important, that future societies compensate victims of our decisions. Who knows what far worse problems they face? There may be millions more equivalents of today's starving children in Somalia or of today's civil war victims in what was Yugoslavia.

The Implications of a Zero Discount Rate

A final flaw in the environmentalist argument in favor of a zero, or very low, discount rate, is that the result would be greatly to speed up economic growth and hence the use of the environment.[18] For if the prospect of an extra £1 of consumption in, say, 50 years' time was regarded today as having the same value now as £1 of consumption today, then it follows that anything greater than £1 of consumption in the future, say £1.01, would be valued more highly than £1 today. And there must be an infinite number of investment projects that could earn such trivial rates of return. So the general adoption of zero discount rates would logically imply that today's consumption ought to be cut to the bone in order that almost all resources could be turned over to investment in lunatic projects that would not stand a chance of being adopted if normal discounting rules were applied. Such a Stalinist policy of starving the present in the interest of "pie in the sky" in the distant future has been attempted in the communist and "ex-communist" countries, and the world has seen the disastrous outcome!

Nor can we escape from this argument by saying that a zero discount rate ought to be applied to environmental projects but not to investment in general. For there is no difference in principle between the benefits that will be obtained in the future from, say, preserving the beauty of the countryside and the benefits that would be obtained in the future from any other productive investment.

Of course it is necessary to estimate what future relative prices will be.[19] We should use the right estimate of the damage that would be done in 100 years' time if we fail to carry out the environmental project. It would be necessary, for example, to allow for "externalities" (i.e., environmental effects that may not pass through the market and do not enter into the calculations of those responsible for them). It would also be necessary to allow for changes in the relative prices of environmental amenities as against other goods and services that may contribute to people's welfare, although some writers would prefer to make this adjustment by using special project-specific discount rates.[20]

It is also necessary to use a correct estimate of the rate of return on new investments in the economy. Now there is general agreement among economists that there are numerous imperfections in the capital market, so that the market rate of interest may not be the socially optimal rate. To allow for this we might want to take account of changes in supply and demand. For example, we might want to assume that the relative value of beautiful countryside will rise over time insofar as it is fixed in amount and insofar as increased leisure may make people demand more of it. But, in the same way, we might want to assume that, with growing incomes, there will be an increasing demand for live music, so that the relative price of live music performances will rise. For the real wages of musicians will probably rise more or less in line with the rest of the economy, whereas it is virtually impossible for them to increase their productivity. (Of course, they might be able to speed up their productivity by cutting out the slow movements from symphonies!)

Furthermore, many people—including the mass of the world's population currently living in developing countries, not to mention millions of people in advanced countries who still live in poverty—might appreciate just getting more ordinary goods and services. The social rate of return on primary education in poor countries, for example, is reported to be about 25 percent. The rate of return in many such countries to investments in providing safe drinking water and sanitation is probably even higher in terms of the addition to the welfare of the people in question, even if it is not always easy to measure it. If a lower, or zero, discount rate were to be used in such countries in order to carry out more investment therein it would mean more investment to reduce the possible harmful effects of global warming in 100 years' time and less to alleviate their current appalling living conditions and help lift them out of acute poverty.

Thus none of the objections to discounting discussed above seems to be valid. Since some limit has to be placed on total investment, if discounting were not to be used future consumption levels would be lower than they otherwise would be, and future generations would therefore be poorer. Indeed if the arguments for zero, or artifically low, discount rates were to be used as a guide to policy it would lead to massive rates of investment in unproductive projects at the cost of totally unacceptable sacrifices of current consumption.

What Discount Rate to Use?

Finally, what discount rate should we use? Every economist knows that the market rate of interest—insofar as one can establish some representative rate—does not accurately reflect either people's preferences or the real rate of return that can be obtained on marginal investments in the economy. After all, economic analysis is well stocked with examples of divergencies between, on the one hand, the outcome of free market forces and the outcomes that would be socially optimal.

Thus although the precise manner and degree of the appropriate adjustment is the subject of much indecisive debate it is likely that the rate of interest determined in the market exceeds the rate that is "optimal" for society as a whole.[21] So for one reason or another public cost-benefit analysis has been obliged to try to identify some rate of discount that is adjusted for various distortions. Several approaches have been adopted and it would be out of place to go into detail here.[22]

One standard approach is to make some assumption about the future rate of growth of consumption and then modify it by some assumption as to the rate at which the marginal utility of consumption falls off as consumption rises. For example, there is some evidence for the view that a rise of 1 percent in consumption could imply a fall of at least 1.5 percent in the marginal utility of further increments in consumption.[23] In that case, if it were thought that consumption would increase by, say, 2 percent per annum over the relevant time period this would lead to a fall in the marginal utility of consumption of 3 percent per annum. This, therefore, would be the minimum discount rate that should be used. We might also want to add some allowance for "pure" time preference, to arrive at the overall discount rate—for example, on the grounds that most people do not expect to be immortal. Estimates of these components of the final overall (consumption) discount rate can vary, of course, but the estimate of about 4 percent proposed by Maurice Scott seems fairly reasonable and also happens to be very much in line with the

194

same author's much later estimates of the average real rate of return on more or less riskless long-term government bonds in Britain and the United States over the last two or three decades.[24]

Of course the rate of return on investments in most developing countries is estimated to be very much higher, corresponding to the fact that capital is much scarcer in such countries. And this should be taken into account in discounting the benefits of environmental projects (as of any projects) in such countries. This is not the place, however, to go into the special problems of project appraisal in developing countries. Here it must suffice to emphasize that insofar as the case set out above for discounting environmental projects along the same lines as any other projects is accepted, it also would have to be accepted that the high discount rate appropriate in developing countries would inevitably curtail the scope for economically defensible investments in environmental projects in such countries.

The conclusion of this chapter, therefore, is that there seem to be no grounds for the widespread view that discounting future costs and benefits in general, or environmental costs and benefits in particular, is "unfair" to future generations. This means that in finding a socially optimal balance between imposing costs on present generations and avoiding future environmental damage, the distant benefits of the latter type of project are rightly discounted at some socially appropriate discount rate. This will certainly be less than the market rates in almost all economies, but not necessarily less than the rates that many governments use in public investment decisions. However, an important consideration in estimating what would be an appropriate rate is the rate of technological progress in the world as a whole that can be expected over the long-run future. This is not something that we can predict with any confidence, but reasons have been given in Chapter 1 for expecting it to be at least as high as it has been over the last few decades.

Conclusions
Toward a Balanced Debate

We have argued that there is a need for the environmental debate to get away from its obsession with the glamorous issues—such as the threat of global catastrophe from global warming or the exhaustion of finite resources—and to take a more balanced view of the choices that have to be made. These choices are extremely difficult, chiefly because there are three major conflicts that have to be faced in this area. They are, first, the conflict between the claims of different environmental concerns on available resources; second, the conflict between the interests of different countries; and, third, the conflict between the interests of different generations.

Instead, it is widely asserted by many extreme environmentalists that the important conflict is between economic growth and the environment. A part of this book, therefore, has been devoted to showing that, far from this being the case, economic growth is a necessary condition for proper protection of the environment. In the longer run it is also probably a sufficient condition. But how long the longer run is depends on what policies are adopted to deal with the environment. This raises difficult problems of identifying and measuring the innumerable ecological, scientific, and economic data that are required to implement appropriate environmental policies.

Economists are well aware that, in general, market imperfections prevent society from giving due concern to environmental protection whether there is economic growth or not. Many environmental economists, scientists, and ecologists are engaged in seeking out the facts necessary to devise appropriate policies to correct these market imperfections and to put values on their costs and benefits. For there are innumerable claims on limited resources, and the first conflict that has to be dealt with is between the various environmental protection activities that society needs to undertake. How much should be spent on cleaning up rivers or beaches, or urban air pollution, or on preventing future climate change, rather than on more houses, hospitals, schools, food, clothing, and all the other items of consumption that enter into people's standards of living? The work being carried out in various scientific and economic institutions designed to help resolve these conflicts is crucially important. It is unfortunate, therefore, that it is the more glamorous environmental issues that grab the headlines and absorb most of the energies and funds available for environmental research.

Of course, the priorities that should be given to alternative uses of resources will depend much on which country we are talking about—an affluent country or an impoverished country? This leads us to the second area of conflict, namely between the rich and the poor. In the poorer countries of the world, what happens to the carbon dioxide concentration in the atmosphere in 100 years' time may not matter much. For it has been shown in the preceding chapters of this book that the real environmental issues facing the world today are those afflicting the majority of the world's population who live in developing countries. These are lack of clean drinking water or decent sanitation, or exposure to intolerably bad air quality in large cities. It is also shown that economic growth is the only sure path along which they can hope to overcome these environmental problems. Of course, appropriate policies are needed there, too. But it is only in the context of rising incomes that such policies stand much chance of being adopted. For otherwise, more urgent claims for food and shelter will swamp claims for better environmental conditions.

Insofar as the needs of developing countries are recognized by extreme environmentalists, they are usually just mentioned, in passing, as being catered to in the now fashionable concept of "sustainable development." This is usually supposed to mean something like "the path of development that ensures that welfare never decreases." But, as shown above, this is a totally redundant concept. The objective of policy should be to maximize social welfare over whatever time period is relevant, and if this involves some decrease in welfare during that period, so what? If that is the way that welfare over the whole period is maximized it is still the optimal policy.

Of course, the selection of the relevant time period leads us to our third conflict of interest. This is between the interests of different generations. But it has been argued in this book that, as far as the environment is concerned, this conflict is nothing like as great as is widely asserted. This is not because we ought to ignore the interests of future generations. How great our obligations to future generations are is a complex philosophical issue to which moral philosophers have only relatively recently paid much attention. It has been shown above that it may be impossible to provide any fully coherent and articulated theory of justice toward future generations. At the same time it has been argued that our moral intuitions in favor of "fairness" toward future generations should provide some check on the extent to which we can feel free to use the resources of the planet as much as we might otherwise like.

But the main reason why the practical consequences of our concern for future generations seem far less dramatic than many eco-doomsters would have us believe is a purely technical one. For these practical consequences depend on how genuine the danger is that continued economic growth will run up against constraints such as climate change or the exhaustion of finite resources. We have shown that in fact these fears are groundless. There is no danger of our running out of finite resources. And the impact of climate change on the standard of living of future generations is likely to be relatively trivial. Biodiversity presents more of a problem, largely because we know so little about the enormous complexity of the interrelationships between different components of the ecosystem, although there is strong—if patchy—evidence that species may be being made extinct at an undesirable rate.

Striking the right balance between the three areas of conflict identified will be extremely difficult—indeed impossible—for they interact. For example, the choice is not just between protecting the environment of future generations and that of the present generation. Within each generation there are conflicting interests. If the costs of greater environmental protection were to be borne, for example, only by the wealthier members of society, they might be more acceptable. But if the costs are to be borne by the mass of the world's population living in developing countries, the "tradeoff" is very different. Even within the more affluent societies there are conflicting interests in different forms of environmental concern. The better-off members of society may be more concerned with climate change or reducing road congestion or providing beautiful lampposts, while the poorer members of society may be more concerned with decent housing or working conditions. Since, in democratic societies, all interests—including minority interests—should be respected, the conflicts of choice here also will be difficult.

Hence we should first downgrade our concern with the glamorous issues, and concentrate instead on the nitty-gritty research required to devise appropriate policies for dealing with genuine environmental issues in rich countries as well as in developing countries. These include, for example, identifying the sources of local water and air pollution, the damage they cause, the costs of reducing the pollution, and the best methods for doing so. They also include the study of methods of dealing with a host of other problems, such as disposing of waste of all kinds, from nuclear waste to used automobile tires, or how to value the importance that people attach to a clean environment, or how best to design internationally feasible policies to prevent overfishing of certain species. As far as developing countries are concerned, priority should be given to the population problem, which is largely responsible for the environmental difficulties in most developing countries, whether it be shortage of clean drinking water or urban degradation or deforestation.

Above all, we should not be panicked into the sort of drastic action urged on us by many environmental activists, such as hastily concocted international agreements to adopt draconian cuts in the use of fossil fuels. It is far more important to dismantle many current policies that subsidize uneconomic use of fossil fuels and to promote further research into energy efficiency and the development of economically viable substitutes. Calls for drastic action may give us all a nice inner glow of self-righteousness but, if they were to be heeded, they would impose totally unjustified burdens on the vast proportion of the world's population.

In short, the message of this book is that we have time to think. What is needed is the will to do so.

Notes

Introduction

1. Mishan, E. J., 1967, and Schumacher, E. F., 1973.
2. Wilson, E. O., 1992, pp. 270/1.
3. Kenny, A., 1994, p. 11.
4. See British submission to the 1972 UN Conference on the Human Environment, Stockholm, 1972; First Report of the Royal Commission on Environmental Pollution, 1972; Warren Springs Laboratory, 1972, and information given in a reply to a Parliamentary question by a Minister for the environment, Mr. Eldon Griffiths, Dec. 22, 1972 (*House of Commons Debates, Col. 1974*).
5. This was the title of the English edition, published by Jonathan Cape, London, 1974. The USA edition, under the title *Two Cheers for the Affluent Society*, was published by St. Martin's Press, New York, in 1975.

Chapter 1

1. Jonathan Porritt in Porritt, J. (ed.), 1990, p. 122.
2. Borcherding, T., 1990.
3. Mishan, E. J., 1967.
4. See for example, Ashby, E. and Anderson, M., 1981; and Brimblecombe, P., 1987.
5. A clear expression of the importance of not imposing excessive sacrifices on the poor of present generations is David Pearce's *Economic Values and the Natural World*, 1993, p. 53.
6. Kenny, A., 1994, p. 10.
7. UNDP, 1991, p. 79.
8. Goldsmith, E., 1988, p. 193.
9. Solow, R. M., 1992a, 3–9.
10. Porritt, J., in Button, J. (ed.), *The Green Fuse*, p. 140.
11. It is unfortunate that support for such a view is given by Sir Crispin Tickell, who surely knows better, in "What We Must Do to Save the Planet," in *New Scientist*, 7.9.92.
12. Quoted, but accompanied by a critical review, in the editorial of *Environmental Values*, vol. 1, no. 3, autumn 1992, p. 190.
13. Fleming, D., ibid., p. 276.

Chapter 2

1. The definition of "developing countries" is, of course, arbitrary. The World Bank has tended to classify countries into "low income" and "middle income" groups, as those groups comprising countries with annual per capita income levels in 1989 at or below $610, and between $610 and $7,620, respectively, and "developing countries" are often defined as comprising these two groups—i.e., countries in which the

201

annual average per capita income is less than $7,620 (see World Bank, 1992, p. xi). On this basis the population of developing countries in 1989 was estimated to be 3,800 million out of a total world population of 4,931 million (World Bank, 1991, p. xiv).

2. *Development and the Environment*, report submitted by a panel of experts convened by the Secretary-General of the United Nations Conference on the Human Environment (Norstedt, Stockholm, 1971).

3. These are the estimates contained in *Global Consultation on Safe Water and Sanitation for the 1990s*, which, as indicated below, were published in 1990 and were lower than other World Bank estimates published in 1988, both for 1980 and for projections to 1990. The former are probably more consistent with another estimate according to which over 1.5 billion people in the world still do not have access to safe drinking water, in Briscoe, J. and de Ferranti, D., 1988.

4. *Global Consultation on Safe Water and Sanitation for the 1990s*, background paper to the Sept. 1990, New Delhi conference of same name sponsored by UNDP and other organizations, and prepared by the Secretariat to the conference, p. 5. Estimates from this document have to be based on the charts contained therein and so are about as rough as the basic reliability of the data justify. The projections quoted above for numbers without access to safe drinking water or satisfactory sanitation in the year 2000 are lower than those made in World Bank, 1988, Annex 1.

5. See Beckerman, W., 1992.

6. Briscoe, J. and De Ferranti, D., 1988, p. 1; a breakdown by these diseases is given in Esrey, S. S., Potash, J. B., Roberts, L. and Shiff, C., 1990, p. vii, but no total is shown. Presumably there is considerable overlap in that people suffering from one of the diseases are also likely to be suffering from one or more of the others.

7. This estimate refers to mortality among children below five years of age. See Esrey et al., 1990, and Snyder, J. D. and Merson, M. H., 1982, pp. 605–13.

8. World Bank, EMTEN/EMENA, 1989c, p. 65.

9. Aziz, K. M. A. et al., 1990, p. 10.

10. Ibid., pp. xii–xiii.

11. World Bank internal memorandum. The WASH survey quoted above is based on a survey of over a hundred detailed studies, many of which found results similar to those quoted here.

12. World Bank Operations Evaluation Department, 1990b, pp. 11 and 12.

13. One of the members of the Royal Commission on Environmental Pollution, of which I was a member from 1970 to 1973, who was a bishop, disputed my view that, because it required victims, sin could not exist in isolation, from which I deduced that bishops have more imagination than I have.

14. The need to take account of human exposure to given air quality conditions has given rise to the recently developed concept of "total exposure assessment" in which an attempt is made to take account of the numbers of people actually exposed to the air pollution conditions described by the various indicators. See a discussion of the concept in GEMS, 1982.

15. The full scientific evidence behind the estimates of the relative pollution effects of alternative activities, notably cooking methods in developed and developing countries, is contained in Smith, K. R., 1987.

16. Of course, this is partly because developing countries are conventionally defined in terms of income levels and happen, at present, to encompass about 75 percent of the world's population. The estimate here is based on Smith, K. R., 1988. The estimates shown above are obtained by expressing, as percentages of the total,

the products of the cells in tables 2 and 3 in this source. They correspond to the results shown graphically in figure 3 of the source.

17. See Smith, K. R., 1987, p. vii.

18. GEMS, 1988, table 3, p. 86. See also World Bank, 1992, p. 52.

19. Smith, K. R., 1987, pp. 18–19 and, for a more extended analysis of the same theme, the same author's "The Risk Transition" (1990).

20. See Ozorio de Almeida, A. L. de, 1991.

21. Residents in the cities are presumably free to move out. Therefore insofar as they do not—at least not as fast as others are coming in—we must presume that even though their welfare is reduced by the inflow of new migrants it is still higher than it would be if they moved back to rural areas. Nevertheless, their welfare will still tend to be reduced by the inflow of newcomers, so the net welfare effect of the inflow will be the rise in the welfare of the latter less the fall in the welfare of the former.

22. UN, 1990, tables A5, A6, and A7.

23. Faiz, A. et al., 1990, p. 28.

24. World Bank, Operations Evaluation Department, 1990b, p. (iv).

25. Faiz, A. et al., 1990, p. 40. Similar accounts can be found for other cities in developing countries. For example, it is reported that the severe traffic problems of Cairo are partly the result of a high percentage of unsurfaced roads, rapid and unmanageable growth of car ownership, and absence of traffic management measures, inadequate parking control, poor traffic signs and signals, and lack of regulatory enforcement. All these variables add to congestion and hence to pollution. (See Leitmann, J., 1991, p. 17, based on material in the World Bank's *Greater Cairo Urban Development Project*, 1982.)

26. Leitmann, J., 1991, p. 23.

27. Faiz, A. et al., 1990, p. 17.

28. For Mexico, ibid. For Sao Paulo, World Bank Operations Evaluation Department, 1990b, p. 10; and for Tunis, World Bank EMENA, 1989b, p. 78.

29. Faiz, A. et al., 1990, p. 16.

30. Phantumvanit, D. and Panayotou, T., 1990, p. 27.

31. Tongpan, S. et al., 1990, p. 6. See also same conference, Phantumvanit, D. and Panayotou, T., 1990, ch. 3, "Poverty and deforestation: a vicious circle."

32. Internal World Bank country economic memorandum on Thailand.

33. Reis, E. J. and Margulis, S., 1991.

34. Leitmann, J., 1991, p. 22.

35. World Bank, 1989a, pp. 64ff.

36. Kumar, S. K. and Hotchkiss, D., 1988, pp. 11 and 28. See also Pasha, H. A. and McGarry, M. G. (eds) 1989, p. 1. In this document it is reported that 45 percent of all child deaths are caused by diarrhea.

37. See, for example, Whittington, D., Xinming, M., and Roche, R., 1990 (esp. pp. 269–80); Whittington, D., Okorafor, A., Okore, A., and McPhail, A., 1990; or WASH Field Report no. 246, 1988, pp. vii and 27.

38. World Bank, 1989a, p. xvi.

Chapter 3

1. An excellent up-to-date survey of some of the reasons for doubting the widespread acceptance of the need to reduce the use of CFCs in order to protect the ozone layer is provided in Singer, F., 1994.

2. *Memoirs of Chateaubriand,* p. 141.

3. The Metropolitan Working Classes' Association for Improving the Public Health, 1947, pp. 6–7.

4. Gavin, H., 1848, p. 20. Dr Gavin was a lecturer in forensic medicine and public health at the Charing Cross Hospital, and a member of the Committees of the Health of Towns and of London Association.

5. See Gavin, H., 1847, p. 33. See also Holland, E. C., 1843, and Hammond, J. L., 1917, ch. 3.

6. Health of Towns Association, 1848, p. 7.

7. OECD, 1990, table 2, p. 40.

8. Farber, K. D. and Rutledge, G., 1989, pp. 19–23.

9. Gordon Hughes argues (1990, p. ii), that insofar as Eastern European economies develop along the lines of the currently advanced Western economies their pollution intensities, and possibly levels, will decline precisely on account of this shift in economic structure that seems to characterize economic growth in almost all countries of the world.

10. For various reasons figures for individual countries are not strictly comparable, so that a more reasonable picture of the income/water supply relationship is provided by grouping countries into broad income bands. Country income levels are at constant (1987) $US. For details of individual countries and sources and definitions, see Beckerman, W., 1992.

11. See, for example, OECD, 1991, figure 9, "Trends in manmade sulphur oxide emissions," p. 37.

12. UNEP/WHO GEMS, 1988, p. 15.

13. See details and sources in Beckerman, W., 1992, table 3.4.

14. The six worst cities, taking the average of 1980–84, in the GEMS ranking, were Teheran, Shenyang, Calcutta, Beijing, Xian, and New Delhi, with Bombay, Kuala Lumpur, and Bangkok not far behind. In these cities SPM and smoke levels exceeded the WHO guideline for the 98th percentile (i.e., the exposure level that should not be exceeded more than 2 percent of the time, or 7 days a year) for anything between 200 days and 300 days per year (UNEP/WHO GEMS, 1988, figure 4.9, p. 33).

15. Up to a point the emission of pollutants from an automobile falls off rapidly as its speed increases, so that a major cause of urban air pollution from automobiles is traffic congestion. See Faiz, A. et al., 1990, tables 19, 20, and 21, pp. 42, 43, and 46.

16. UNEP/WHO GEMS, 1988, p. 44.

17. Ibid., p. 43. Even here, however, there are notable exceptions, namely Singapore.

18. UNEP/WHO GEMS, 1988, p. 60.

19. Ibid., p. 60.

20. See evidence in Beckerman, W., 1974. This source also documents improvements in air and water quality in the 1960s and early 1970s in a number of developed countries as well as the pollution abatement policies being introduced around that time in the countries in question, pp. 124–40.

21. Ashby, E. and Anderson, M., 1981, p. 116, and Brimblecombe, P., 1987, p. 170.

22. See World Bank, 1990a, p. 35 et seq.

23. Ibid., figure IV-1, p. 79.

24. World Bank, EMTEN/EMENA, 1989c, pp. 9 and 10.

25. UNEP/WHO GEMS, 1988, pp. 38–57.

26. For example, in Bangkok tighter standards on emissions were introduced as far back as 1979, but it has proved impossible fully to monitor and hence enforce

these standards in a city in which the number of vehicles has grown rapidly to its present level of well over 2 million. Tighter restrictions were introduced in subsequent years and further reductions in permitted lead and sulphur levels are to be introduced in 1992 and 1993, but given the extra expenditures that this will require by the petroleum refining and distribution industries, together with the increased monitoring burden, it is far from certain that the newer standards will be fully implemented. (See internal World Bank memo by Christopher Redfern on "Thailand: Environment," May 9, 1991.)

27. One recent authoritative discussion of the international political implications of global action to deal with global environmental threats, notably climate change, is Chapter 5 of Skolnikoff, E. B., 1993.

Chapter 4

1. Mishan, E. J., 1972.

2. Brown, L., 1991, pp. 353–4.

3. Sir Crispin Tickell, 1993.

4. In spite of the rapturous reception accorded to the study in many circles, two eminent experts who studied it very carefully concluded that ". . . on examination, we find that the most important parts of the model are naïve in conception, amateurish in construction, and make negligible—and warped—use of empirical data. . . . The notion that this model might seriously be used for forecasting long-term trends in resource utilization is absurd" (Kay, J. A. and Mirrlees, J. A., 1975).

5. Montefiore, H., 1971.

6. 2 Kings 2: 19–23.

7. The estimates of the non-fuel mineral resources shown below originate with the U.S. Bureau of Mines, where they are defined to "include demonstrated resources that are currently economic, marginally economic, and some of those that are currently subeconomic." The Club of Rome used the same source for most of the minerals on their list except for their figure of coal reserves, the source of which is not clear (not that this matters, because there is no dispute that we are not likely to run out of coal reserves in the foreseeable future). The estimates for fuels are from table 2, p. 5 of Dennis Anderson's Feb. 1991 paper "Global Warming and Economic Growth," for the World Bank's 1992 *World Development Report*.

8. The sources used for this table were (i) *reserves*: 1970 reserves as in Meadows, D. et al., 1972, pp. 56–9; 1989 reserves of metals from *The World Almanac*, 1990, p. 130 (these data are taken from the U.S. Bureau of Mines estimates); (ii) *consumption*: metals from *Metal Bulletin's Prices and Data* (Metal Bulletin Books Ltd, Surrey, UK), 1990, p. 255 and passim; various unit conversions were carried out to make them comparable with reserves figures; (iii) *fuel* reserves and consumption from Dennis Anderson, Feb. 1991, op. cit. (iv) *food output per head*: UNCTAD *Handbook of International Trade and Development Statistics*, 1989, p. 456, table 6.5 (data taken from an FAO data tape).

9. For the items other than fuel the consumption figures for 1989 covered only the first nine months of the year and excluded the Soviet bloc countries. This will not significantly affect the estimated cumulative 1970–89 total, of course.

10. Billion barrels of oil equivalent (Bboe); data relate to 1990 reserves and rounded estimates of cumulative 1970 through 1990 consumption.

11. See the story in Moore, S., 1992.

12. Schumacher, E. F., 1973, p. 118.

13. World Bank, 1992, table A.10, p. 205.

14. Solow, R. M., 1974a.

15. See French, A., 1964.

16. Jevons, W. S., 1866.

17. World Bank, 1992, p. 205.

18. See references in World Bank, 1972, pp. 38–9.

19. Beckerman, W., 1972.

20. Estimates made in 1973 by the Commodities Research Unit, London, on the basis of data on concentrations of metals in the earth's surface given in the *Encylopaedia Britannica*.

21. For full list of sources see Beckerman, W., 1974, note 9 to ch. 8, p. 274.

22. World Bank, 1992, pp. 122–3.

23. Ibid., figure 6.8, p. 123.

24. Beckerman, W., 1972.

25. The Club of Rome's *Limits to Growth* made a big deal out of its computerized systems analysis that was designed by its main originator, Jay Forrester, to handle feedback mechanisms. It was ironic therefore that it completely failed to take account of these economic feedbacks, as was pointed out at the time by various commentators, notably John Maddox, the editor of *Nature*, in "Is the end of the world really nigh?," 1972.

26. Beckmann, P., 1973, p. 68 et seq.

27. Ibid., p. 89.

28. Beckerman, W., 1972.

29. This point was well put in a scathing review of *The Limits to Growth*, by Carl Kaysen, 1972.

30. Department of the Environment, 1992, figure 5.8, p. 61.

31. Bryant, C. and Cook, P., 1992, Annex table A.1.

32. Quoted in Moore, S., 1992, p. 101.

33. Quotation ibid, p. 102, from Avery, D. T., 1991.

Chapter 5

1. Midgley, M., 1993, p. 7.

2. Myers, N., 1993, p. 74.

3. Passmore, J., 1974, p. 116.

4. Singer, P., 1986, p. 221.

5. Wilson, E. O., 1992, p. 331.

6. Farnsworth, N. and Soejarto, D., 1985.

7. Farnsworth, N., 1988.

8. The Myers view on this is quoted in Pearce, D., 1991.

9. Wilson, E. O., 1992, p. 332.

10. Ibid., pp. 332 and 335.

11. Passmore, J., 1974, pp. 124–5.

12. Simon, J., 1986. Among the sources of widespread alarm about species extinction were the *1980 Global Report to the President* of the USA, which led to an influential study document by the Congressional Office of Technology Assessment, and a statement by Thomas Lovejoy of the World Wildlife Fund, the data for which were drawn chiefly from Norman Myers's *The Sinking Ark*.

13. Simon, J., 1986.

14. Wilson, E. O., 1992, p. 268.
15. Whitmore, T. C. and Sayer, J. A. (eds), 1992.
16. Simberloff, D., 1992, p. 85.
17. Heywood, V. H. and Stuart, S. N., 1992, p. 93 and passim.
18. Brown, K. S. and Brown, G. G., 1992, p. 128.
19. Ibid., pp. 107–8.
20. Reid, W. V., 1992, pp. 55–6.
21. Quoted by Julian Simon, 1986, A fuller survey of the whole species extinction problem is contained in Simon, J. and Wildavsky, A. (eds), 1994. A survey of weaknesses in the methods used to predict mass species extinction is also given in Mann, C., 1991.
22. Wilson, E. O., 1992, p. 330.
23. Ehrlich, P. and Wilson, E. O., 1991.
24. *Atlantic Monthly*, Jan. 1992, pp. 47–8.
25. Ibid.
26. *The Economist*, 19.3.94, Survey on "The Future of Medicine," p. 15. The quotation is a report of predictions made by Dr Daniel Cohen, director of the French center that was responsible for publishing, in 1993, the complete map of a human genome.
27. As David Pearce (1991) explains: "The role of substitutes for plant-based drugs is thus crucial. Many modern drug manufacturers tend to focus more on the production of synthetic drugs using recent advances in molecular biology and biotechnology. Put another way, their willingness to pay for retention of tropical forests as repositories of potential pharmaceuticals could be very low."
28. See a succint survey of the way protectionist motives enter into the trade-environment connection by Bhagwati, J., 1993.

Chapter 6

1. Reported in *Atlantic Monthly*, Oct. 1990, p. 46.
2. Boehmer-Christiansen, Sonja A., 1994, pp. 400–2.
3. *Climate Change 1992*, Supplementary Report to the IPCC Scientific Assessment, CUP, 1992, p. 19.
4. In fact, with the aid of the analysis of isotope Oxygen-18 obtained from drilling cores from the ocean floor it has been possible to reconstruct the climatic history of the Earth for the last 100 million years. And this shows enormous fluctuations in temperature that cannot be satisfactorily explained: ". . . the available evidence suggests that the onset of the next glacial is, if anything, overdue. In fact it may already have been under way for 6,000 years!" (Ellsaesser, H. W., 1990, p. 23); see also Berger, A., 1988, pp. 624–57.
5. See White, J. W. C., 1993, p. 186, and *The Times Magazine*, 28.4.93, which summarizes earlier reports in *Nature*.
6. IPCC, 1992, p. 16.
7. Ibid., figure 2, p. 18.
8. Lindzen, R. S., 1990, p. 7; and 1992.
9. See Balling, R. J., 1992, ch. 7, and Charlson, R. J. and Wigley, T. M. L., 1994, pp. 28–35.
10. Quoted by Wildavsky in his Introduction to Balling, R. J., 1992, p. xxvii.
11. IPCC, 1990, p. 19.

12. See Mason, Sir John, 1989, table 2, p. 428; Lindzen, R. S., 1990, p. 9 and section 3, p. 10; and Mitchell, J. F. B., 1989: ". . . the major shortcoming is our poor understanding of the processes governing the formation and radiative properties of clouds" (p. 136). See also Michaels, P. J., 1990.

13. Wigley, T. M. L., 1994, p. 709.

14. Balling, R. J., 1992, table 4, p. 68.

15. Mason, Sir John, 1989, p. 421, and Lindzen, R. S., 1990. See also devastating statistical criticism of the proposition that data for the past century provide evidence of an upward trend in world temperature that can be associated with CO_2 concentrations in Solow, A. R. and Broadus, J. M., 1989, pp. 449–53; and Solow, A. R., 1991a, esp. pp. 17–25.

16. Important evidence for this includes records of the freezing over of Lake Konstanz in Switzerland that go back to the year 875 AD, which show the main frequency of freezing over to have taken place in the 15th and 16th centuries, with a declining frequency since then. See Solow, A. R., 1991a. See also Ellsaesser, H. W., 1990.

17. Schlesinger, M. E. and Jiang, X., 1991, pp. 219–21. Of course, as the authors point out, the impossibility of allowing for natural climatic influences means that a simple use of the observed CO_2/temperature change relationship over the past is a very uncertain guide to what the "pure" underlying CO_2/temperature relationship really is.

18. See Taylor, K. E. and Penner, J. E., 1994, and Wigley, T. M. L., 1994.

19. Balling, R. J., 1992, p. 110.

20. Department of the Environment, 1991, Executive Summary, p. (i).

21. Balling, R. J., 1992, p. 80.

22. In game theory terms there is no way of striking the balance between more or less certain costs and highly conjectural benefits that is required in order to enter the net benefit in the relevant element in the "payoff" matrix.

23. For an excellent survey of this field see Griffin, James, 1986, ch. V.

Chapter 7

1. Schelling, T. C., 1990, p. 76.

2. See White, R., 1990, p. 23.

3. The estimates of an approximately zero net effect on agricultural output made by the Environmental Protection Agency (in Smith, J. B. and Tirpak, D. A. (eds), 1988, pp. 21–2) have been confirmed in a more recent and very detailed study, breaking down the USA into a large number of regions and using alternative climate models (see Adams, R. et al., 1990, vol. 345, pp. 219–24).

4. See Cline, W. R., 1991, p. 23.

5. Nordhaus, W. D., 1990 (1991).

6. Sen, A., 1981.

7. See Ryan, S., 1994.

8. Cline, W. R., 1989, p. 18.

9. Department of the Environment, 1991, para. 2 of "overall conclusions."

10. Report of IPCC Working Group I, op. cit., June 1990, p. 18.

11. The best known and most authoritative estimates are probably those of W. Nordhaus, of Yale University, which have been published in sources already quoted and, very recently, in *Science*, vol. 258, Nov. 1992. A survey of various estimates

by Fankhauser, S., 1994, shows other estimates only very slightly higher than Nordhaus's.

12. This is a fairly obvious point of course and has been made in several places, such as Beckerman, W., 1990, p. 12. One particularly useful study, in the course of which this point has been made, is that by Barker, T., Baylis, S., and Madsen, P., 1993, pp. 296–308. Recent detailed estimates of the welfare effects of carbon taxes, taking into account various possible forms in which the revenues may be rebated to the economy are given in Shah, A. and Larsen, B., 1993.

13. Cline, W. R., 1992.

14. For details see Beckerman, W. and Malkin, J., 1994.

15. Ausubel, J. H., 1991, p. 649.

16. Schlesinger, M. E. and Jiang, X., 1991, p. 221.

17. Balling, R. J., 1992, pp. 137–41.

18. See Burniaux, J. M. et al., 1992, Section V.

Chapter 8

1. Meadows, D. et al., 1972, a report to the Club of Rome.

2. Robbins, L., 1971.

3. Mishan, E. J., 1967, p. xvi.

4. Mishan, E. J., 1971, p. 49.

5. Tickell, Sir Crispin, 1991.

6. Pigou, A. C., 1932, ch. 1, para. 5.

7. Ibid.

8. Ibid., para. 8.

9. UNDP, 1991, p. 27.

10. World Bank, 1991, p. xiv.

11. le Fanu, J., 1993, p. 13.

12. I have made estimates of the adjustment that would be needed to growth rates of GNP in 13 countries if allowance were to be made for changes in leisure in Beckerman, W., 1978.

13. Beckerman, W., 1974, ch. 3.

14. Dasgupta, P. and Weale, M., 1992, esp. table 3, p. 124.

15. Dasgupta, P., 1990.

16. UNDP, 1991, p. 1.

17. Ibid., p. 3. There are of course serious conceptual problems with aggregate indicators of overall human development or welfare. One is the lack of any sound theoretical basis for assessing the relative weight to be given to the different components of any such index. Indeed some of the components of welfare may be incommensurable with each other. The most that can be said here is that, while recognizing the conceptual problems associated with these composite indexes, they are highly correlated with national income per head. Thus, while economic growth may not be everything in life, there is overwhelming evidence to the effect that it is accompanied by increases in human welfare defined more widely.

18. Lefèbvre, H., 1958.

19. Crosland, C. A. R., 1956, ch. 2, and 1962, p. 99.

20. Mishan, E. J., 1967, p. 120.

21. Hirsch, F., 1977.

22. This is not to say that such a policy has never been pursued in any country, because it is arguable that the Stalinist policy of forcing the buildup of heavy industry at the expense of consumption levels represented just such a choice between present and future consumption.

23. An early exposition of the problem by a pioneer in this field, Allen Kneese, is his *Economics and the Environment*, 1977, ch. 5. A very recent brief survey is contained in ch. 1 of Cairncross, F., 1991, and a recent detailed survey is given in Winpenny, J. T., 1991.

24. David Pearce in the course of an interview reported in *Environmental Action* (a South African review "for leaders of Business and Public Policy"), Jan/Feb 1992, p. 12.

25. See the classic statement of this doctrine by Gilbert, M. and Jaszi, G., 1946.

Chapter 9

1. Dasgupta, P. and Mäler, K.-G., 1994a; 1994b, p. 12.

2. The legal status of Agenda 21 is far from clear, although it was later enshrined in a resolution of the Second Committee of the General Assembly of the U.N. (at its 51st meeting of 16 December 1992). But this only urged governments and international bodies to take the action necessary to follow up the agreements reached in Rio, and there is no question of countries that do not take much notice of its being brought before the International Court of Justice! After all, most countries in the world are constantly in breach of various more binding commitments into which they have entered concerning human rights without ever being pursued in the courts or penalized in any way.

3. See, for example, Pearce, D. W., Markandya, A., and Barbier, E., 1989, p. 1; Solow, R. M., 1992; Pezzey, J., 1992a, p. 1.

4. Brooks, H., 1992, p. 30.

5. See criticism along these lines by Dasgupta, P. and Mäler, K-G., 1990, p. 106, in which they take specific issue with a definition of SD by Pearce, Barbier, and Markandya, which required no decline in the natural capital stock. This condition differs significantly from one proposed by the same authors but with their names in a different order, namely in Pearce, Markandya, and Barbier, 1989, p. 3. It is interesting that changing the order of the authors changed their definition of "sustainable development." I presume that they could not reach agreement and so took it in turns as to whose definition was adopted.

6. Even at a technical level, whether some project or development program is sustainable or not depends on numerous assumptions—e.g., concerning availability of inputs, foreign loans, and so on.

7. Little, I. M. D. and Mirrlees, J. A., 1990, p. 365.

8. World Commission on Environment and Development, 1987.

9. An excellent recent survey is contained in Appendix 1 of Pezzey, J., 1992a.

10. See Pezzey, J., 1992a; 1992b, pp. 321–62.

11. Pearce, D. W., 1993, p. 48.

12. On p. 48 of Pearce et al., 1989, this maintenance of the stock of natural capital seems to be the concept of "sustainable development" to which the authors subscribe (in that particular publication), though wider concepts were also given their due.

13. We abstract here from the question of whether, at the margin, the person derives as much welfare from a unit of consumption as from a unit of income devoted to investment.

14. This example does not depend at all on any assumptions about the person's rate of time preference.

15. Pigou, A. C., 1932, p. 89. The link between economic welfare and distribution is forcibly expressed in, for example, Graaff, J. de V., 1957, p. 92. Distributional considerations are even included in standard techniques of cost-benefit analysis pioneered by Ian Little and J. A. Mirrlees (see, in particular, Little, I. M. D. and Mirrlees, J. A., 1974). I myself have published estimates of growth rates of national income in nine countries adjusted for changes in their internal income distributions, and others had already done so before me (see Beckerman, W., 1978, ch. 4, "The Adjustment of Growth Rates for Changes in Income Distribution."

16. Some of the difficulties surrounding the problem of our obligations to future generations are briefly discussed by Pasek, J., 1992.

17. As proposed by Dasgupta, P. and Heal, G. M., 1979, p. 262.

18. One interesting attempt to relate alternative ethical views concerning intergenerational justice is in d'Arge, R. C., Schultze, W. D., and Brookshire, D. S., 1982.

19. See, for example, Partridge, E. (ed.), 1981. One distinguished philosopher who has made extensive criticisms along these lines is Derek Parfit, as in Parfit, D., 1984, Appendix F.

20. We might, however, use a slightly lower discount rate to allow for the reduced risk of our not surviving long enough to see the fruits of our savings.

21. And how temporary is the temporary decline in welfare that is permitted under the Pearce definition? If we cannot specify this precisely the condition is totally nonoperational. By this I do not mean to suggest that we should give a precise number of years. What is required is a specification of the precise criteria by which we can determine whether any particular "temporary" decline in welfare is optimal. Economists define the optimum output of any commodity as that at which the marginal social cost of producing it equals the marginal social benefit. This definition does not tell us exactly how much of each commodity should be produced in terms of kilograms or gallons or any other units. But it gives a precise and operational definition. By contrast definitions of sustainable development that include vague qualifications about the acceptability of "temporary" declines in social welfare, devoid of any criteria for deciding how temporary is temporary, are totally nonoperational.

22. Pezzey, J., 1992, p. 11.

23. Nagel, T., 1979, p. 3.

24. A relatively recent paper by R. M. Solow which contains also the key references to contributions made by Hartwick, Weitzman, Dixit, and others is Solow, R. M., 1986.

25. Solow, R. M., 1974, p. 30. More specifically, here, and elsewhere, Solow demonstrates that, with growing population and technical progress, constant consumption per head may not be desirable. Elsewhere, he also explicitly states that "there are social goals other than sustainability" (in Solow, R. M., 1992b, p. 20).

26. See, for example, the generally excellent article by Common, M. and Perrings, C., 1992, where they write (p. 10): "Economists have always had to work hard to find a rationalization for the principle of constant consumption. In this instance, the rationalization was provided by Solow, who used the egalitarian arguments of Rawls (1971) to propose a 'Rawlsian' maximum approach to the intertemporal distribution of consumption."

27. Various other methods have been used to attempt to measure capital stocks and their depreciation, such as the use of fire insurance surveys. Or estimates have been made of the typical length of life of specific types of building or machinery or

capital equipment and so on. But nobody would pretend that such estimates provide more than rough orders of magnitude at best.

28. I explained the theory and backed it up with the facts in Beckerman, W., 1974, ch. 8, "Resources for Growth." For more recent data see also Beckerman, W., 1992, op. cit., Annex 2.

29. The Environment Directorate of the OECD, and the World Bank, frequently produce authoritative studies of economic valuation of environmental costs and benefits, including, for example, Munasinghe, M., 1993; Pezzey, J., 1992a; and Peskin, H. and Lutz, E., 1990. See also Cairncross, F., 1991, and Winpenny, J. T., 1991, and the papers included in Part II of Costanza, R. (ed.), 1991.

30. These are among the tasks of the Convention on Biodiversity signed by over 150 countries at the 1992 UN Conference on Environment and Development at Rio de Janeiro.

Chapter 10

1. One distinguished philosopher who has analyzed this problem with great sophistication, namely Derek Parfit, discusses the case of a moderate amount of depletion of natural resources that is not enough to prevent people living more than two centuries later having a much higher quality of life than we do now. He writes, "Can we claim that these people have a *right* to an *even higher* quality of life? I believe that, on any plausible theory about rights, the answer would be no" (Parfit, D., 1984, p. 365). Of course, Parfit is not excluding here the possibility that a moral theory not based on *rights* might give a different answer.

2. I am abstracting here from the well-known conceptual problems of comparing economic welfare over long periods of time.

3. Sen, A., 1987, p. 2.

4. Sen, A., 1973, p. 6. And elsewhere he put the implication of this even more bluntly: "In short, a society or an economy can be "Pareto optimal" and still be perfectly disgusting" (1970, p. 22). In its intergenerational context Dasgupta and Heal say that "... a programme can be intertemporally efficient and yet be perfectly ghastly" (Dasgupta, P. and Heal, G. M., 1979, p. 257).

5. This aspect of optimality is well explored in a series of papers by Richard B. Howarth and Richard B. Norgaard, notably "Intergenerational resource rights, efficiency, and social optimality" (1990), and by Richard B. Norgaard in "Sustainability and the economics of assuring assets for future generations" (1992).

6. See, in particular, Daly, H. E., 1992.

7. The limited, but nevertheless valuable role of philosophical considerations in the environmental context is well set out by Williams, B., 1992, p. 60.

8. The New English Bible, OUP, 1970, p. 2.

9. Hay, D. 1989, p. 19. Hay addresses himself more specifically to the Christian attitude to long-range environmental problems in Hay, D., 1990. See Thomas, K., 1984, ch. 1, for a masterly survey of the theological basis of the strongly anthropocentric bias in Christianity, and the extent to which this differs from certain other religions.

10. Passmore, J., 1974.

11. For a recent survey of some of the difficulties, see Pasek, J., 1992.

12. The implications of this problem have been explored with great subtlety by Derek Parfit, notably in *Reasons and Persons*, 1984.

13. Parfit, D., 1983, p. 169.

14. Jan Narveson first advanced this view in his pioneering article "Utilitarianism and New Generations" (1967). In a later article he expressed the person-affecting view as follows: "Duties must always be duties to someone: if no person is affected by an action, then that action (or inaction) cannot be a violation or fulfillment of a duty" (Narveson, J., 1978).

15. Broome, J., 1992, pp. 125 et seq., and Heyd, D., 1992. See also a survey of this particular problem in Pasek, J., 1993.

16. In other words, it may be argued that while the proposition that harm is only done if actual people are harmed is a sound ethical judgement *assuming the existence of a given population*, it is totally inapplicable where the size and identity of the population depends on our actions. In such circumstances, it might be argued, we should reject the whole framework of the person-affecting assumption.

17. Griffin, J., 1982, p. 369.

18. As John Stuart Mill himself pointed out, the utilitarian principle "has had a large share in forming the moral doctrines even of those who most scornfully reject its authority. Nor is there any school of thought that refuses to admit that the influence of action on happiness is a most material and even predominant consideration in many of the details of morals, however unwilling to ackowledge it as the funadamental principle of morality, and the source of moral obligation" (Mill, J. S., 1962, p. 254).

19. As Jonathan Glover himself indicates, ibid., p. 4. As regards intergenerational justice in particular, it has been alleged by Sumner, L. W., 1973, that average utilitarianism does incorporate such a bias in favor of present generations, but this is highly debatable. In fact, one of the most prominent contemporary defenders of utilitarianism, J. J. C. Smart, specifically asks: "Why should not future generations matter as much as present ones? To deny it is to be temporally parochial" (Smart, J. J. C. and Williams, B., 1973, p. 64).

20. Of course, the way the world is behaving these days, it is quite possible that the end of mankind will arrive before a hundred years have elapsed.

21. For a full exposition of this see Sen, A., 1973, pp. 16ff.

22. This is of course widely recognized in the literature, but an authoritative statement of this particular limitation on utilitarianism by an economist is in Mirrlees, J. A., 1982, pp. 80–81. A detailed recent discussion of this problem, among others, is contained in Heyd, D., 1992.

23. Partha Dasgupta suggested some time ago that it is arguable ". . . that according to broad utilitarian tenets, all obligations, and indeed all moral reasons for doing anything, are grounded upon the *existence* of persons who would benefit or be injured by the effects of one's actions," so that one might not feel logically obliged to take account of the addition to total utility made by the extra people at the expense of the utility of the existing people. (See Dasgupta, P., 1971, p. 117.)

24. Parfit, D., 1984.

25. Barry, B., 1989, p. 161.

26. Ibid., p. 189.

27. Rawls, J., 1972.

28. Ibid., p. 137.

29. Ibid. p. 278. I advanced this objection to the use of the "original position" device in the context of intergenerational justice in 1983 (see Beckerman, W., 1983, p. 15). Brian Barry made the same point more clearly as follows: ". . . if we know

who the people at the gathering are, the choice of principles must already have somehow been made . . . there may be different numbers of generations under alternative arrangements" (Barry, B., 1989, p. 194).

30. This is known as his "difference principle."

31. See also Barry, B., 1989, pp. 189–202, and Solow, R. M., 1974, pp. 29–45.

32. Rawls, J., 1972, pp. 284 and 286.

33. For example, Rawls develops other criteria that might be adopted for justice between generations, such as the "just savings" rule. However, there are difficulties with this rule as well, but they lie outside the scope of this book.

34. As Brian Barry puts it, "The point here is that we should think not of a choice made by a particular generation at a single point in time but of a pattern of collaboration across many generations in a common scheme of justice. Although, in the nature of the case, successive generations cannot take part in any system of mutual benefit, they can all play their parts in a system accepted by all as just. The principle of fair play, which says that there is an obligation to do one's bit to sustain just institutions, thus operates here even in the absence of any possibility of mutual benefit" (Barry, B., 1989, p. 200).

Chapter 11

1. In writing this chapter I have greatly benefited from discussions with J. Broome, I. M. D. Little, and M. Fg. Scott. (In particular John Broome's own work in this field has done much to clarify the misunderstanding that exists between economists and philosophers as regards the discounting issue.) Needless to say they are in no way responsible for the contents of this chapter or any errors therein.

2. See, for example, the literature referred to in notes 6 and 8 below, and an extensive survey of the problem in Price, C., 1993.

3. Partridge, E. (ed.), 1981.

4. Rawls, J., 1972, p. 295.

5. Of course, it may be morally undesirable to "do unto others as you would have them do unto you." For example, they may have different tastes.

6. Parfit, D., 1984, Appendix F. The same point is reproduced in Cowen, T. and Parfit, D., 1992, ch. VII.

7. Dasgupta and Heal argue that pure time preference would be appropriate if it is believed that "there is a positive chance that future generations will not exist" (see Dasgupta, P. S. and Heal, G. M., 1979, p. 262, and the same point is made by Dasgupta in Dasgupta, P. S., 1982, p. 275). The possibility of extinction of the human race corresponds to the case I have referred to above concerning the *risk*, for an individual, of not surviving long enough to enjoy the benefit of one's investments.

8. The relevant literature is full of quotations (usually the same ones) from famous economists about the irrationality of pure time preference. For example, Robert Goodin has reminded us that "Economist [Frank] Ramsey remarks that to '. . . discount later enjoyments in comparison with earlier ones . . . is a practice which is ethically indefensible and arises merely from the weakness of the imagination . . .' and Harrod blasts our 'time preference' as a 'polite expression for rapacity and the conquest of reason by passion' " (Goodin, R., 1978). Pigou wrote: ". . . our telescopic faculty is defective and we, therefore, see future pleasures, as it were, on a diminished scale . . . it implies that people distribute their resources between the present, the near future, and the remote future on the basis of a wholly irrational preference . . . .

The inevitable result is that efforts directed towards the remote future are starved relatively to efforts directed towards the present" (Pigou, A. C., 1932, pt. I, ch. II, p. 25). See also Dasgupta, P. and Heal, G. M., 1979, ch. 9, p. 261. An excellent survey of this literature is contained in Price, C., 1993.

9. There are of course various formal treatments of the optimal savings (and investment) rate for society as a whole, which we do not attempt to summarize here. This section is devoted to considering the application to society of the particular line of argument presented in the previous section concerning what is optimal for an individual.

10. Cowen, T. and Parfit, D., 1992.

11. Ibid., p. 151.

12. Allowing, of course, for well-known market distortions, such as taxes or subsidies, and externalities.

13. One could go further; not only does the rationality or otherwise of their choice have little direct connection with its morality, but it is arguable that the procedure they are adopting is in fact perfectly rational. For it would be irrational for them to waste time and energy in an effort to make precise calculations of the exact degree of risk involved in each investment or the exact amount by which their marginal utility would decline if they became richer. Rational choice includes the choice of how far it is worth sacrificing time and resources into making marginally better decisions.

14. Parfit, D., 1984, p. 483.

15. This point is clearly set out in Mishan, E. J., 1981, pp. 499–513.

16. Some interpretations of utilitarianism might fit this position, for utilitarianism is not concerned with equality of utilities per se, only with their sum total. This only requires that the *marginal utility* that people derive from marginal increases in income are equal, but this does not necessarily imply that their total incomes have to be equal. Some poor people, for example, may be worse at converting extra income into extra utility than are some rich people.

17. In all such cases, the actual Pareto improvement is not a *sufficient* condition for an improvement in social welfare.

18. This argument is very clearly set out by Pearce, D., Markandya, A., and Barbier, E., 1989, who emphasize that this point "reduces considerably the force of the arguments to the effect that conventionally determined discount rates should be lowered . . . to accommodate environmental considerations" (p. 30). See also Beckerman, W., 1991, pp. 78–79.

19. An excellent discussion of the extent to which we can replace discounting at different rates by changing the relative prices of the items to be discounted is provided in Price, C., 1993, ch. 21.

20. This would be the approach preferred, for example, by Broome, J., 1992.

21. A recent discussion of the relation between the socially optimal rate of time preference and the rate of return at the margin on private investments is contained in ch. 6 of Cline, W. R., 1992. Cline concludes that the correct social rate of time preference ought to be of the order of 1 percent. If the arguments presented in this chapter are correct, Cline's view is mistaken.

22. A survey of the whole field in relation to environmental policy is contained in Pearce et al., 1989.

23. See Little, I. M. D. and Mirrlees, J. A., 1990, p. 240, and Scott, M. Fg., 1977, p. 231. Much higher estimates are recorded in Price, C., 1993, p. 233. Dasgupta, P.

and Mäler, K-G., 1994, suggest a figure of 2.5 for the relevant coefficient, which would mean an overall consumption discount rate, even assuming zero "pure" time preference, of about 5 percent per annum.

24. See Scott, M. Fg., 1993, no. 1.

Bibliography

Adams, R. et al., "Global climate change and US agriculture" *Nature* (17 May 1990).

Ashby, Sir Eric (later Lord), and Anderson, M., *The Politics of Clean Air* (Clarendon Press, Oxford, 1981).

Ausubel, J. H., "Does climate still matter?" *Nature* (April 1981).

Avery, D. T., *Global Food Progress* (Hudson Institute, Stanford, 1991).

Aziz, K. M. A. et al., *Water Supply, Sanitation and Hygiene Education*, Report of a Health Impact Study in Mirzapur, Bangladesh (UNDP-World Bank Water and Sanitation Program, Washington, D.C., 1990).

Balling, R. J. Jr., *The Heated Debate* (Pacific Research Institute for Public Policy, San Francisco, 1992).

Barker, T., Baylis, S. and Madsen, P., "A UK carbon/energy tax" *Energy Policy* (March 1993).

Barry, B., *Theories of Justice* (Harvester-Wheatsheaf, London, 1989).

Beckerman, W., "Economists, scientists and environmental catastrophe" *Oxford Economic Papers* (Nov. 1972).

―――― *In Defence of Economic Growth* (Cape, London, 1974; US edition *Two Cheers for the Affluent Society*, St. Martin's Press, New York, 1975).

―――― *Measures of Leisure, Equality and Welfare* (OECD, Paris, 1978).

―――― "Human resources: are they worth preserving?" in P. Streeten and H. Maier (eds) (1983).

―――― *Pricing for Pollution* (Institute of Economic Affairs, London, 2nd edn. 1990)

―――― "Global warming: a sceptical economic assessment" in D. Helm (ed.) (1991).

―――― *Economic Development and the Environment: Conflict or Complementarity* (World Bank Background Paper no. 24 to the World Development Report, Washington D.C., 1992).

―――― and Malkin, J. "How much does global warming matter?" *The Public Interest* (Winter 1994).

Beckmann, P., *Eco-Hysterics and the Technophobes* (Golem Press, Boulder, Colorado, 1973).

Behrman, J. and Srinivasan, T. N. (eds), *Handbook of Development Economics*, vol. 3 (North Holland, Amsterdam, 1994).

Berger, A., "Milankovitch theory and climate" *Review of Geophysics* (vol. 26, no. 4, 1988).

Bhagwati, J., "The case for free trade" *Scientific American* (Nov. 1993).

Block, W. E. (ed.), *Economics and the Environment* (Fraser Institute, Vancouver, Canada, 1990).

Borcherding, T., "Natural resources and transgenerational equity," in W. E. Block (ed.) (1990).

Boehmer-Christiansen, S. A. "A scientific agenda for climate policy?" *Nature*, vol. 372 (Dec. 1994).

Brimblecombe, P., *The Big Smoke* (Routledge, London, 1987).

Briscoe, J. and de Ferranti, D., *Water for Rural Communities* (World Bank, Washington, D.C., 1988).

Brooks, H., "Sustainability and technology" *Science and Sustainability* (International Institute for Applied Systems Analysis, Vienna, 1992).

Broome, J., *Counting the Cost of Global Warming* (White Horse Press, Cambridge, 1992).

Brown, K. S., and Brown, G. G., "Habitat alteration and species loss in Brazilian forests" in T. C. Whitmore and J. A. Sayer (eds) (1992).

Brown, L., "Is economic growth sustainable?" *Proceedings of the World Bank Annual Conference on Development Economics* (Washington, D.C., 1991).

Bryant, C., and Cook, P., "Environmental issues and the national accounts" *Economic Trends* (Nov. 1992).

Burniaux, J-B. et al., *The Costs of Reducing CO_2 Emissions: Evidence from Green* (OECD Economics Department Working Papers no. 115, Paris, 1992).

Cairncross, F., *Costing the Earth* (Economist Books, London, 1991).

Charlson, R. J., and Wigley, T. M. L., "Sulfate aerosol and climatic change" *Scientific American* (Feb. 1994).

Chateaubriand, Vicomte de, *Memoirs* (Penguin 1965).

Cline, W. R., *Political Economy of the Greenhouse Effect* (Institute of International Economics, Washington, D.C., preliminary draft Aug. 1989).

_____ *The Economics of Global Warming* (Institute of International Economics, Washington, D.C., 1992).

Common, M., and Perrings, C., "Towards an ecological economics of sustainability" *Ecological Economics* (vol. 6, 1992).

Costanza, R. (ed.), *Ecological Economics: The Science and Management of Sustainability* (Columbia University Press, 1991).

Cowen, T., and Parfit, D., "Against the social discount rate" in P. Laslett and J. S. Fishkin (eds) (1992).

Crosland, C. A. R., *The Future of Socialism* (Cape, London, 1956).

_____ *The Conservative Enemy* (Cape, London, 1962).

d'Arge, R. C., Schultze, W. D., and Brookshire, D. S., "Carbon dioxide and intergenerational choice" *American Economic Review* (May 1982).

Daly, H. E., *Steady State Economics* (Earthscan, 2nd edn. London, 1992).

Dasgupta, P. S., "On optimum population size" in A. Mitra (ed.) (1971).

_____ "Resource depletion, research and development, and the social discount rate" in R. C. Lind (ed.) (1982).

_____ "Well-being and the extent of its realisation in poor countries" *Economic Journal* (vol. 100 Supplement, 1990).

_____ and Heal, G. M., *Economic Theory and Exhaustible Resources* (CUP, 1979).

_____ and Mäler, K-G., "The environment and emerging development issues" *Proceedings of the World Bank Annual Conference on Development Economics, 1990* (Washington, D.C., 1990).

_____ and _____ "Poverty, institutions, and the environmental-resource base" in J. Behrman and T. N. Srinivasan (eds) (1994a).

_____ and _____ *Poverty, Institutions, and the Environmental-Resource Base*, World Bank Environment Paper no. 9 (Washington, D.C. 1994b).

_____ and Weale, M., "On measuring the quality of life" *World Development* (Jan. 1992).

218

Department of the Environment, United Kingdom Climate Change Impacts Review Group, *The Potential Effects of Climate Change in the United Kingdom* (HMSO, London, 1991).

Department of the Environment, *The UK Environment* (HMSO, London, 1992).

Dornbusch, R. and Poterba, J. M. (eds) *Global Warming: Economic Policy Responses* (MIT Press, Cambridge, Mass., 1991).

Ehrlich, P. R., and Wilson, E. O., "Biodiversity studies: science and policy," *Science* (Aug. 1991).

Ellsaesser, H. W., "A different view of the climatic effect of CO_2—updated" *Atmósfera* (vol. 3, 1990).

Esrey, S. S., Potash, J. B., Roberts, L., and Shiff, C., *WASH Technical Report No. 66* (report for the Office of Health, Bureau for Science and Technology, Washington, D.C., July 1990).

Faiz, A., Sinha, K., Walsh, M., and Varma, A., *Automotive Air Pollution* (World Bank Working Paper WPS 492, Aug. 1990).

Fankhauser, S., "The economic costs of global warming damage: a survey" *Global Environmental Change* (forthcoming 1994).

Farber, K. D., and Rutledge, G., "Pollution abatement and control expenditures" *Survey of Current Business* (U.S. Dept. of Commerce, Washington, D.C., June 1989).

Farnsworth, N., "Screening of plants for new medicines," in E. O. Wilson (ed.) (1988).

_____ and Soejarto, D., "Potential consequences of plant extinction in the United States on the current and future availability of prescription drugs" *Economic Botany* (vol. 39, no. 3, 1985).

Fellner, W., and Haley, B. (eds), *Readings in the Theory of Income Distribution* (Blakiston Co., Philadelphia, 1946).

French, A., *The Growth of the Athenian Economy* (London, 1964).

Gavin, H., *Unhealthiness of London and the Necessity of Remedial Measures* (London, 1847).

_____ *Sanitary Ramblings* (London, 1848).

GEMS (Global Environment Monitoring System of the United Nations) *Assessment of Urban Air Quality* (1988).

_____ *Estimating Human Exposure to Air Pollutants* (WHO Offset Publication no. 69, 1982).

Gilbert, M., and Jaszi, G., "National product and income statistics as an aid in economic problems" in W. Fellner and B. Haley (eds) (1946).

Glover, J. (ed.), *Utilitarianism and Its Critics* (Macmillan, New York, and London, 1990).

Goldsmith, E., *The Great U-Turn, De-Industrialising Society* (Green Books, Devon, 1988).

Goodin, R., "Uncertainty as an excuse for cheating our children," *Policy Sciences* (vol. 10, 1978).

Graaff, J. de V., *Theoretical Welfare Economics* (CUP, 1957).

Griffin, J., "Bentham and modern utilitarianism" *Revue Internationale de Philosophie* (vol. 131, no. 3, 1982).

Griffin, J., *Well-being* (OUP, 1986).

Hammond, J. L., *The Town Labourer* (London, 1917).

Hay, D., *Economics Today* (Apollos, 1989).

_____ *Christians in the Global Greenhouse* (The Tyndale Bulletin, 1990).

Health of Towns Association, *Report of the Sub-committee on the Questions Addressed to the Principal Towns of England and Wales* (London, 1848).

Helm, D. (ed.), *Economic Policy Towards the Environment* (Blackwell, 1991).

Helm, J. L. (ed.), *Energy, Production, Consumption and Consequences* (National Academy Press, Washington, D.C., 1990).

Heyd, D., *Genethics: Moral Issues in the Creation of People* (Univ. of California Press, 1992).

Heywood, V. H., and Stuart, S. N., "Species extinction in tropical forests" in T. C. Whitmore and J. A. Sayer (eds) (1992).

Hirsch, F., *Social Limits to Growth* (Routledge, 1977).

Holland, E. C., *The Vital Statistics of Sheffield* (1843).

Howarth, R. B. and Norgaard, R. B., "Intergenerational resources rights, efficiency, and social optimality," *Land Economics* (Feb. 1990).

Hughes, G., "Are the costs of cleaning up Eastern Europe exaggerated?" Paper for the World Bank and the Commission of the European Communities (Nov. 1990).

IPCC (Intergovernmental Panel on Climate Change), *Climate Change: the IPCC Scientific Assessment* (CUP, 1990).

―――― *Climate Change 1992: The IPCC Supplementary Report to the IPCC Scientific Assessment* (CUP, 1992).

Jevons, W. S., *The Coal Question* (London, 1866).

Kay, J. A., and Mirrlees, J. M., "The desirability of natural resource depletion" in D. W. Pearce (ed. with the assistance of J. Rose) (1975).

Kaysen, C. "The computer that printed out W*O*L*F*" *Foreign Affairs* (July 1972).

Kenny, A., "The Earth is fine: the problem is the greens," *Spectator* (12 March 1994).

Kneese, A., *Economics and the Environment* (Penguin, 1977).

Kumar, S. K., and Hotchkiss, D., *Consequences of Deforestation for Women's Time Allocation, Agricultural Production, and Nutrition in Hill Areas of Nepal* (Research Report no. 69, International Food Policy Research Institute, Washington, D.C., 1988).

Laslett, P., and Fishkin, J. S., *Justice Between Age Groups and Generations* (Yale University Press, 1992).

le Fanu, J., "Peddling toxic shocks" *The Times* (19 Oct. 1993).

Lefèbvre, H., *Critique de la vie quotidienne* (L'Arche, Paris, 1958).

Leitmann, J., *Energy-Environment Linkages in the Urban Sector* (World Bank Discussion Paper, April 1991).

Lind, R. C. (ed.), *Discounting for Time and Risk in Energy Policy* (Resources for the Future, Washington, D.C., 1982).

Lindzen, R.S., "Greenhouse warming: science v. consensus" *Proceedings of the Mid-West Energy Conference* (Chicago, 1989).

―――― "Some coolness concerning global warming" *Bulletin of the American Meteorological Society* (3 Jan. 1990).

―――― "Global warming: the origins and nature of alleged scientific consensus" (paper presented to the OPEC seminar on the environment, Vienna, April 1992).

Little, I. M. D., and Mirrlees, J. A., *Project Appraisal and Planning for Developing Countries* (Heinemann, 1974).

―――― "Project appraisal and planning twenty years on" *Proceedings of the World Bank Annual Conference on Development Economics 1990* (World Bank, 1990).

Maclean, D., and Brown, P. G. (eds), *Energy and the Future* (Rowman and Littlefield, New Jersey, 1983).

Maddox, J., "Is the end of the world really nigh?," *Sunday Times* (4 June 1972).

Mann, C., "Extinction: are ecologists crying wolf?," *Science* (Aug. 1991).

Mason, Sir John, "The greenhouse effect" *Contemporary Physics* (vol. 30, no. 6, 1989).

Meadows, D. et al., *The Limits to Growth* (Universe Books, New York, 1972).

Metropolitan Working Classes' Association for Improving Public Health, *Drainage and Sewerage* (London, 1847).

Michaels, P. J., "The greenhouse effect and global change: review and reappraisal" *International Journal of Environmental Studies* (1990).

Midgley, M., "The end of anthropocentrism" (paper presented to annual conference of the Royal Institute of Philosophy, Cardiff, 1993).

Mill, J. S., *Utilitarianism* (Fontana edition, ed. Mary Warnock, London, 1962).

Mirrlees, J. A., "The economic uses of utilitarianism" in A. Sen and Bernard Williams (eds) (1982).

Mishan, E. J., *The Costs of Economic Growth* (Staples Press, London, 1967).

_____ "Making the future safe for mankind" *The Public Interest* (Summer 1971).

_____ "Industry's impact on the environment" *Financial Times* (7 July 1972).

_____ *Introduction to Normative Economics* (OUP, 1981).

Mitchell, J. F. B., "The greenhouse effect and climate change" *Review of Geophysics* (Feb. 1989).

Mitra, A. (ed.), *Economic Theory and Planning: Essays in Honour of A. K. Das Gupta* (OUP, 1971).

Montefiore, The Rt. Rev. Hugh (Bishop of Kingston-upon-Thames at time in question), "Man's hope of survival" *Observer* (19 Dec. 1971).

Moore, S., "So much for 'scarce resources' " *The Public Interest* (Winter 1992).

Munasinghe, M., *Towards Sustainable Development: The Role of Environmental Economics and Valuation* (World Bank Environment Paper no. 3, 1993).

Myers, N., "Biodiversity and the precautionary principle" *Ambio* (May 1993).

Nagel, T., *Mortal Questions* (CUP, 1979).

Narveson, J., "Utilitarianism and new generations" *Mind* (vol. 76, 1967).

_____ "Future people and us" in R. I. Sikora and B. Barry (eds) (1978).

Nordhaus, W. D., "To slow or not to slow: the economics of the greenhouse effect" (draft of Feb. 1990, a shorter version of which was subsequently published in the *Economic Journal*, July 1991).

Norgaard, R. B., *Sustainability and the Economics of Assuring Assets for Future Generations* (World Bank Policy Research Working Paper, Jan. 1992).

OECD, *Pollution Abatement and Control Expenditure in OECD Member Countries* (Paris, 1990).

_____ *The State of the Environment* (Paris, 1991).

Ozorio de Almeida, A. L. de, *The Civilization of the Amazon* (Texas University Press, 1991).

Parfit, D., "Energy policy and the further future: the identity problem," in D. Maclean and P. G. Brown (eds) (1983).

_____ *Reasons and Persons* (OUP, 1984).

Partridge, E. (ed.), *Reponsibilities to Future Generations* (Prometheus Books, New York, 1981).

Pasek, J., "Obligations to future generations: a philosophical note" *World Development* (vol. 20, no. 4, 1992).

_____ *Environmental Policy and the "Identity Problem"* (CSERGE Working Paper, University College London and University of East Anglia, 1993).

Pasha, H. A., and McGarry, M. G. (eds), *Rural Water Supply and Sanitation in Pakistan: Lessons from Experience* (World Bank Technical Paper no. 105, June 1989).

Passmore, J., *Man's Responsibility for Nature* (Duckworth, London, 1974).

221

Pearce, D. W., "An economic approach to saving the tropical forests," in D. Helm (ed.) (1991).

―――― Economic Values and the Natural World (Earthscan, London, 1993).

―――― Markandya, A., and Barbier, E., Blueprint for a Green Economy (Earthscan, London, 1989).

Peskin, H., and Lutz, E., A Survey of Resources and Environmental Accounting in Industrialized Countries (World Bank, 1990).

Pezzey, J., Sustainable Development Concepts: An Economic Analysis (World Bank Environment Paper no. 2, 1992a).

―――― "Sustainability: an interdisciplinary guide" Environmental Values (vol. 1, 1992b).

Phantumvanit, D. S., and Panayotou, T., Natural Resources for a Sustainable Future: Spreading the Benefits (1990 TDRI Year-End Conference, synthesis paper no. 1, Bangkok, Dec. 1990).

Pigou, A. C., The Economics of Welfare (Macmillan, 4th edn, 1932).

Porritt, J. (ed.), Friends of the Earth Handbook (Macdonald Optima, 1990).

Price, C., Time, Discounting and Value (Blackwell, Oxford, 1993).

Rawls, J., A Theory of Justice (OUP, 1972).

Reid, W. W., "How many species will there be?," in T. C. Whitmore and J. A. Sayer (eds) (1992).

Reis, E. J., and Margulis, S., "Options for slowing Amazon jungle-clearing," in R. Dornbush and J. Poterba (eds) (1991).

Robbins, (Lord) Lionel, "Growth and anti-growth," Financial Times (2 Dec. 1971).

Royal Commission on Environmental Pollution, First Report (HMSO, 1971).

Ryan, Sean, "Scientists dismiss global warming leading to floods" Sunday Times (27 March 1994).

Schelling, T. C., "Global environment forces," in J. L. Helm (ed.) (1990).

Schlesinger, M. E., and Jiang, X., "Revised projections of future greenhouse warming" Nature (March 1991).

Schumacher, E. F., Small Is Beautiful (Blond Briggs, London, 1973).

Scott, M. Fg., "The test rate of discount and changes in base-level income in the United Kingdom" Economic Journal (June 1977).

―――― "Real interest rates: past and future" National Institute Economic Review (no. 143, Feb. 1993).

Sen, A., Collective Choice and Social Welfare (Holden-Day, San Francisco, 1970).

―――― On Economic Inequality (OUP, 1973).

―――― Poverty and Famines: An Essay on Entitlement and Deprivation (Clarendon Press, Oxford, 1981).

―――― On Ethics and Economics (Blackwell, 1987).

―――― and Williams, B. (eds), Utilitarianism and Beyond (CUP, 1982).

Shah, A., and Larsen, B., Global Warming, Carbon Taxes and Developing Countries (World Bank Public Economics Division, 1993).

Sikora, R. I., and Barry, B. (eds), Obligations to Future Generations (Temple University Press, Philadelphia, 1978).

Simberloff, D., "Do species-area curves predict extinction in fragmented forests?," in T. C. Whitmore and J. A. Sayer (eds) (1992).

Simon, J., "Disappearing species, deforestations and data," New Scientist (15 May 1986).

―――― and Wildavsky, A. (eds), The State of Humanity, (Blackwell, Oxford, 1994).

Singer, F., "Ozone depletion" *The National Interest* (Summer 1994).

Singer, P., "All animals are equal" in P. Singer (ed.) (1986).

_____ *Applied Ethics* (Oxford Readings in Philosophy, OUP, 1986).

Skolnikoff, E. B., *The Elusive Transformation* (Princeton University Press, 1993).

Smart, J. J. C., and Williams, B., *Utilitarianism: For and Against* (CUP, 1973).

Smith, J. B., and Tirpak, D. A. (eds), *The Potential Effects of Global Climate Change on the United States* (report to the U.S. Congress by the Environmental Protection Agency, 1988).

Smith, R. K., *Biofuels, Air Pollution, and Health* (Plenum Press, New York and London, 1987).

_____ "Air pollution: assessing total exposure in developing countries" *Environment* (Dec. 1988).

_____ "The risk transition" *International Environmental Affairs* (Summer 1990).

Snyder, J. D., and Merson, M. H., "The magnitude of the global problem of acute diarrhoeal disease: a review of active surveillance data" *Bulletin of the World Health Organisation* (vol. 60, 1982).

Solow, A. R., "Is there a global warming problem?" in R. Dornbusch and J. Poterba (eds) (1991a).

_____ "The story of Lake Konstanz" *Journal of Climate* (1991b).

_____ and Broadus, J. M., "On the detection of greenhouse warming" *Climatic Change* (1989).

Solow, R. M., "The economics of resources or the resources of economics" *American Economic Review*, Papers and Proceedings (May 1974a).

_____ "Intergenerational equity and exhaustible resources," *Review of Economic Studies* (Symposium, 1974b).

_____ "On the intergenerational allocation of natural resources" *Scandinavian Journal of Economics* (vol. 86, 1986).

_____ "Sustainability: an economist's perspective," *National Geographic and Exploration* (8(1), 1992a).

_____ "An almost practical step towards sustainability" (lecture on the occasion of the Fortieth Anniversary of Resources for the Future, Washington, D.C., Oct. 1992b).

Streeten, P., and Maier, H., *Human Resources, Employment and Development* (Macmillan, London, 1983).

Sumner, L. W., "Classical utilitarianism and the population optimum," in R. L. Sikora and B. Barry (eds) (1978).

Taylor, C. C. W. (ed.) *Ethics and the Environment* (Corpus Christi College, Oxford, 1992).

Taylor, K. E. and Penner, J. E., "Responses of the climate system to atmospheric aerosols and greenhouse gases" *Nature*, vol. 369 (June 1994).

Thomas, Sir Keith, *Man and the Natural World* (Penguin, London, 1994).

Tickell, Sir Crispin, "What we must do to save the planet," *New Scientist* (7 Sept. 1992).

_____ "The diversity of life" (lecture to the Isis Society, Oxford, 18 March 1993).

Tongpan, S. et al., *Deforestation and Poverty: Can Commercial and Social Forestry Break the Vicious Circle?* (1990 TDRI Year-End Conference, Research Report no. 2, Bangkok, 1990).

UN *World Urbanization Prospect* (New York, 1990).

UNDP *Global Consultation on Safe Water and Sanitation for the 1990s*

_____ *Human Development Report 1991* (OUP, 1991).

UNEP/WHO GEMS *Assessment of Urban Air Quality* (1988).

Warren Springs Laboratory, *National Survey of Air Pollution* (HMSO, 1972).

BIBLIOGRAPHY

WASH Field Report no. 246, *Willingness to Pay for Water in Newala District, Tanzania* (Report sponsored by the AID, Washington, D.C., Oct. 1988).

White, J. W. C., "Don't touch that dial" *Nature*, vol. 364 (July 1993).

White, R., "The great climate debate" *Scientific American* (July 1990).

Whitmore, T. C., and Sayer, J. A. (eds), *Tropical Deforestation and Species Extinction* (Chapman and Hall, New York, 1992).

Whittington, D., Okorafor, A., Okore, A., and McPhail, A., *Cost Recovery Strategy for Rural Water Delivery in Nigeria* (World Bank Urban Development Working Paper, WPS 369, 1990).

Whittington, D., Xinming, M., and Roche, R., "The value of time spent on collecting water: some estimates for Ukunda, Kenya" *World Development* (vol. 18, no. 2, 1990).

Wigley, T. M. L., "Outlook becoming hazier" *Nature*, vol. 369 (June 1994).

Williams, B., "Must a concern for the environment be centered on human beings?," in C. C. W. Taylor (ed.) (1992).

Wilson, E. O. (ed.), *Biodiversity* (National Academy Press, Washington, D.C., 1988).

‗‗‗‗‗ *The Diversity of Life* (Penguin, 1992).

‗‗‗‗‗ and Ehrlich, P. R.: see under Ehrlich, P. R. (1991).

Winpenny, J. T., *Values for the Environment* (HMSO, 1991).

World Bank, *Report on "The Limits to Growth"* (mimeographed, Sept. 1972).

‗‗‗‗‗ *Annual Sector Review of Water Supply and Sanitation* (Nov. 1988).

‗‗‗‗‗ *Philippines: Environment and Natural Resources Management Study* (World Bank Country Study, 1989a).

‗‗‗‗‗ EMENA *Tunisia—Country Environmental Study and National Action Plan* (Nov. 1989b).

‗‗‗‗‗ EMTEN/EMENA *Les Problèmes de l'Environment en Algerie* (1989c).

‗‗‗‗‗ *Brazil: The New Challenge of Adult Health* (World Bank Country Study, 1990a).

‗‗‗‗‗ Operations Evaluation Department, *Environmental Aspects of Selected Bank-Supported Projects in Brazil: The World Bank and Pollution Control in Sao Paulo* (Sept. 1990b).

‗‗‗‗‗ *Social Indicators of Development 1990* (Johns Hopkins University Press, Baltimore, 1991).

‗‗‗‗‗ *World Development Report 1992: Development and the Environment* (OUP, 1992).

World Commission on Environment and Development, *Our Common Future* (OUP, 1987).

Index

225

About the Author

Wilfred Beckerman is an Emeritus Fellow of Balliol College in Oxford, England, and was a member of the Royal Commission on Environmental Pollution from 1970 to 1973. This book is a sequel to his *Two Cheers for the Affluent Society*, of which Russell Lewis wrote in the *London Daily Telegraph*, "Fortunately each age has its passionate believers in sanity and reason, and Wilfred Beckerman, an economist both numerate and literate, is the perfect foil to those who let their enthusiasm for the environment run away with them."

Cato Institute

Founded in 1977, the Cato Institute is a public policy research foundation dedicated to broadening the parameters of policy debate to allow consideration of more options that are consistent with the traditional American principles of limited government, individual liberty, and peace. To that end, the Institute strives to achieve greater involvement of the intelligent, concerned lay public in questions of policy and the proper role of government.

The Institute is named for *Cato's Letters*, libertarian pamphlets that were widely read in the American Colonies in the early 18th century and played a major role in laying the philosophical foundation for the American Revolution.

Despite the achievement of the nation's Founders, today virtually no aspect of life is free from government encroachment. A pervasive intolerance for individual rights is shown by government's arbitrary intrusions into private economic transactions and its disregard for civil liberties.

To counter that trend, the Cato Institute undertakes an extensive publications program that addresses the complete spectrum of policy issues. Books, monographs, and shorter studies are commissioned to examine the federal budget, Social Security, regulation, military spending, international trade, and myriad other issues. Major policy conferences are held throughout the year, from which papers are published thrice yearly in the *Cato Journal*. The Institute also publishes the quarterly magazine *Regulation*.

In order to maintain its independence, the Cato Institute accepts no government funding. Contributions are received from foundations, corporations, and individuals, and other revenue is generated from the sale of publications. The Institute is a nonprofit, tax-exempt, educational foundation under Section 501(c)3 of the Internal Revenue Code.

CATO INSTITUTE
1000 Massachusetts Ave., N.W.
Washington, D.C. 20001